KB276179

How to
Master Skills for the
TOEFL iBT
Writing
Intermediate

Authors

Michael A. Putlack   MA in History, Tufts University, Medford, MA, USA
Expert test developer of TOEFL®, TOEIC®, and TEPS

Will Link   MA in English Literature, Florida State University, Tallahassee, FL, USA
Co-author of *How to Master Skills for the TOEFL® iBT Listening Intermediate*

Stephen Poirier   Candidate for PhD in History, University of Western Ontario, Canada
Certificate of Professional Technical Writing, Carleton University, Canada

How to Master Skills for the
TOEFL® iBT Writing Intermediate

Publisher: Kyudo Chung
Editorial Director: Dongho Lee
Editors: Hwagohn Kim, Jun Hwang
Proofreader: Michael A. Putlack
Translation: Kyungran Lee
Cover Design: Hyejung Sohn
Interior Design: Jee-eun Yun
Electronic Production: Keumjoo Kim

First Published in October 2007
By Darakwon, Inc.
Darakwon Bldg., 211, Munbal-ro, Paju-si, Gyeonggi-do 10881
Republic of Korea
Tel: 02-736-2031 (Ext. 250)
Fax: 02-732-2037

Price: ₩17,000

ISBN 978-89-5995-229-8
978-89-5995-234-2 (set)

www.darakwon.co.kr

[Components] Main Book / 1 Audio CD
& Free MP3 Download / Answer Book

20 19 18 17 16 15 14   22 23 24 25 26

How to
Master Skills ^{for the}

TOEFL® iBT
Writing

Intermediate

Michael A. Putlack | Will Link | Stephen Poirier

DARAKWON

Contents

Introduction

A. Information on the TOEFL® iBT

The Format of the TOEFL® iBT

Section	Number of Questions	Timing	Score

Reading	• 3~5 Passages
	  − approximately 700 words each
	  − 12~14 questions per passage
		60~100 min.	30 points

Listening	• 2~3 Conversations
	  − 12~25 exchanges each (3 min.)
	  − 5 questions per conversation
	• 4~6 Lectures
	  − 500~800 words each (3~5 min.)
	  − 6 questions per lecture
		60~90 min.	30 points

BREAK		10 min.	

Speaking	• 2 Independent Tasks
	(preparation: 15 sec. / response: 45 sec.)
	❶ 1 personal experience
	❷ 1 personal choice/opinion
	
	• 2 Integrated Tasks: Read-Listen-Speak
	(preparation: 30 sec. / response: 60 sec.)
	❶ 1 campus situation topic
	  − reading: 75~100 words (45 sec.)
	  − conversation: 150~180 words (60~80 sec.)
	❷ 1 academic course topic
	  − reading: 75~100 words (45 sec.)
	  − lecture: 150~220 words (60~90 sec.)
	
	• 2 Integrated Tasks: Listen-Speak
	(preparation: 20 sec. / response: 60 sec.)
	❶ 1 campus situation topic
	  − conversation: 180~220 words (60~90 sec.)
	❷ 1 academic course topic
	  − lecture: 230~280 words (90~120 sec.)
		20 min.	30 points

Writing	• 1 Integrated Task: Read-Listen-Write (20 min.)
	  − reading: 230~300 words (3 min.)
	  − lecture: 230~300 words (2 min.)
	  − a summary of 150~225 words
	
	• 1 Independent Task (30 min.)
	  − a minimum 300-word essay
		50 min.	30 points

B. Information on the Writing Section

The Writing section of the TOEFL® iBT measures test takers' ability to use writing to communicate in an academic environment. This section has two writing tasks. For the first writing task, you will read a passage and listen to a lecture and then answer a question based on what you have read and heard. For the second writing task, you will answer a question based on your own knowledge and experience.

1. Types of Writing Tasks

(1) Integrated Writing Task

- Read – You will read a short text of about 230~300 words on an academic topic for 3 minutes. You may take notes on the reading passage.
- Listen – After reading the text, you will listen to a lecture discussing the same topic from a different perspective for about 2 minutes. You may take notes on the lecture.
- Write – You will have 20 minutes to write a 150- to 225-word summary in response to the following kinds of questions:

Casting Doubt

_ Summarize the points made in the lecture, being sure to explain how they cast doubt on specific points made in the reading passage.

_ Summarize the points made in the lecture, being sure to explain how they challenge specific claims/arguments made in the reading passage.

cf. This question type accounts for almost all the questions that have been asked on the TOEFL® iBT so far.

Problem–Solution

_ Summarize the points made in the lecture, being sure to specifically explain how they answer the problems raised in the reading passage.

(2) Integrated Writing Task

You will have 30 minutes to write an essay of at least 300 words in response to the following kinds of questions:

Agree / Disagree

_ Do you agree or disagree with the following statement? *[A sentence or sentences that present an issue]* Use specific reasons and examples to support your answer.

cf. This question type accounts for almost all the essay topics that have been asked on the TOEFL® iBT so far.

Preference

_ Some people say X. Others believe Y. Which opinion do you agree with? Use specific reasons and examples to support your answer.

_ Some people do X. Others people do Y. Which do you think is better? Use specific reasons and examples to support your opinion.

2. Writing Scoring Rubrics

(1) Integrated Task (Question 1)

Your response to the Integrated Task will be scored according to these criteria:

Score	Task Description
5	A response at this level is a well-organized summary of the lecture in connection with the reading. The response includes important points made in the lecture and appropriately explains how they are related to important points made in the reading. It shows appropriate language structure and usage, with only occasional minor errors which do not interfere with conveying information and connections.
4	A response at this level contains most of the important points from the lecture and the reading and is generally good in relating the information from the lecture to that of the reading. But it may omit some points or explain them imprecisely. It may also show noticeable minor language errors or an occasional lack of clarity.
3	A response at this level includes some important information from the lecture and connects it with the relevant information from the reading. But it may omit one key point made in the lecture and shows only limited understanding of the information. Some content or connections between ideas may be incomplete or incorrect; errors in grammar or usage make some sentences unclear.
2	A response at this level does not include sufficient relevant information from the lecture and the reading and is not successful in relating the information from the lecture to that from the reading. It is characterized by language errors or expressions that make it difficult for the reader to understand key ideas or to follow connections among ideas.
1	A response at this level contains little or no important points from the lecture and fails to relate information from the lecture and the reading. It is poorly written and contains so many language errors that it is difficult to understand it.
0	A response at this level only copies sentences from the reading, is not related to the topic, is written in a language other than English, or is blank.

(2) Independent Task (Question 2)

Your essay for the Independent Task will be scored according to these criteria:

Score	Task Description
5	An essay at this level effectively responds to the topic and task by clearly stating an opinion and is easy to understand. It is well organized and shows unity, progression, and coherence. It is well developed with clearly appropriate examples, reasons, and/or details, and it displays a good command of language, including a variety of sentence structures and well-suited choices of words and idioms to express ideas.
4	An essay at this level responds to the topic and task well, but some points may not be fully supported. It is generally well organized and shows unity, progression, and coherence with only occasional redundancy or lack of clarity. It also is generally well developed with appropriate examples, reasons, and/or details, and it demonstrates a good use of language, including various sentence structures and range of vocabulary with occasional language errors that do not obscure the meaning.
3	An essay at this level responds to the topic and task on a basic level with somewhat developed examples, reasons, and/or details. It shows unity, progression, and coherence in spite of occasional, unclear connections among ideas. It is also characterized by correct but limited use of grammar and vocabulary, including errors in sentence formation and word choice that may make some sentences unclear or difficult to understand.
2	An essay at this level displays limited development in response to the topic and task, with inappropriate or insufficient supporting details. It has poor organization or connections among ideas and is marked by obviously inappropriate word choice or word forms and an accumulation of errors in grammar and/or usage.
1	An essay at this level responds to the task confusingly. It lacks any organization and development. It contains little or no detail or details that are not related to the task, and it shows serious and frequent errors in grammar and usage.
0	An essay at this level only contains words from the topic, is not related to the topic, is written in a language other than English, or is blank.

How to Use This Book

How to Master Skills for the TOEFL® iBT Writing Intermediate is designed to be used either as a textbook for a TOEFL® iBT writing preparation course or as a tool for individual learners who are preparing for the TOEFL® test on their own. With a total of 16 units, this book is organized to prepare you for the test by providing you with a comprehensive understanding of the test and thorough practice of essential skills and question types to address the writing tasks on the TOEFL® iBT. Each unit provides a step-by-step program that can enhance your writing ability as well as familiarize you with the question types asked on the TOEFL® iBT. At the back of the book are a list of essential essay topics and two actual tests of the Writing section of the TOEFL® iBT.

PART 1   Integrated Writing

❶ Note Taking & Outlining

In this section, you will practice taking notes while reading an academic passage and listening to a lecture on the same topic. Also, you will practice identifying and expressing the main arguments from both the reading and the lecture on a sentence level.

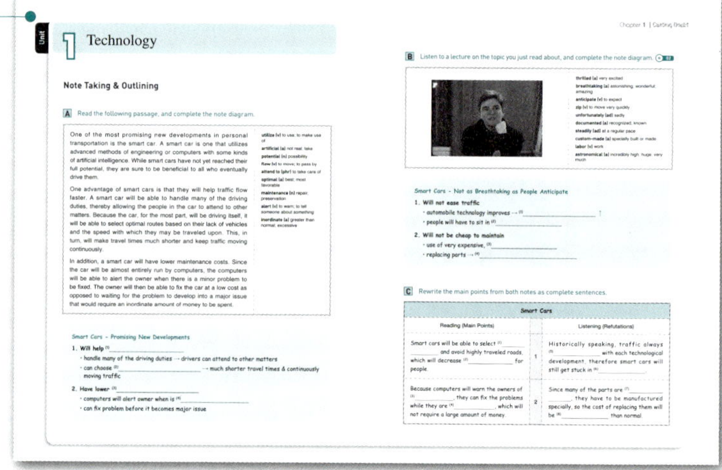

❷ Paraphrasing & Summarizing

This section helps you to practice paraphrasing some important information from the reading and lecture in your own words as well as summarizing both the reading passage and the lecture.

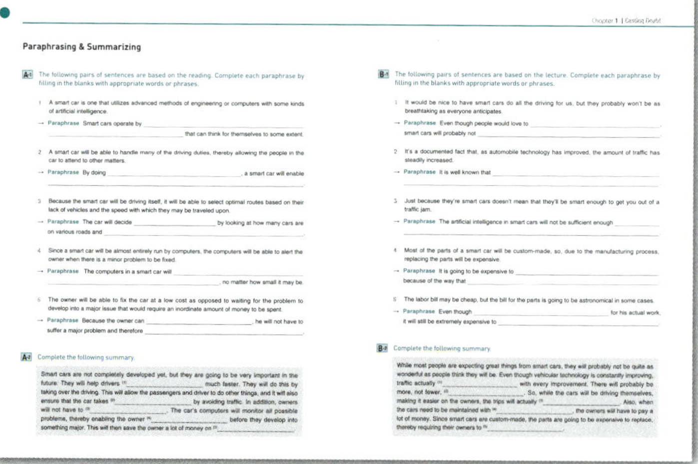

❸ Synthesizing & Organizing

This section allows you to practice combining the main arguments from both the reading and the lecture in one sentence. It also provides you with a useful template for writing a response.

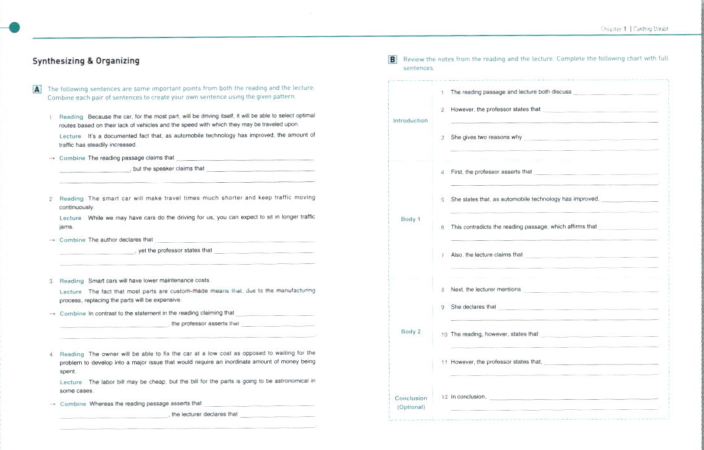

❹ Writing & Checking

In this part, you will read the academic passage and listen to the lecture once again and will be asked to write a completely new response on your own. You can evaluate your response with the given checklist.

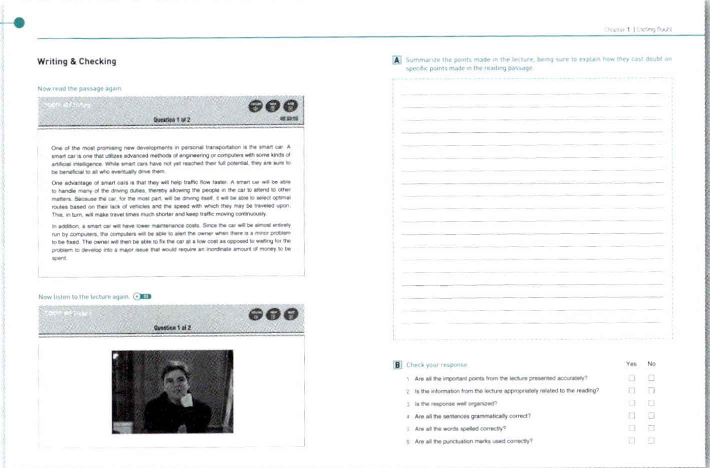

❺ Understanding the Topic | Brainstorming

These sections help you understand the essay topic and brainstorm your ideas about the topic. In the Understanding the Topic section, you will learn what kinds of questions you should ask to understand the topic appropriately. In the Brainstorming section, you can practice brainstorming your ideas in a structured way by using a mind map.

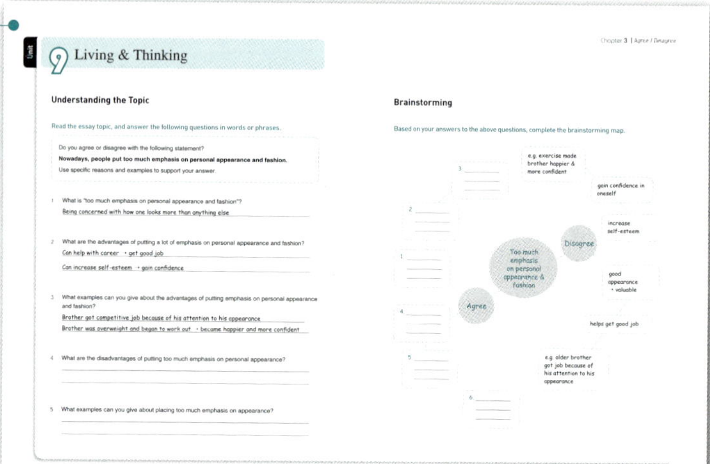

❻ Outlining | Writing the Thesis Statement & Topic Sentences

These sections help you practice making an outline of your ideas and translating them into sentences. In the Outlining section, you will practice organizing your brainstormed ideas into a logical sequence. In the Writing the Thesis Statement & Topic Sentences section, you will practice writing the most important sentences in an essay—the thesis statement, topic sentences, and the summary sentence(s).

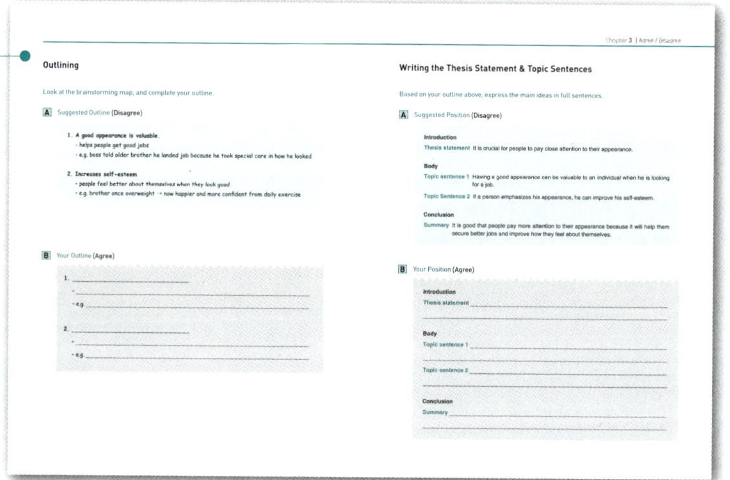

❼ Writing the Details

This section will ask you to complete your essay based on your outline. You should support your thesis statement and topic sentences with details, such as general statements, reasons, and examples.

❽ Completing & Checking Your Essay

This part offers a new essay topic on which you should write an essay. You have to plan your time to write the essay in 30 minutes. You can evaluate your essay with the given checklist.

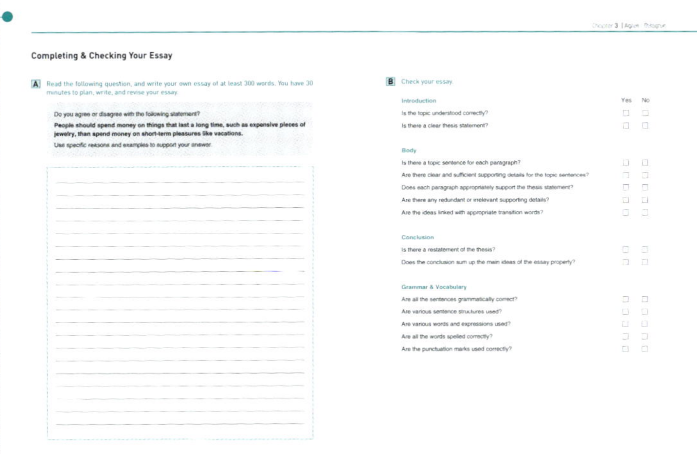

❾ Essential Essay Topics

This part provides you with a list of essential essay topics reconstructed from the ones that have so far been asked on the TOEFL® iBT. By practicing writing your essays on these topics, you will effectively prepare yourself for the Independent Writing of the TOEFL® iBT.

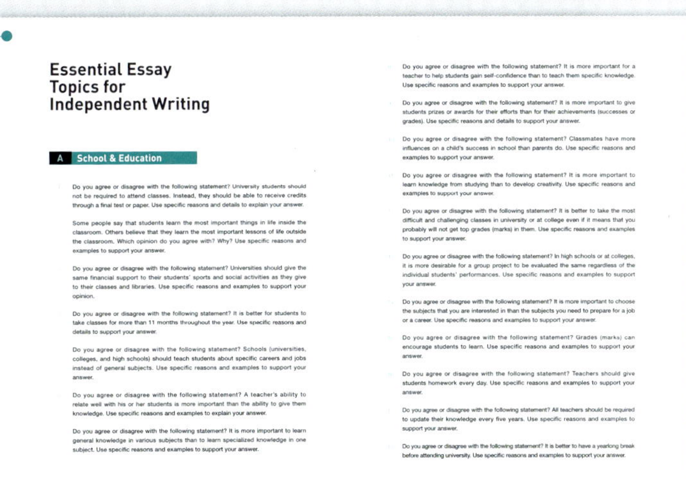

❿ Actual Tests

This part offers two full practice tests that are modeled on the Writing section of the TOEFL® iBT. These tests will familiarize you with the actual test format of the TOEFL® iBT.

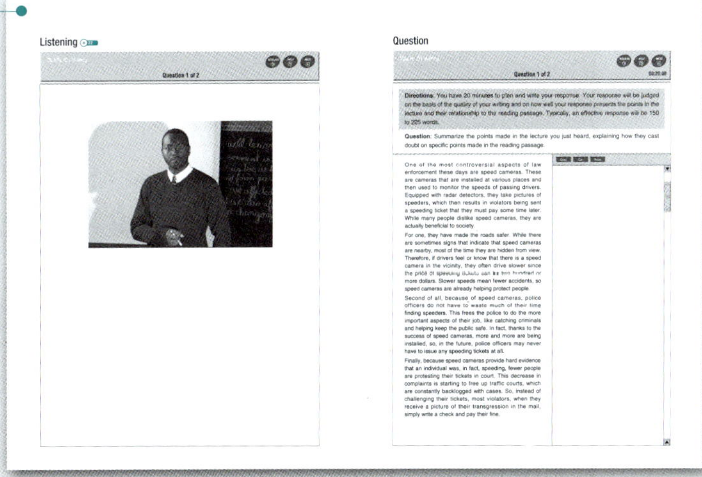

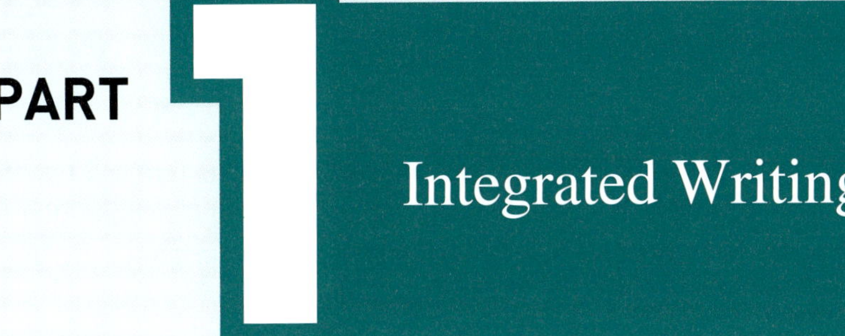

PART
1
Integrated Writing

Overview

■ Introduction

The Integrated Writing Task on the TOEFL® iBT has two parts. The first part is a reading passage, and the second part is a listening lecture that is related to the reading passage. After reading and listening, you must then answer a question related to the passage and lecture.

Reading

The reading passage, which covers an academic topic, is typically 230-300 words long, and the reading time is 3 minutes. There is typically an introduction paragraph to begin the passage. Then the reading passage provides some main points in the body. There may or may not be a short conclusion.

Listening

The listening lecture is typically 230-300 words long and takes about 2 minutes. The lecture begins with a short introduction and then follows by providing counterpoints that relate to the topic. These points typically cast doubt upon or challenge the arguments that were made in the reading passage. Sometimes, they may provide solutions to the problems posed in the reading.

Writing

The ideal response provides information on all the points and counterpoints that are given in the reading and the lecture. The summary should be about 150-225 words long although it may be longer. You should not give your opinion in the summary.

■ Question Types

1. Casting Doubt

- Summarize the points made in the lecture, being sure to explain how they cast doubt on specific points made in the reading passage.

- Summarize the points made in the lecture, being sure to explain how they challenge specific claims/arguments made in the reading passage.

  cf. This question type accounts for almost all of the questions that have been asked on the TOEFL® iBT so far.

2. Problem-Solution

- Summarize the points made in the lecture, being sure to specifically explain how they answer the problems raised in the reading passage.

1. Casting Doubt

You should mention all three points and counterpoints. You should relate each point and its counterpoint one at a time, providing the reasons why each counterpoint disagrees with the point in the reading passage.

2. Problem-Solution

You should note the individual solutions that the lecture provides for each problem. The professor will mention why each solution will work. You should be sure to include the reasons for these solutions in your response.

■ Key Strategies

1. Note Taking & Outlining

_ Take notes on each point in the reading passage and listening lecture.
_ Focus on the main ideas, not the minor ones.
_ Create an outline to show how each point and counterpoint relate to one another.

2. Paraphrasing & Summarizing

_ Do not repeat the words of the reading passage exactly as they are written.
_ Paraphrase the sentences from the reading passage and listening lecture.
_ Summarize the reading passage and listening lecture in your own words.

3. Synthesizing & Organizing

_ Recognize how the points and counterpoints are related to one another.
_ Be sure to mention all three of the points and counterpoints in your response.
_ Organize your response by including an introduction and, when appropriate, a short conclusion.

4. Writing & Checking

_ Write your response from the notes and outline that you wrote.
_ Be sure to include an introduction, body, and conclusion. However, the conclusion is optional.
_ Check over your writing to make sure that you did not make any mistakes.

Sample iBT Question

Directions Now you will see the reading passage for 3 minutes. Remember that it will be available to you again while you are writing. Immediately after the reading time ends, the lecture will begin, so keep your headset on until the lecture has ended.

Reading

<table><tr><td>TOEFL iBT Writing</td><td>VOLUME　HELP　NEXT</td></tr><tr><td>Question 1 of 2</td><td>00:03:00</td></tr></table>

One of the most controversial topics in education these days is the way to pay teachers their salaries. Many people favor determining teachers' salaries based on merit. In other words, teachers will be paid according to how well they teach and how well their students do in the classroom. This is an idea that should be implemented for a number of reasons.

First, this is a very fair way of paying teachers. Nowadays, teachers are paid primarily based upon seniority. The longer the person has been teaching, the more money the teacher receives. However, this is not fair. Now, the best teachers can receive the higher salaries they deserve even if they have not been teaching for very long. Also, ineffective teachers will receive lower salaries even if they have been employed for ten or twenty years.

Second of all, paying teachers on a merit basis will encourage most of them to perform better. They will actually begin to compete with one another, which will improve the quality of the education they provide for their students. They will all improve when competing against one another. Likewise, they will begin to develop better teaching methods in an effort to perform better in the classroom.

Finally, if the teachers are trying and working harder, then the students themselves will benefit greatly. The fact that the teachers are providing better lessons means that students will learn much better. Also, the students themselves will likely be inspired to study harder when they see just how hard their teachers are working.

It is obvious that a merit-pay-based system will have several benefits both for teachers and students. All school systems should consider implementing this method as soon as possible.

Listening

Script

Male Professor: I know that paying teachers based upon some sort of merit system sounds great. However, it actually has a number of disadvantages. You might not have considered them, so let me fill you in.

To begin with, who is going to determine the merit of each teacher? The principal, most likely. While most principals will do this in an honest fashion, some may not. First, the principal might use the merit-based policy to control many of the teachers. The teachers may have to follow the principal's rules or find their salaries getting cut. Also, the principal may show favoritism towards various teachers and ignore good teachers instead to give pay raises to his friends. We can't allow that to happen.

Here's another point. Okay, yes, teachers will most likely try harder and develop new teaching methods and strategies. But they probably won't share any effective strategies with their colleagues. After all, they'll want to earn more money than them. This isn't what education should be about. Education is about sharing knowledge, not hoarding it. And you're also likely to see less cooperation among teachers. All of this new competition is bound to create rivalries between faculty members.

Finally, this plan might have a negative effect on the students themselves. Since part of the merit-pay system will be determined by grades, teachers will be likely not to give failing or low grades to bad students. We'll probably see countless instances of grade inflation. Also, some teachers will probably pass students who should be kept back a grade. This will be doing the student a disservice and shouldn't happen.

As you can see, a merit-pay system would have a number of disadvantages. School systems should think hard before they implement them.

Question Summarize the points made in the lecture you just heard, explaining how they cast doubt on the points made in the reading.

<table>
<tr><td>TOEFL iBT Writing</td><td>  </td></tr>
<tr><td colspan="2" align="center">Question 1 of 2</td></tr>
</table>

00:20:00

Sample Answer

[Introductory sentence] The reading passage supports the idea of paying teachers according to how well they perform. [Topic sentence] However, the professor provides several reasons why merit pay is a bad idea.

[Refutation 1] First of all, the professor claims that the principal will probably determine the merit of each teacher. He claims that some principals may be biased when they determine who the best and worst teachers are. He asserts that bad principals may force teachers to follow their rules or suffer bad evaluations. [Relation 1] Since the best teachers will get high salaries while the worst get low ones, he fears some principals may show favoritism to certain teachers when determining salaries.

[Relation 2] Second, the professor acknowledges that teachers may try harder and develop better teaching methods. [Refutation 2] However, he doubts they will share their good methods with others. He says all the teachers will be competing against each other. He also believes there will be rivalries between teachers, so the overall quality of teaching might not rise.

[Refutation 3] Finally, the professor thinks that teachers might not fail bad students. Also, he thinks teachers will harm the students by passing them when they should be failing them. Therefore, many students will not see positive benefits from the merit-pay system. [Relation 3] This point disproves the reading passage's contention that students will try harder when they see their teachers working hard.

Chapter 1

Casting Doubt

1 Technology

Note Taking & Outlining

A Read the following passage, and complete the note diagram.

One of the most promising new developments in personal transportation is the smart car. A smart car is one that utilizes advanced methods of engineering or computers with some kinds of artificial intelligence. While smart cars have not yet reached their full potential, they are sure to be beneficial to all who eventually drive them.

One advantage of smart cars is that they will help traffic flow faster. A smart car will be able to handle many of the driving duties, thereby allowing the people in the car to attend to other matters. Because the car, for the most part, will be driving itself, it will be able to select optimal routes based on their lack of vehicles and the speed with which they may be traveled upon. This, in turn, will make travel times much shorter and keep traffic moving continuously.

In addition, a smart car will have lower maintenance costs. Since the car will be almost entirely run by computers, the computers will be able to alert the owner when there is a minor problem to be fixed. The owner will then be able to fix the car at a low cost as opposed to waiting for the problem to develop into a major issue that would require an inordinate amount of money to be spent.

utilize (v) to use; to make use of

artificial (a) not real; fake

potential (n) possibility

flow (v) to move; to pass by

attend to (phr) to take care of

optimal (a) best; most favorable

maintenance (n) repair; preservation

alert (v) to warn; to tell *someone* about *something*

inordinate (a) greater than normal; excessive

Smart Cars - Promising New Developments

1. **Will help** (1)_______________________
   - handle many of the driving duties → drivers can attend to other matters
   - can choose (2)_______________________ → much shorter travel times & continuously moving traffic

2. **Have lower** (3)_______________________
   - computers will alert owner when is (4)_______________________
   - can fix problem before it becomes major issue

B Listen to a lecture on the topic you just read about, and complete the note diagram. 🔊 02

thrilled (a) very excited

breathtaking (a) astonishing; wonderful; amazing

anticipate (v) to expect

zip (v) to move very quickly

unfortunately (ad) sadly

documented (a) recognized; known

steadily (ad) at a regular pace

custom-made (a) specially built or made

labor (v) work

astronomical (a) incredibly high; huge; very much

Smart Cars - Not as Breathtaking as People Anticipate

1. Will not ease traffic
- automobile technology improves → (1)_________________________ ↑
- people will have to sit in (2)_____________________________

2. Will not be cheap to maintain
- use of very expensive, (3)_______________________________
- replacing parts → (4)_____________________________________

C Rewrite the main points from both notes as complete sentences.

Smart Cars		
Reading (Main Points)		Listening (Refutations)
Smart cars will be able to select (1)_________ _________ and avoid highly traveled roads, which will decrease (2)_______________ for people.	1	Historically speaking, traffic always (5)_______________ with each technological development, therefore smart cars will still get stuck in (6)_______________.
Because computers will warn the owners of (3)_______________, they can fix the problems while they are (4)_______________, which will not require a large amount of money.	2	Since many of the parts are (7)_______________ _______, they have to be manufactured specially, so the cost of replacing them will be (8)_______________ than normal.

Paraphrasing & Summarizing

A-1 The following pairs of sentences are based on the reading. Complete each paraphrase by filling in the blanks with appropriate words or phrases.

1   A smart car is one that utilizes advanced methods of engineering or computers with some kinds of artificial intelligence.

→ **Paraphrase** Smart cars operate by ____

____ that can think for themselves to some extent.

2   A smart car will be able to handle many of the driving duties, thereby allowing the people in the car to attend to other matters.

→ **Paraphrase** By doing ____, a smart car will enable

____.

3   Because the smart car will be driving itself, it will be able to select optimal routes based on their lack of vehicles and the speed with which they may be traveled upon.

→ **Paraphrase** The car will decide ________________________ by looking at how many cars are

on various roads and ____.

4   Since a smart car will be almost entirely run by computers, the computers will be able to alert the owner when there is a minor problem to be fixed.

→ **Paraphrase** The computers in a smart car will ____

____, no matter how small it may be.

5   The owner will be able to fix the car at a low cost as opposed to waiting for the problem to develop into a major issue that would require an inordinate amount of money to be spent.

→ **Paraphrase** Because the owner can ________________________, he will not have to

suffer a major problem and therefore ____.

A-2 Complete the following summary.

Smart cars are not completely developed yet, but they are going to be very important in the future. They will help drivers (1)________________________ much faster. They will do this by taking over the driving. This will allow the passengers and driver to do other things, and it will also ensure that the car takes (2)________________________ by avoiding traffic. In addition, owners will not have to (3)________________________. The car's computers will monitor all possible problems, thereby enabling the owner (4)________________________ before they develop into something major. This will then save the owner a lot of money on (5)________________________.

B-1 The following pairs of sentences are based on the lecture. Complete each paraphrase by filling in the blanks with appropriate words or phrases.

1   It would be nice to have smart cars do all the driving for us, but they probably won't be as breathtaking as everyone anticipates.

→   **Paraphrase** Even though people would love to _______________________________,
smart cars will probably not _______________________________.

2   It's a documented fact that, as automobile technology has improved, the amount of traffic has steadily increased.

→   **Paraphrase** It is well known that _______________________________
_______________________________.

3   Just because they're smart cars doesn't mean that they'll be smart enough to get you out of a traffic jam.

→   **Paraphrase** The artificial intelligence in smart cars will not be sufficient enough _______________
_______________________________.

4   Most of the parts of a smart car will be custom-made, so, due to the manufacturing process, replacing the parts will be expensive.

→   **Paraphrase** It is going to be expensive to _______________________________
because of the way that _______________________________.

5   The labor bill may be cheap, but the bill for the parts is going to be astronomical in some cases.

→   **Paraphrase** Even though _______________________________ for his actual work,
it will still be extremely expensive to _______________________________.

B-2 Complete the following summary.

While most people are expecting great things from smart cars, they will probably not be quite as wonderful as people think they will be. Even though vehicular technology is constantly improving, traffic actually (1)_______________________ with every improvement. There will probably be more, not fewer, (2)_______________________. So, while the cars will be driving themselves, making it easier on the owners, the trips will actually (3)_______________________. Also, when the cars need to be maintained with (4)_______________________, the owners will have to pay a lot of money. Since smart cars are custom-made, the parts are going to be expensive to replace, thereby requiring their owners to (5)_______________________.

Synthesizing & Organizing

A The following sentences are some important points from both the reading and the lecture.
Combine each pair of sentences to create your own sentence using the given pattern.

1   **Reading** Because the car, for the most part, will be driving itself, it will be able to select optimal routes based on their lack of vehicles and the speed with which they may be traveled upon.

   Lecture It's a documented fact that, as automobile technology has improved, the amount of traffic has steadily increased.

→ **Combine** The reading passage claims that ____

___________________________ , but the speaker claims that ___________________________

____ .

2   **Reading** The smart car will make travel times much shorter and keep traffic moving continuously.

   Lecture While we may have cars do the driving for us, you can expect to sit in longer traffic jams.

→ **Combine** The author declares that ____

___________________________ , yet the professor states that __________________________

____ .

3   **Reading** Smart cars will have lower maintenance costs.

   Lecture The fact that most parts are custom-made means that, due to the manufacturing process, replacing the parts will be expensive.

→ **Combine** In contrast to the statement in the reading claiming that _______________________

______________________________________ , the professor asserts that __________________

____ .

4   **Reading** The owner will be able to fix the car at a low cost as opposed to waiting for the problem to develop into a major issue that would require an inordinate amount of money being spent.

   Lecture The labor bill may be cheap, but the bill for the parts is going to be astronomical in some cases.

→ **Combine** Whereas the reading passage asserts that ___________________________________

____ , the lecturer declares that ________________

____ .

B Review the notes from the reading and the lecture. Complete the following chart with full sentences.

Introduction	1 The reading passage and lecture both discuss ________________________. 2 However, the professor states that ________________________ ________________________. 3 She gives two reasons why ________________________ ________________________.
Body 1	4 First, the professor asserts that ________________________ ________________________. 5 She states that, as automobile technology has improved, ________________________ ________________________. 6 This contradicts the reading passage, which affirms that ________________________ ________________________. 7 Also, the lecture claims that ________________________ ________________________.
Body 2	8 Next, the lecturer mentions ________________________. 9 She declares that ________________________ ________________________. 10 The reading, however, states that ________________________ ________________________. 11 However, the professor states that, ________________________ ________________________.
Conclusion (Optional)	12 In conclusion, ________________________ ________________________.

Writing & Checking

One of the most promising new developments in personal transportation is the smart car. A smart car is one that utilizes advanced methods of engineering or computers with some kinds of artificial intelligence. While smart cars have not yet reached their full potential, they are sure to be beneficial to all who eventually drive them.

One advantage of smart cars is that they will help traffic flow faster. A smart car will be able to handle many of the driving duties, thereby allowing the people in the car to attend to other matters. Because the car, for the most part, will be driving itself, it will be able to select optimal routes based on their lack of vehicles and the speed with which they may be traveled upon. This, in turn, will make travel times much shorter and keep traffic moving continuously.

In addition, a smart car will have lower maintenance costs. Since the car will be almost entirely run by computers, the computers will be able to alert the owner when there is a minor problem to be fixed. The owner will then be able to fix the car at a low cost as opposed to waiting for the problem to develop into a major issue that would require an inordinate amount of money to be spent.

Now listen to the lecture again. 03

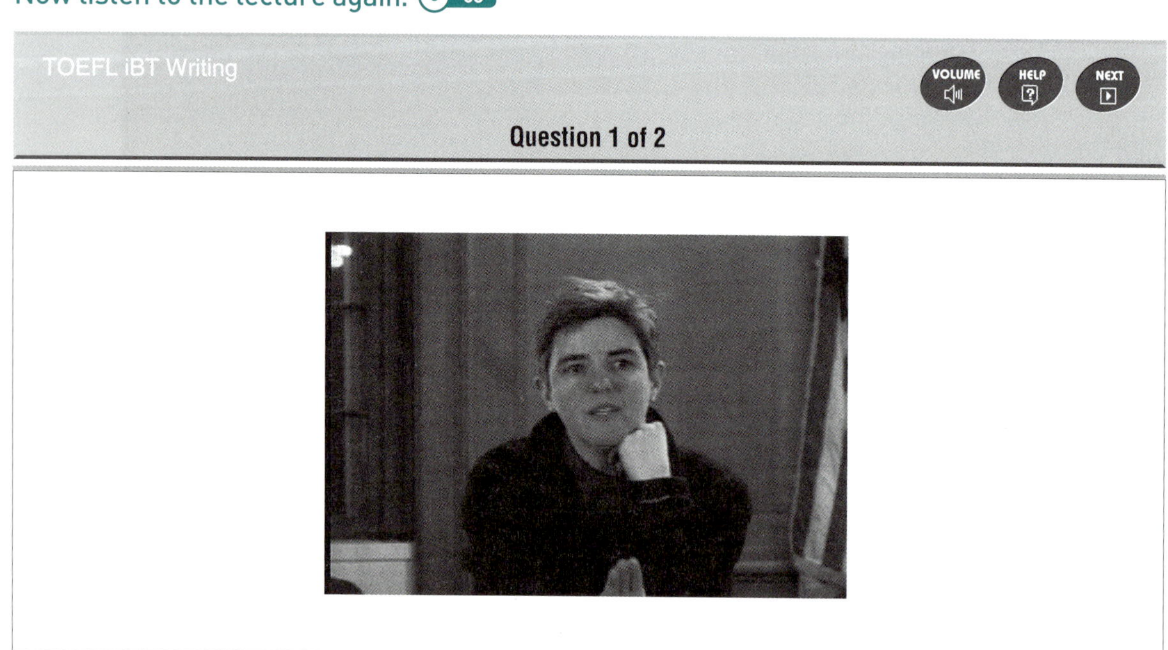

A Summarize the points made in the lecture, being sure to explain how they cast doubt on specific points made in the reading passage.

B Check your response.

		Yes	No
1	Are all the important points from the lecture presented accurately?	☐	☐
2	Is the information from the lecture appropriately related to the reading?	☐	☐
3	Is the response well organized?	☐	☐
4	Are all the sentences grammatically correct?	☐	☐
5	Are all the words spelled correctly?	☐	☐
6	Are all the punctuation marks used correctly?	☐	☐

 # Environment I

Note Taking & Outlining

A   Read the following passage, and complete the note diagram.

Many environmentalists are wary of allowing the introduction of new species into an ecosystem. Ecosystems are fragile, and invasive species can often cause many problems when they are introduced where they do not belong. In fact, when they invade a new ecosystem, they often have several harmful effects.

For one, the introduction of new species can ruin the local ecosystem in many ways. First, it can act as a predator and eat other local species, thereby causing their extinction. Another way is that it can consume too much of a valuable local food source. This consumption can cause other animals not to be able to eat as much as they are accustomed to. The result may be a decrease in the number of native species.

Another way that nonnative species can be harmful is by causing the people who live in that area to suffer from financial losses. An example of this is the mesquite tree in the American Southwest. It thrives in areas with little water. However, because it soaks up the water from the ground, nearby grasses do not get enough and die. This causes local ranchers to lose money since they have to pay extra for animal feed. Also, the mesquite tree regenerates easily, so farmers must pay large amounts of money to remove the trees from their land.

wary of (phr) cautious about; suspicious of

fragile (a) easily destroyed or broken

invasive (a) moving into a place where one does not belong

ruin (v) to destroy

predator (n) an animal that kills and eats other animals

consume (v) to eat; to take in

be accustomed to (phr) to be used to

thrive (v) to prosper

regenerate (v) to grow back; to renew

Invasive Species - Harmful to the Environment

1. **Ruin the local ecosystem**
   - can be a predator and (1)________________________ → make them become extinct
   - can consume too many natural resources → native species do not have (2)________________

2. **Cause local individuals to suffer financial losses → e.g. mesquite trees**
   - (3)________________________ from the ground → grasses die from a lack of water
   - (4)________________________ → farmers must pay a lot of money to remove the trees

B Listen to a lecture on the topic you just read about, and complete the note diagram. 🔘 **04**

detrimental (a) harmful

beneficial (a) helpful; useful

celebrated for (phr) famous for

extinction (n) dying out; annihilation; extermination

wildlife (n) animals

excessive (a) too much

graze (v) to eat grass in a field

harmless (a) not harmful or dangerous; innocuous

devour (v) to eat completely

pesticide (n) poison that kills insects

Invasive Species - Not Always Harmful

1. Do not harm their new ecosystems

- (1) _________________ in Kansas → has not caused any species to go extinct
- (2) _________________ in Texas → have not killed any native species

2. Can be beneficial → e.g. (3) _________________

- devours many insects → keeps the bug population down
- farmers do not need (4) _________________ → poisons will not hurt humans

C Rewrite the main points from both notes as complete sentences.

Invasive Species		
Reading (Main Points)		Listening (Refutations)
Invasive species can (1) _________________ by killing all the native species or (2) _________________ .	1	Many invasive species, like (5) _________________ _________________ , do not have any negative effects on their new ecosystems because they do not (6) _________________ .
Some nonnative species like (3) _________________ can cause (4) _________________ because of its killing of local plant life or the cost of paying for its removal.	2	Some invasive species, like (7) _________________ _____ , which kills bugs and keeps farmers from (8) _________________ that can be harmful to humans, can actually be helpful to people.

Paraphrasing & Summarizing

A-1 The following pairs of sentences are based on the reading. Complete each paraphrase by filling in the blanks with appropriate words or phrases.

1   Ecosystems are fragile, and invasive species can often cause many problems when they are introduced where they do not belong.

→ **Paraphrase** When ________________________________ go to a new place, they can often cause many problems because ________________________________.

2   An invasive species can act as a predator and eat other local species, thereby causing their extinction.

→ **Paraphrase** Some nonnative species ________________________________, occasionally to the point of ________________________________.

3   The fact that invasive species eat all of the food can cause other animals not to be able to eat as much as they are accustomed to.

→ **Paraphrase** Some native species ________________________________ because invasive species are ________________________________.

4   Another way that nonnative species can be harmful is by causing the people who live in that area to suffer from financial losses.

→ **Paraphrase** Some invasive species are detrimental because ________________________________ ________________________________.

5   The mesquite tree regenerates easily, so farmers must pay large amounts of money to remove the trees from their land.

→ **Paraphrase** It is expensive ________________________________ from a plot of land since they ________________________________.

A-2 Complete the following summary.

Because ecosystems can (1)________________________, most environmentalists do not want animal or plant species introduced to a new area. For example, invasive species might act as (2)________________________ and kill all of a local species. Or they might simply eat (3)________________________, which will cause these animals to starve to death. Other invasive species cause (4)________________________. An example of this is the mesquite tree. This tree kills all the local grass, so farmers need to purchase more food for their animals. The trees are also hard to (5)________________________, so farmers have to spend a lot of money paying for their removal.

B-1 The following pairs of sentences are based on the lecture. Complete each paraphrase by filling in the blanks with appropriate words or phrases.

1   Although we've discussed a lot of harmful invasive species, please remember that they are not always detrimental to the local ecosystem.

→ **Paraphrase** While many invasive species ____ , this is not always the case.

2   Everyone knows that Kansas is famous for wheat and Texas is celebrated for cows.

→ **Paraphrase** It is well known that ____

____ .

3   Cows are not predators, so no animals have been killed by them while they graze.

→ **Paraphrase** Cows are harmless creatures that __________________________________

____ .

4   A perfect case of a beneficial invasive species is that of the cane toad, which was introduced for farmers down in Florida, among other places.

→ **Paraphrase** The cane toad in Florida, one of the places the animal was introduced, ___________

____ .

5   Since the toads eat so many insects, farmers don't have to use any pesticides that could be dangerous to humans.

→ **Paraphrase** Because cane toads ____ , there is no need to ____ .

B-2 Complete the following summary.

Many people believe that all invasive species harm their new environments, but that is not necessarily true. Some nonnative plants and animals do not (1)__________________________ . Two examples of this are (2)__________________________ . The wheat has never killed another local species. Likewise, the cows simply graze in their fields and do not harm others. Also, some invasive species can actually (3)__________________________ . (4)__________________________ is one such example. It kills many insects that eat farmers' crops. Also, its presence means that farmers do not have to resort to using (5)__________________________ on their crops. In this case, the cane toad has truly improved the local environment.

Synthesizing & Organizing

A The following sentences are some important points from both the reading and the lecture. Combine each pair of sentences to create your own sentence using the given pattern.

1 **Reading** First, a nonnative species can act as a predator and eat other local species, thereby causing their extinction.

   Lecture For example, wheat has not caused the extinction of any local wildlife.

   → **Combine** The reading declares that ____ _______________________________, but the professor claims that _______________________ ____.

2 **Reading** Another way is that invasive species can consume too much of a valuable local food source.

   Lecture And cows, of course, are not predators, so no animals have been killed by them while they graze.

   → **Combine** While the author of the reading passage claims that _________________________ _______________________________________ the lecturer states that ___________________ ____.

3 **Reading** The mesquite tree's killing of local grasses causes local ranchers to lose money since they have to pay extra for animal feed.

   Lecture Cane toads devour many harmful insects, so they keep the bug population down.

   → **Combine** In opposition to the claim that ____ _______________________________, the professor asserts that _______________________ ____.

4 **Reading** Also, the mesquite tree regenerates easily, so farmers must pay large amounts of money to remove the trees from their land.

   Lecture Also, since the toads eat so many insects, farmers don't have to use any pesticides that could be dangerous to humans.

   → **Combine** Contrasting the reading's assertion that _________________________________ _______________________________, the professor believes that _______________________ ____.

B Review the notes from the reading and the lecture. Complete the following chart with full sentences.

Introduction	1 The reading passage and lecture both talk about ____________________, but they disagree as to ____________________. 2 The professor believes that ____________________ ____________________. 3 However, the reading passage believes ____________________.
Body 1	4 The lecturer first states that ____________________ ____________________. 5 He claims that ____________________. 6 The reading, however, disagrees and claims that ____________________ ____________________. 7 Also, they sometimes eat all of an area's food supply, which ____________________ ____________________.
Body 2	8 The professor also asserts that ____________________ ____________________. 9 He cites the example of ____________________. 10 He claims that ____________________ ____________________. 11 However, the reading claims that ____________________ ____________________. 12 The reading states that ____________________ ____________________. 13 It is also expensive to ____________________.
Conclusion (Optional)	14 Clearly, ____________________ ____________________.

Writing & Checking

Now read the passage again.

Many environmentalists are wary of allowing the introduction of new species into an ecosystem. Ecosystems are fragile, and invasive species can often cause many problems when they are introduced where they do not belong. In fact, when they invade a new ecosystem, they often have several harmful effects.

For one, the introduction of new species can ruin the local ecosystem in many ways. First, it can act as a predator and eat other local species, thereby causing their extinction. Another way is that it can consume too much of a valuable local food source. This consumption can cause other animals not to be able to eat as much as they are accustomed to. The result may be a decrease in the number of native species.

Another way that nonnative species can be harmful is by causing the people who live in that area to suffer from financial losses. An example of this is the mesquite tree in the American Southwest. It thrives in areas with little water. However, because it soaks up the water from the ground, nearby grasses do not get enough and die. This causes local ranchers to lose money since they have to pay extra for animal feed. Also, the mesquite tree regenerates easily, so farmers must pay large amounts of money to remove the trees from their land.

Now listen to the lecture again. 05

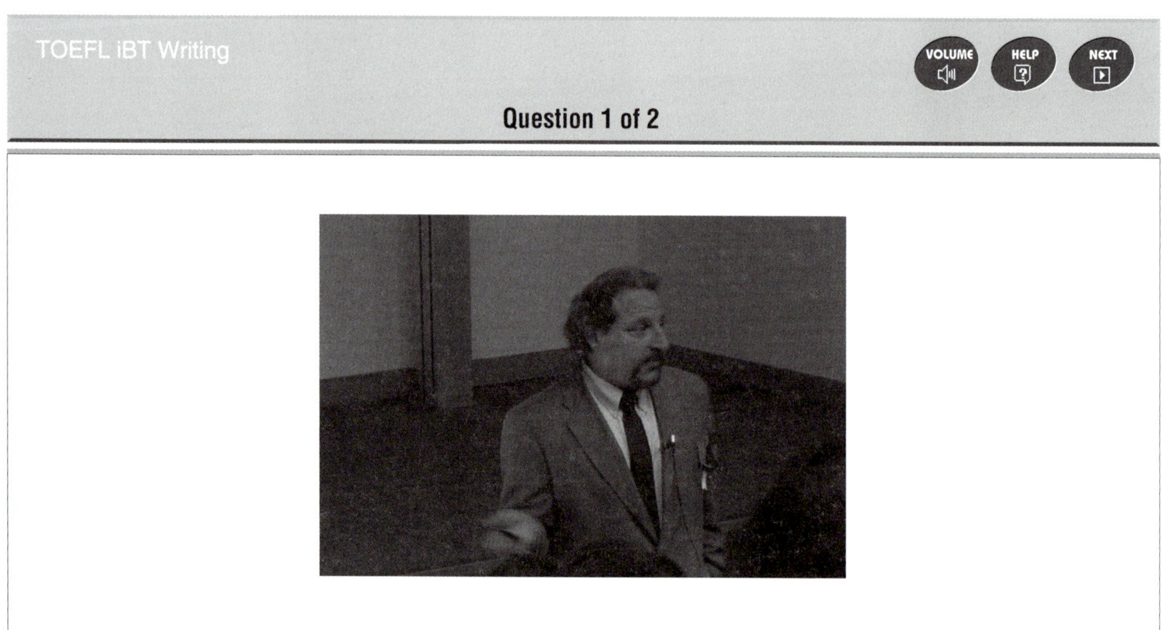

A Summarize the points made in the lecture, being sure to explain how they cast doubt on specific points made in the reading passage

B Check your response.

		Yes	No
1	Are all the important points from the lecture presented accurately?	☐	☐
2	Is the information from the lecture appropriately related to the reading?	☐	☐
3	Is the response well organized?	☐	☐
4	Are all the sentences grammatically correct?	☐	☐
5	Are all the words spelled correctly?	☐	☐
6	Are all the punctuation marks used correctly?	☐	☐

3 Sociopolitics

Note Taking & Outlining

A Read the following passage, and complete the note diagram.

A contentious issue in American politics is whether or not to raise the gasoline tax. Many people support it because they believe it will help the economy. However, their beliefs are erroneous since raising the gas tax would definitely have negative effects on the economy.

To begin with, an increase in the gas tax would disrupt the economy. Many people rely upon their cars to get to work. By raising the gas tax just a few percentage points, the government would be making people's commutes to work cost more. In many cases, they cannot afford this extra expense. In addition, if people are spending more money on gasoline, then they will spend less money purchasing other products. Since the American economy runs on consumer spending, a decrease in spending could greatly damage the economy.

Second of all, an increase in the gasoline tax would hurt those with low incomes. Naturally, it would make their gasoline more expensive, and these people simply do not have the money they would need to pay the tax. Also, since many people with low incomes live in areas with no public transportation, they might not be able to afford to go out or even make it to their workplaces. At best, they would suffer increased financial hardship.

contentious (a) controversial; causing disagreement

erroneous (a) incorrect; wrong; misleading

rely upon (phr) to depend on

commute (n) the trip from one's home to one's workplace

run on (phr) to need; to depend on

hurt (v) to harm; to damage

income (n) wages; earnings

transportation (n) ways to move from one place to another

make it (phr) to get somewhere in time

hardship (n) difficulty

Raising the Gasoline Tax - A Bad Economic Idea

1. **Would disrupt the economy**
   - could hurt (1)_________________________ → make it difficult to afford commuting to work
   - people spend less on other products → could damage (2)_________________________

2. **Would hurt people with low incomes**
   - gasoline becomes (3)_________________________ → poor people cannot afford it
   - no (4)_________________________ → people cannot get to work or go out

B Listen to a lecture on the topic you just read about, and complete the note diagram. 🔘 06

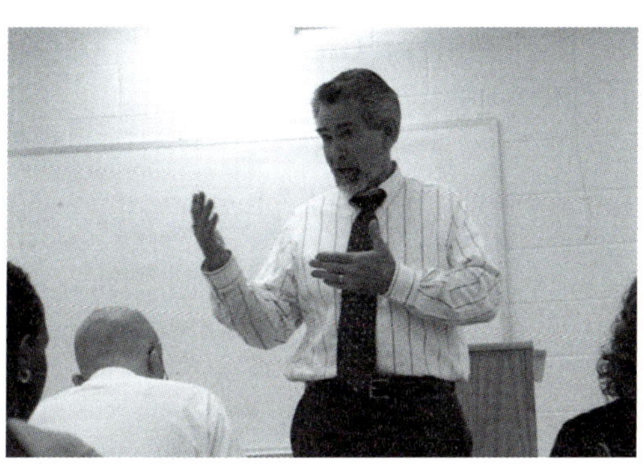

touchy (a) sensitive
refer to (phr) to speak about; to mention
disrupt (v) to interfere with
complex (a) complicated; intricate
dramatically (ad) severely; significantly; radically
tremendous (a) very large
infrastructure (n) a transportation network
affect (v) to influence
tax break (n) relief from paying higher taxes
rebate (n) a repayment; a refund

Raising the Gasoline Tax - No Harm to the Economy

1. Would not disrupt the economy
- economy is (1)______________________ → gasoline tax cannot hurt it
- other factors are damaging economy → (2)______________________ and infrastructure

2. Can help poor people
- give (3)______________________ to people with low incomes
- charge less at (4)______________________ → people with low incomes save money

C Rewrite the main points from both notes as complete sentences.

Raising the Gasoline Tax		
Reading (Main Points)		**Listening (Refutations)**
Increasing the gasoline tax would be bad for America because it would increase the prices of (1)______________ and also (2)________________, which would harm the economy.	1	A rise in the gasoline tax would not hurt the economy since (5)________________ ____________ to be affected by it and also because there are other problems like (6)________________ that are causing economic damage.
Raising the gasoline tax would harm people with low incomes since they would not be able to (3)____________ and do not have access to good (4)____________.	2	While a gasoline tax would hurt people with low incomes, the government could (7)________________ or (8)________ ____________ for gasoline at gas stations.

Paraphrasing & Summarizing

A-1 The following pairs of sentences are based on the reading. Complete each paraphrase by filling in the blanks with appropriate words or phrases.

1   Their beliefs are erroneous since raising the gas tax would definitely have negative effects on the economy.

→ **Paraphrase** People who think ____

____ are wrong.

2   By raising the gas tax just a few percentage points, the government would be making people's commutes to work cost more.

→ **Paraphrase** If ____,

it will make ____ for everyone.

3   If people are spending more money on gasoline, then they will spend less money purchasing other products.

→ **Paraphrase** ____ will cause people to

____ .

4   Raising the gasoline tax would make gasoline more expensive, and people with low incomes simply do not have the money they would need to pay the tax.

→ **Paraphrase** People who ____ would not

be able to afford gas if ____ .

5   Since many people with low incomes live in areas with no public transportation, they might not even be able to afford to go out or even make it to their workplaces.

→ **Paraphrase** Those with low salaries who ________________________________ will

not have enough money to ____ .

A-2 Complete the following summary.

Although some people believe the government should increase the gasoline tax, it would actually
(1)____. First, many people use their cars to drive to work. Raising
the gas tax would make these trips (2)________________________. And then people would
spend less money (3)________________________. The American economy needs people to buy
things, or else it will start getting bad. Also, a high gasoline tax would be bad for people who
(4)________________________. They might not even be able to afford to (5)________________________.
Since they cannot take public transportation, it would be difficult for them to get around.

B-1 The following pairs of sentences are based on the lecture. Complete each paraphrase by filling in the blanks with appropriate words or phrases.

1   I must say that I'm strongly in favor of raising the gas tax for a number of reasons.

→ **Paraphrase** In my view, there are many reasons _______________________________

____ .

2   Our economy is way too complex for just one factor to hurt the economy.

→ **Paraphrase** Due to ____ ,

one factor alone cannot ____ .

3   There are many other factors, like health care and fixing the nation's infrastructure, that are already doing tremendous economic damage.

→ **Paraphrase** Many other things, such as _______________________________________

____ , are already harming the economy.

4   The government could give tax breaks to people whose incomes are below a certain level.

→ **Paraphrase** The government could __________________________________ on people

who ____ .

5   The government could also allow people with lower incomes to pay less money when they go to fill up their cars.

→ **Paraphrase** It might be possible to _______________________________________

____ .

B-2 Complete the following summary.

The professor fully supports (1)_______________________________ for a couple of different reasons. First, he does not agree with arguments that a higher gas tax would harm the economy. Since the American economy is so (2)_______________________ , it would be impossible for an increased gas tax to damage it. Likewise, issues like (3)_______________________________ are already causing lots of damage to the economy. Second, while people with (4)_______________ _______________________ would be hurt by an increased tax, there are ways to avoid this pain. The government could give them (5)_______________________ to compensate them for the increase in taxes. Or they could simply pay less when they go to fill up their cars.

Synthesizing & Organizing

A The following sentences are some important points from both the reading and the lecture. Combine each pair of sentences to create your own sentence using the given pattern.

1 **Reading** By raising the gas tax just a few percentage points, the government would be making people's commutes to work cost more.

Lecture For one thing, our economy is way too complex for just one factor to hurt the economy.

→ **Combine** The reading passage declares that ____

____ , but the professor claims that ____________________

____ .

2 **Reading** In addition, if people are spending more money on gasoline, then they will spend less money purchasing other products.

Lecture Also, there are many other factors, like health care expenses and fixing the nation's infrastructure, that are already doing tremendous economic damage.

→ **Combine** The reading claims that ____

____ , yet the professor claims that ____________________

____ .

3 **Reading** Naturally, it would make their gasoline more expensive, and these people simply do not have the money they would need to pay the tax.

Lecture For example, the government could give tax breaks to people whose incomes are below a certain level.

→ **Combine** In response to the claim that ____

____ , the professor states that ______________________

____ .

4 **Reading** Also, since many people with low incomes live in areas with no public transportation, they might not even be able to afford to go out or even make it to their workplaces.

Lecture Or the government could also allow people with lower incomes to pay less money when they go to fill up their cars.

→ **Combine** While the reading asserts that, ____

____ , the lecturer maintains that ____________________

____ .

B Review the notes from the reading and the lecture. Complete the following chart with full sentences.

Introduction	1 The professor firmly disagrees with the reading passage, which states that _____ ____. 2 Instead, the professor feels that ________________________________ ____.
Body 1	3 To begin with, the reading passage declares that ___________________ ____. 4 The author also mentions that ___________________________________ ____. 5 Since the American economy _____________________________________ _______________________________, it would start to go into decline. 6 However, the professor believes _________________________________ ____. 7 Plus, a gas tax's effects cannot compare to ______________________ _______________________, which are already damaging the current economy.
Body 2	8 The reading also states that ___________________________________ ____. 9 The professor mentions that ___________________________________ ____. 10 He also thinks that ____ ____.
Conclusion (Optional)	11 The professor and the reading passage _________________________ ____.

Writing & Checking

Now read the passage again.

A contentious issue in American politics is whether or not to raise the gasoline tax. Many people support it because they believe it will help the economy. However, their beliefs are erroneous since raising the gas tax would definitely have negative effects on the economy.

To begin with, an increase in the gas tax would disrupt the economy. Many people rely upon their cars to get to work. By raising the gas tax just a few percentage points, the government would be making people's commutes to work cost more. In many cases, they cannot afford this extra expense. In addition, if people are spending more money on gasoline, then they will spend less money purchasing other products. Since the American economy runs on consumer spending, a decrease in spending could greatly damage the economy.

Second of all, an increase in the gasoline tax would hurt those with low incomes. Naturally, it would make their gasoline more expensive, and these people simply do not have the money they would need to pay the tax. Also, since many people with low incomes live in areas with no public transportation, they might not be able to afford to go out or even make it to their workplaces. At best, they would suffer increased financial hardship.

Now listen to the lecture again. 07

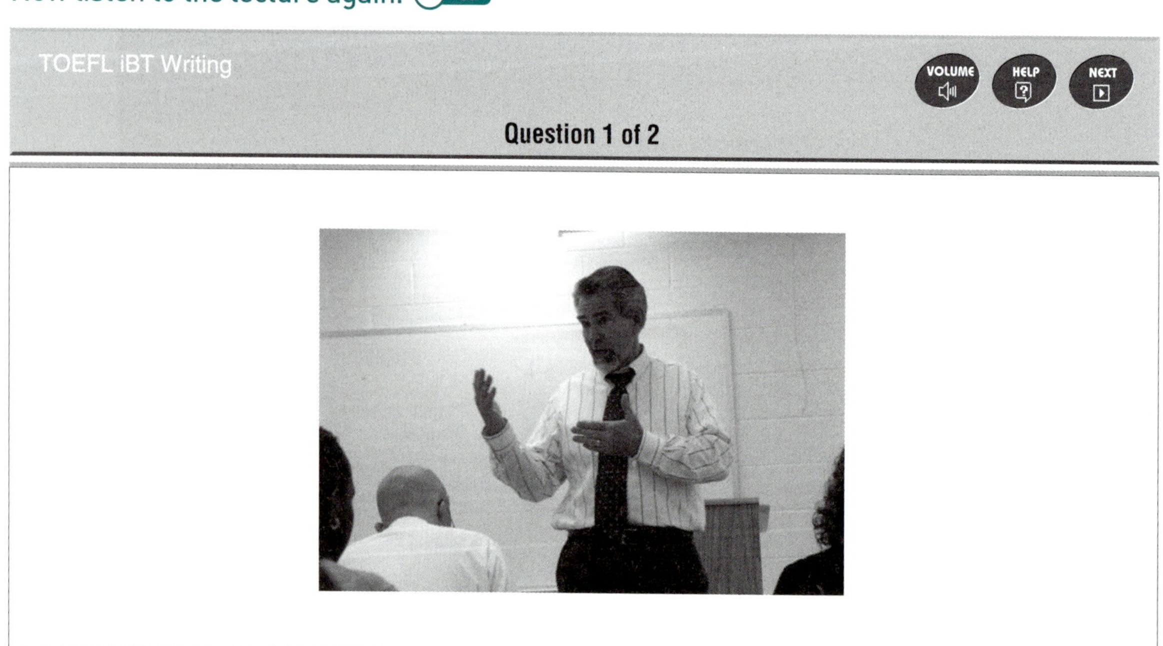

A Summarize the points made in the lecture, being sure to explain how they cast doubt on specific points made in the reading passage.

B Check your response.

		Yes	No
1	Are all the important points from the lecture presented accurately?	☐	☐
2	Is the information from the lecture appropriately related to the reading?	☐	☐
3	Is the response well organized?	☐	☐
4	Are all the sentences grammatically correct?	☐	☐
5	Are all the words spelled correctly?	☐	☐
6	Are all the punctuation marks used correctly?	☐	☐

4 Environment II

Note Taking & Outlining

A Read the following passage, and complete the note diagram.

Because of the dangers of forest fires, some park rangers have started promoting a new way to take care of forests. Their method is called prescribed burning. What they do is actually start fires in forests to burn down various kinds of trees or other plant life. Unfortunately, prescribed burning is not an effective method for a number of different reasons.

First, fires are extremely difficult to control. While park rangers insist that they take tremendous precautions, it is still possible for a prescribed burning to rage out of control. This has actually happened in some cases. Because the rangers could not control the fire, it caused much more damage than a regular forest fire would have. In fact, fire is unpredictable. Rangers may want to burn one area but instead end up burning additional places because of the unpredictability of forest fires.

In addition, prescribed burning is not cheap. It costs a large amount of money to start and control a forest fire. There are numerous people and machines involved in this process, so salaries and equipment costs must be paid. Moreover, when fires start burning uncontrollably, it costs even more money to reign them back in. All things considered, prescribed burning has many disadvantages and should not be practiced.

promote (v) to support; to endorse

prescribed (a) arranged; managed

insist (v) to claim; to state

tremendous (a) great; very large

precaution (n) a safety measure

rage (v) to burn

unpredictable (a) random; unknown

end up V-ing (phr) to wind up V-ing

numerous (a) a lot of; a large number of

reign *something* back in (phr) to get *something* back in control

Prescribed Burning - An Ineffective Alternative to Forest Fires

1. **Difficult to control**
   - can rage out of control → can burn more areas than (1)______________________
   - (2)______________________ → may start to burn other unintended places

2. **Very expensive**
   - must pay for (3)______________________
   - can cost more when fires begin (4)______________________

B Review the notes from the reading and the lecture. Complete the following chart with full sentences.

<table>
<tr><td rowspan="1">Introduction</td><td>1 The lecturer claims that _______________________ , yet the reading passage declares the opposite.

2 The professor gives several reasons to _______________________ .</td></tr>
<tr><td rowspan="1">Body 1</td><td>3 First, in contrast to the claim that _______________________ , the professor says that _______________________ .

4 He also claims that _______________________ .

5 Also, the professor states that _______________________ .

6 This is countered by the reading assertion that _______________________ .</td></tr>
<tr><td rowspan="1">Body 2</td><td>7 Second, the lecturer declares that _______________________ .

8 Meanwhile, the reading says that _______________________ .

9 The reading also states that _______________________ .

10 However, the professor mentions that _______________________ .</td></tr>
<tr><td rowspan="1">Conclusion (Optional)</td><td>11 The professor and reading clearly disagree with one another with regards to ___ _______________________ .</td></tr>
</table>

Writing & Checking

Now read the passage again.

Because of the dangers of forest fires, some park rangers have started promoting a new way to take care of forests. Their method is called prescribed burning. What they do is actually start fires in forests to burn down various kinds of trees or other plant life. Unfortunately, prescribed burning is not an effective method for a number of different reasons.

First, fires are extremely difficult to control. While park rangers insist that they take tremendous precautions, it is still possible for a prescribed burning to rage out of control. This has actually happened in some cases. Because the rangers could not control the fire, it caused much more damage than a regular forest fire would have. In fact, fire is unpredictable. Rangers may want to burn one area but instead end up burning additional places because of the unpredictability of forest fires.

In addition, prescribed burning is not cheap. It costs a large amount of money to start and control a forest fire. There are numerous people and machines involved in this process, so salaries and equipment costs must be paid. Moreover, when fires start burning uncontrollably, it costs even more money to reign them back in. All things considered, prescribed burning has many disadvantages and should not be practiced.

Now listen to the lecture again.  09

A Summarize the points made in the lecture, being sure to explain how they cast doubt on specific points made in the reading passage.

B Check your response.

	Yes	No
1 Are all the important points from the lecture presented accurately?	☐	☐
2 Is the information from the lecture appropriately related to the reading?	☐	☐
3 Is the response well organized?	☐	☐
4 Are all the sentences grammatically correct?	☐	☐
5 Are all the words spelled correctly?	☐	☐
6 Are all the punctuation marks used correctly?	☐	☐

5 Education

Note Taking & Outlining

A   Read the following passage, and complete the note diagram.

These days, many schools and research institutions find themselves relying more and more upon educational videos and DVDs. While some purists, preferring to use books, are vehemently against this trend, the reliance upon visual materials is actually a positive thing.

First of all, educational materials are useless if the audience does not pay attention to them. The twenty-first century is a visual age. Students are much more used to watching videos and DVDs than to reading books. By relying upon visual aids, educators are more likely to capture the attention of students. Also, videos and DVDs are more easily able to explain difficult processes or ideas through the use of graphics or computer animation. This quality makes difficult topics much easier to understand, a definite merit that will help students further their education.

Also, videos and DVDs are much cheaper than books. Many visual aids sell for less than ten dollars while books may cost two or three times that amount. Since many students are on tight budgets, this economic benefit will help them considerably. Additionally, many schools only have to purchase one video or DVD as opposed to buying thirty or forty or more copies of the same book. By purchasing visual materials, schools can save considerable amounts of money, which they can use to buy other important materials.

purist (n) a traditionalist; a person opposed to change

vehemently (ad) passionately; very strongly

reliance (n) dependence

visual (a) related to sight

capture the attention of (phr) to cause *someone* to pay attention

process (n) a method; a way

merit (n) an advantage

on tight budgets (phr) without much money to spend

considerably (ad) significantly; greatly

purchase (v) to buy

as opposed to (phr) instead of

Educational Visual Aids - Effective Educational Tools

1. **21ˢᵗ century = a visual age**
   - students - used to (1)________________________ → help to capture their attention
   - videos & DVDs - explain concepts with (2)________________ → easier to understand

2. **Are not expensive**
   - are much cheaper than books → good for students on (3)________________
   - schools can (4)________________ → use money on other purchases

B Listen to a lecture on the topic you just read about, and complete the note diagram. 🔊 **10**

inform (v) to tell
educate (v) to teach; to inform
limit (v) to restrict
impart (v) to provide; to convey
contain (v) to have; to include
design (v) to construct; to create
simplified (a) shortened; made easier
pricey (a) expensive
annoying (a) bothersome

Educational Visual Aids - Not as Good as People Believe

1. Provide limited information
- are incomplete because of (1)_______________________________
- are designed for entertainment → cannot explain difficult topics &
  are (2)_______________________________

2. Are not really cheaper
- (3)_______________________________ → expensive ($50-100)
- must purchase DVD player and TV → additional expenses of (4)_______________________

C Rewrite the main points from both notes as complete sentences.

Educational Visual Aids		
Reading (Main Points)		Listening (Refutations)
Educational visual aids can both (1)_________ _______________ and (2)_______________ _________ by using computer graphics or animation.	1	Visual aids often provide limited information due to (5)_______________, and they often rely upon (6)_______________ _______________.
Visual aids are (3)_______________, which can be helpful to students on tight budgets, and schools only need (4)_________ ______, so they can spend their money on other necessities.	2	Educational visual aids can be (7)_________ _______________ than books and also require expensive DVD players and TVs, equipment that can sometimes (8)_________ _______________.

Paraphrasing & Summarizing

A-1 The following pairs of sentences are based on the reading. Complete each paraphrase by filling in the blanks with appropriate words or phrases.

1 While some purists, preferring to use books, are vehemently against this trend, the reliance upon visual materials is actually a positive thing.

→ **Paraphrase** Despite the fact that ____
_______________________________________, they are actually beneficial to use.

2 By relying upon visual aids, educators are more likely to capture the attention of students.

→ **Paraphrase** Teachers can ____
if they ____.

3 Videos and DVDs are more easily able to explain difficult processes or ideas through the use of graphics or computer animation.

→ **Paraphrase** Since they use graphics and animation, visual aids can _______________
____.

4 Many visual aids sell for less than ten dollars while books may cost two or three times that amount.

→ **Paraphrase** The price of books ____
____.

5 By purchasing visual materials, schools can save considerable amounts of money, which they can use to buy other important materials.

→ **Paraphrase** Because schools will _________________________________ by purchasing visual aids, they can use the money to ____.

A-2 Complete the following summary.

The use of (1)_____________________ like DVDs and videotapes is something positive even though some people oppose them. The first reason given is that most students are used to watching videos instead of reading books. Therefore, the teachers can (2)_____________________ more easily. Also, these visual aids can make difficult concepts (3)_____________________ by using graphics and animation. Second of all, the price of visual aids is much lower than that of books. This is good for students (4)_____________________ and for schools since the schools can buy just one DVD or tape and use the leftover money for (5)_____________________.

B-1 The following pairs of sentences are based on the lecture. Complete each paraphrase by filling in the blanks with appropriate words or phrases.

1   I must inform you that books are still much better than watching visual aids.

→ **Paraphrase** It is preferable to ____

____ ______.

2   The video is likely to be incomplete and not contain all the necessary information.

→ **Paraphrase** Visual materials ____

____.

3   Visual materials are often designed more for entertainment than education.

→ **Paraphrase** Entertaining, not educating, is ______________________________________

____.

4   Tapes and disks of movies are often rather cheap, but this isn't the case for educational materials.

→ **Paraphrase** Educational visual materials are ____________________________________

____.

5   Even if you own the DVD, you still have to purchase the DVD player and television set, which aren't cheap.

→ **Paraphrase** Without ____

______________ ____, you cannot watch a DVD.

B-2 Complete the following summary.

The professor feels that (1) ________________________ is a much preferable alternative to watching visual materials like DVDs and videotapes. First, she states that visual materials often provide (2) ________________________ because they have to be so short. Books, on the other hand, hold much more information. Also, visual materials tend to simplify things since they are more interested in (3) ________________________ instead of educating them. Also, the professor says that books are actually cheaper than DVDs and videotapes. The reason is that (4) ________________________ ________________ can be much more expensive than movies. Also, a person with a DVD needs to purchase (5) ________________________, which will cost more money to keep up.

Synthesizing & Organizing

A The following sentences are some important points from both the reading and the lecture. Combine each pair of sentences to create your own sentence using the given pattern.

1 **Reading** By relying upon visual aids, educators are more likely to capture the attention of students.

   Lecture Therefore, the video is likely to be incomplete and not contain all the necessary information.

   → **Combine** The author of the reading declares that _______________________________

   _____________________________________; however, the professor counters by saying that

   ____.

2 **Reading** Also, videos and DVDs are more easily able to explain difficult processes or ideas through the use of graphics or computer animation.

   Lecture In addition, visual materials are often designed more for entertainment than education.

   → **Combine** The reading mentions that ____

   ___________________________________, yet the professor believes ___________________

   ____.

3 **Reading** Many visual aids sell for less than ten dollars while books may cost two or three times that amount.

   Lecture Educational visual aids are almost always very pricey, costing between fifty to one hundred dollars.

   → **Combine** In contrast to the reading, which states that _________________________________

   _________________________________, the professor claims that ___________________

   ____.

4 **Reading** By purchasing visual materials, schools can save considerable amounts of money, which they can use to buy other important materials.

   Lecture Also, even if you own the DVD, you still have to purchase the DVD player and television set, which aren't cheap.

   → **Combine** While the reading passage mentions that _____________________________________

   _________________________________, the professor states that ___________________

   ____.

B Review the notes from the reading and the lecture. Complete the following chart with full sentences.

<table>
<tr><td rowspan="2">Introduction</td><td>1 The lecturer declares that ____.</td></tr>
<tr><td>2 This is in direct contrast to the reading passage, which claims ____.</td></tr>
<tr><td rowspan="5">Body 1</td><td>3 First, the lecturer states that ____.</td></tr>
<tr><td>4 She says that videos are only a couple of hours long, so ____.</td></tr>
<tr><td>5 The author of the reading, meanwhile, claims that ____.</td></tr>
<tr><td>6 Also, the reading states that ____.</td></tr>
<tr><td>7 The professor, however, says that ____.</td></tr>
<tr><td rowspan="4">Body 2</td><td>8 Second of all, the lecturer declares ____. The reading, however, claims the opposite.</td></tr>
<tr><td>9 Also, the lecturer says that ____, yet the reading claims ____.</td></tr>
<tr><td>10 The reading further says that ____.</td></tr>
<tr><td>11 But the lecturer states that ____.</td></tr>
<tr><td>Conclusion
(Optional)</td><td>12 The professor and reading passage stand on opposite sides of the debate over ____.</td></tr>
</table>

Writing & Checking

<table><tr><td>TOEFL iBT Writing   VOLUME   HELP   NEXT

Question 1 of 2   00:03:00</td></tr></table>

These days, many schools and research institutions find themselves relying more and more upon educational videos and DVDs. While some purists, preferring to use books, are vehemently against this trend, the reliance upon visual materials is actually a positive thing.

First of all, educational materials are useless if the audience does not pay attention to them. The twenty-first century is a visual age. Students are much more used to watching videos and DVDs than to reading books. By relying upon visual aids, educators are more likely to capture the attention of students. Also, videos and DVDs are more easily able to explain difficult processes or ideas through the use of graphics or computer animation. This quality makes difficult topics much easier to understand, a definite merit that will help students further their education.

Also, videos and DVDs are much cheaper than books. Many visual aids sell for less than ten dollars while books may cost two or three times that amount. Since many students are on tight budgets, this economic benefit will help them considerably. Additionally, many schools only have to purchase one video or DVD as opposed to buying thirty or forty or more copies of the same book. By purchasing visual materials, schools can save considerable amounts of money, which they can use to buy other important materials.

Now listen to the lecture again. 🔘 11

<table><tr><td>TOEFL iBT Writing   VOLUME   HELP   NEXT

Question 1 of 2</td></tr></table>

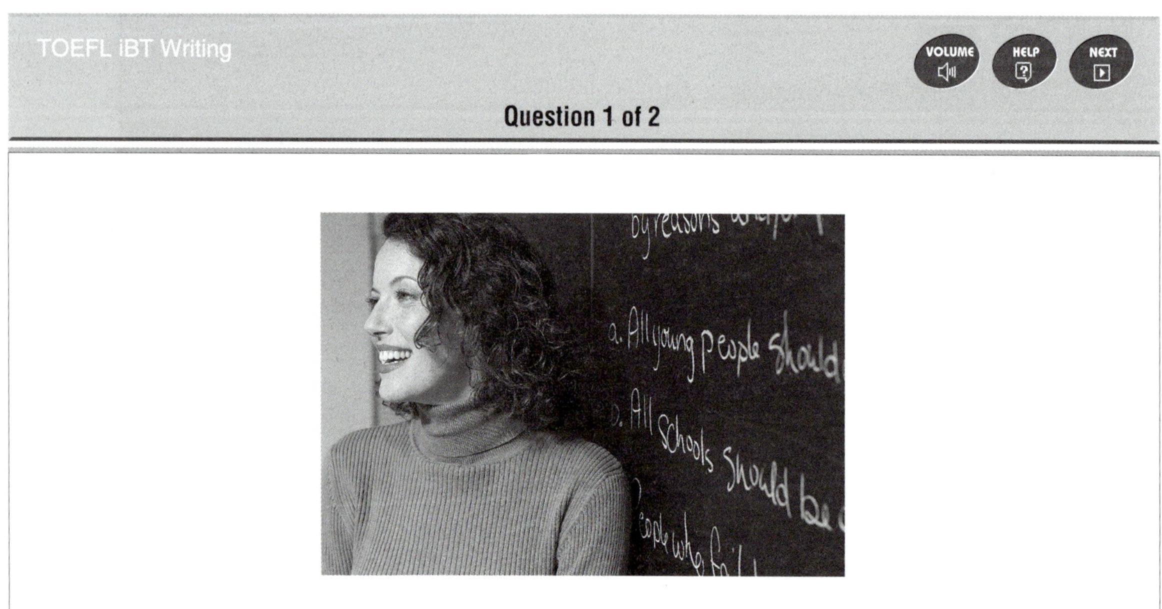

A Summarize the points made in the lecture, being sure to explain how they cast doubt on specific points made in the reading passage.

B Check your response.   Yes   No

1   Are all the important points from the lecture presented accurately?   ☐   ☐

2   Is the information from the lecture appropriately related to the reading?   ☐   ☐

3   Is the response well organized?   ☐   ☐

4   Are all the sentences grammatically correct?   ☐   ☐

5   Are all the words spelled correctly?   ☐   ☐

6   Are all the punctuation marks used correctly?   ☐   ☐

Chapter 2

Problem-Solution

Unit 6 _ Business
Unit 7 _ Education
Unit 8 _ Environment

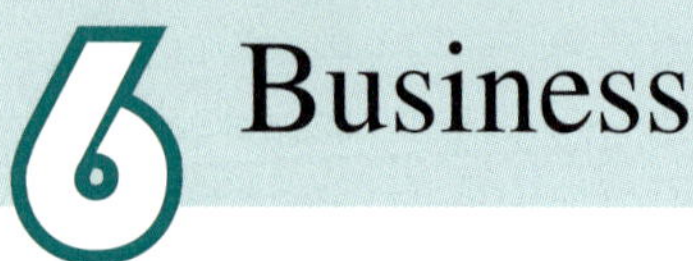

Business

Note Taking & Outlining

A Read the following passage, and complete the note diagram.

In recent years, companies have begun noticing that a large percentage of their employees are not waiting until their sixties to retire. Instead, they are opting for early retirement and are leaving the workforce while they are still in their fifties. After conducting several studies, companies have recognized a couple of reasons for this sudden spate of early retirements by their employees.

To begin with, many employees who are in their fifties have been working for the same employer and doing the same jobs for many years or even decades. What happens is that they simply become burned out from doing the same tasks over and over again. Furthermore, they discover that their daily routines are no longer challenging but have instead become incredibly boring for them.

Second of all, many older people compare themselves with their company's younger employees. When this comparison happens, the results are typically not favorable. Older employees are simply unable to maintain the same pace as younger ones; therefore, the older individuals see themselves accomplishing less work than their younger colleagues. In addition, older workers begin to feel as if they are a burden on the company and are not contributing as much as they could. This self-accusing feeling then encourages them to depart their company and take early retirement.

notice (v) to see; to observe

retire (v) to stop working, usually because of one's age

opt for (phr) to choose; to select

workforce (n) personnel; manpower

spate (n) an increase; a wave

decade (n) ten years

burned out (phr) exhausted; worn out

favorable (a) positive

maintain (v) to keep

burden (n) a weight; an onus

contributing (a) helping; assisting

Early Retirement of Employees in Their Fifties

1. Have worked for the same company for many years
- become (1)_____________________ from doing their jobs
- discover their (2)_____________________ are boring

2. Compare themselves with younger employees
- (3)_____________________ than younger ones
- feel like they are (4)_____________________

B Listen to a lecture on the topic you just read about, and complete the note diagram. 🔊 **12**

underutilize (v) to use less than one should
elderly (a) old; aging
population (n) the number of people living in a certain area
be willing to-V (phr) to want to-V
accomplish (v) to achieve
worn out (phr) extremely tired or exhausted
a range of (phr) various; a variety of
task (n) a job
consult (v) to discuss with; to talk with
draw upon (phr) to use; to utilize

Ways to Ensure Elderly Employees' Usefulness

1. Give them part-time jobs
- would not have to come in every day → won't [1]_______________________
- will have fresh minds → won't [2]_______________________

2. Utilize their experience
- provide them with [3]_______________________
- consult them more often → makes them [4]_______________________ & can draw upon their experience

C Rewrite the main points from both notes as complete sentences.

Early Retirement for Elderly Employees		
Reading (Problems)		Listening (Solutions)
Employees at the same jobs for many years become [1]_______________ and also [2]_______________ by doing the same tasks again and again.	1	It is recommended that companies hire elderly employees on [5]_______________ to keep them from becoming too [6]_______________ and to keep them interested in their work.
Older employees believe that they [3]_______________ than younger employees and therefore feel they are [4]_______________.	2	Companies need to utilize [7]_______________ by giving them various tasks and also [8]_______________ on a more regular basis.

Paraphrasing & Summarizing

A-1 The following pairs of sentences are based on the reading. Complete each paraphrase by filling in the blanks with appropriate words or phrases.

1 In recent years, companies have begun noticing that a large percentage of their employees are not waiting until their sixties to retire.

→ **Paraphrase** Nowadays, it has come to companies' attention that ______________________________

______________________________ .

2 Many employees who are in their fifties have been working for the same employer and doing the same jobs for many years or even decades.

→ **Paraphrase** ______________________________ have remained employed by their companies and made to do the same tasks for ______________________________ .

3 What happens is that older employees simply become burned out from doing the same tasks over and over again.

→ **Paraphrase** Doing the same jobs repeatedly makes older workers ______________________________

______________________________ .

4 Many older people compare themselves with their company's younger employees.

→ **Paraphrase** Elderly employees are often ______________________________

______________________________ .

5 Older employees are simply unable to maintain the same pace as younger ones; therefore, the older individuals see themselves accomplishing less work than their younger colleagues.

→ **Paraphrase** The elderly have trouble ______________________________ , which gives them the feeling that ______________________________ .

A-2 Complete the following summary.

Companies have long wondered why many of their workers began (1) ______________________________ as opposed to their sixties, and now they have a couple of reasons as to why. First, many elderly employees (2) ______________________________ after doing the same jobs day after day for very long periods of time. They simply quit because they cannot handle the boredom of their work. Second, elderly workers recognize that they are (3) ______________________________ by younger employees, which causes their opinions of their value to the company to decline. Realizing they are not (4) ______________________________ as they could be and that they are (5) ______________________________ their employers with their presence, they simply quit their jobs.

B-1 The following pairs of sentences are based on the lecture. Complete each paraphrase by filling in the blanks with appropriate words or phrases.

1 I'd like to continue talking about how society underutilizes its elderly population.

→ **Paraphrase** Let me carry on with some examples as to ________________________________ ________________________________.

2 A large number of elderly people would be willing to work part-time.

→ **Paraphrase** Lots of older people would ________________________________ ________________________________.

3 Letting the elderly work part-time would keep their minds fresh, which means that they wouldn't become bored with their work.

→ **Paraphrase** By only working part-time, ________________________________ ________________________________.

4 I know all of you young people think that you know everything, but your experiences are nothing compared to those of a fifty- or sixty-year-old person.

→ **Paraphrase** Many people in their teens and twenties ________________________________, but ________________________________ in comparison to those more than twice their age.

5 Being consulted by the company would not only make elderly workers feel wanted but would also draw upon their many years of experience working at the company.

→ **Paraphrase** The effects of being consulted would be ________________________________ and also ________________________________ that have built up by their long years or employment.

B-2 Complete the following summary.

The professor believes that it is pointless for people in their fifties to retire and not work anymore, so she provides some suggestions to get people to (1)________________________. She thinks that instead of working full-time, elderly people should be allowed to (2)________________________. This measure would keep the employees (3)________________________ to do their jobs. Also, companies should try to involve their elderly employees in more activities and ask them for (4)________________________ on various things. This effort would give elderly workers the confidence they require and, at the same time, also help their companies by having them rely upon people with (5)________________________.

Synthesizing & Organizing

A The following sentences are some important points from both the reading and the lecture. Combine each pair of sentences to create your own sentence using the given pattern.

1   **Reading**   What happens is that older employees simply become burned out from doing the same tasks over and over again.

    Lecture   However, a large number would be willing to work part-time.

→ **Combine** The author of the reading passage claims that ________________________________

________________________________ , so the professor suggests ________________________________

____ .

2   **Reading**   Furthermore, older employees discover that their daily routines are no longer challenging but have instead become incredibly boring for them.

    Lecture   Also, letting the elderly work part-time would keep their minds fresh, which means that they wouldn't become bored with their work.

→ **Combine** The problem in the reading is that ________________________________

________________________________ , so the professor suggests that ________________________________

____ .

3   **Reading**   Older employees are simply unable to maintain the same pace as younger ones; therefore, the older individuals see themselves accomplishing less work than their younger colleagues.

    Lecture   For example, companies could give elderly employees a wider range of duties instead of making them repeat tasks over and over.

→ **Combine** In the reading, the author suggests that ________________________________

________________________________ ; however, the professor suggests ________________________________

____ .

4   **Reading**   In addition, older workers begin to feel as if they are a burden on the company and are not contributing as much as they could.

    Lecture   And the companies could consult with their elderly employees more often.

→ **Combine** The author of the reading passage mentions that ________________________________

________________________________ , so the lecturer mentions that ________________________________

____ .

B Review the notes from the reading and the lecture. Complete the following chart with full sentences.

Introduction	1 The reading passage mentions a couple of reasons as to ______________________ ____ . 2 The professor provides a couple of solutions for _______________________ ____ .
Body 1	3 The first problem the reading mentions is that ______________________ ____ . 4 So the professor believes ____ ____ . 5 Also, working part-time will keep the elderly from __________________ ____ .
Body 2	6 Another problem leading to early retirement is that ________________ ____ . 7 Therefore, the professor suggests that ______________________________ ____ . 8 Additionally, companies could consult elderly employees ____________ ____ . 9 By doing so, companies could make their older employees feel as though _____ ____ .
Conclusion (Optional)	10 In conclusion, ____ ____ .

Writing & Checking

Now read the passage again.

In recent years, companies have begun noticing that a large percentage of their employees are not waiting until their sixties to retire. Instead, they are opting for early retirement and are leaving the workforce while they are still in their fifties. After conducting several studies, companies have recognized a couple of reasons for this sudden spate of early retirements by their employees.

To begin with, many employees who are in their fifties have been working for the same employer and doing the same jobs for many years or even decades. What happens is that they simply become burned out from doing the same tasks over and over again. Furthermore, they discover that their daily routines are no longer challenging but have instead become incredibly boring for them.

Second of all, many older people compare themselves with their company's younger employees. When this comparison happens, the results are typically not favorable. Older employees are simply unable to maintain the same pace as younger ones; therefore, the older individuals see themselves accomplishing less work than their younger colleagues. In addition, older workers begin to feel as if they are a burden on the company and are not contributing as much as they could. This self-accusing feeling then encourages them to depart their company and take early retirement.

Now listen to the lecture again. 13

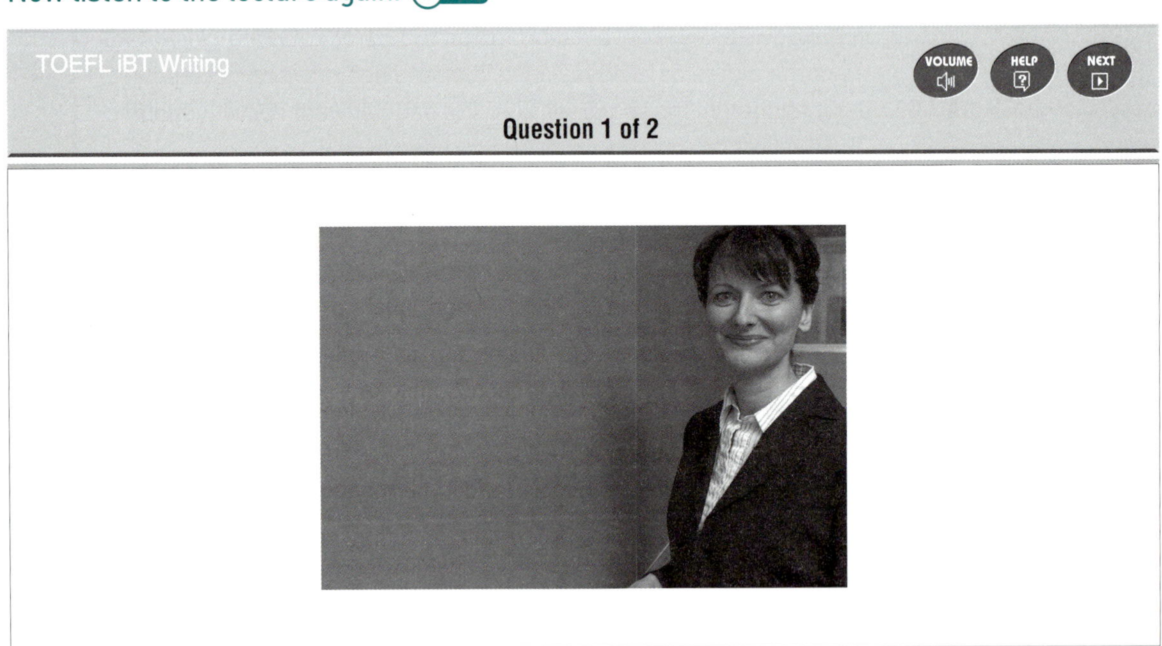

A Summarize the points made in the lecture, being sure to specifically explain how they answer the problems raised in the reading passage.

B Check your response.

		Yes	No
1	Are all the important points from the lecture presented accurately?	☐	☐
2	Is the information from the lecture appropriately related to the reading?	☐	☐
3	Is the response well organized?	☐	☐
4	Are all the sentences grammatically correct?	☐	☐
5	Are all the words spelled correctly?	☐	☐
6	Are all the punctuation marks used correctly?	☐	☐

7 Education

Note Taking & Outlining

A Read the following passage, and complete the note diagram.

Nowadays, many universities are raising their students' tuition. In some cases, the raises are quite substantial. While many students are not pleased with these increases, there are some legitimate reasons for the hikes.

First, universities are constantly striving to upgrade their educational quality. Since fewer people are attending college these days, schools must fight for all the students they can get. One ideal way to attract students is to ensure that the school provides them with an outstanding education. Also, by increasing the school's academic rank, the school will attract both more students and better ones. Since it costs money to enhance the quality of education, the school's budget must increase. Therefore, tuition must also go up.

Second, many universities are finding themselves short of cash these days. This is particularly true of state universities, which often depend upon the state for the majority of their budgets. Unfortunately, many states are cutting general funding to schools. Most particularly hard hit are the funds for the general management of the university. While not necessarily a glamorous job, it is crucial to the well-being of the school. Without sufficient general management funds, many schools would be facing serious problems, so they need to compensate for the lost funds in other ways. It is therefore obvious why schools are increasing tuition every year.

substantial (a) large; considerable

legitimate (a) reasonable; justifiable; valid

hike (n) an increase; a raise

constantly (ad) continuously

strive (v) to struggle; to attempt

ensure (v) to guarantee

outstanding (a) excellent; extremely good

enhance (v) to improve

compensate for (phr) to make up for

glamorous (a) exciting; attractive

University Tuition Increases

1. **Need to improve school to attract students**
   - must provide (1)________________________ → costs more money
   - must increase (2)________________________ → need higher budget

2. **Are often short of cash**
   - (3)________________________ getting funding cut → must make up for lost cash
   - (4)________________________ losing funds → schools facing serious problems

B   Listen to a lecture on the topic you just read about, and complete the note diagram. 🔊 14

offset (v) to counterbalance
augment (v) to increase; to improve
tie (n) a connection
corporation (n) a company; a business
benefit (v) to profit
state-of-the-art (a) modern; high-tech
faculty (n) the members of a teaching staff
the inside track (phr) an advantage
recruit (v) to employ; to hire
contribute to (phr) to assist; to help
a win-win situation (phr) an occasion where both parties do well

Universities Don't Need Money to Raise Quality

1. **Other ways to improve school**
   - professors - lecture better and develop (1)____________________________
   - students – (2)___________________________ in and out of class

2. **Ties with corporations**
   - schools get (3)_________________________ → useful to students and faculty
   - companies can (4)________________ from school body

C   Rewrite the main points from both notes as complete sentences.

University Tuition Increases		
Reading (Problems)		Listening (Solutions)
Schools need more money to improve (1)________________ and increase the school's (2)_____________ if they want to attract more and better students.	1	In order to improve the school, professors can improve (5)______________ while students can do better both in the classroom and (6)_________________.
Schools are getting (3)________________ cut as well as seeing less funding go to their general management, so they have to make up for this loss with (4)______________.	2	Schools should increase (7)____________ ___________ so that they may receive free, exceptional facilities while the corporations will be able to (8)__________ ________ who learned with those facilities.

Paraphrasing & Summarizing

A-1 The following pairs of sentences are based on the reading. Complete each paraphrase by filling in the blanks with appropriate words or phrases.

1 While many students are not pleased with tuition increases, there are some legitimate reasons for these hikes.

→ **Paraphrase** ____ even though schools have some good reasons for ____ .

2 Since fewer people are attending college these days, schools must fight for all the students they can get.

→ **Paraphrase** ____

________________________ since not as many students are going to school as there used to be.

3 By increasing the school's academic rank, the school will attract both more students and better ones.

→ **Paraphrase** Good students will be more interested in ____

____ .

4 Unfortunately, many states are cutting general funding to schools, meaning that the schools must compensate for these lost funds in other ways.

→ **Paraphrase** Because ____ ,

the schools need to ____ .

5 While not necessarily a glamorous job, the general management of the university is crucial to the well-being of the school.

→ **Paraphrase** The department that ____ ,

but, without it, the school would ____ .

A-2 Complete the following summary.

Even though students at universities are not pleased about (1)________________________________ , the schools have some good reasons for doing so. First, they have to improve themselves academically to (2)________________________ , especially since fewer students are going to college nowadays. This requires money. So does raising the school's (3)________________________________ , which will in turn attract better students to the school. Also, a lot of schools receive funding from (4)________________________________ . However, they are receiving less funding nowadays. Also, (5)________________________________ at these schools need enough money to run properly, or else the school will suffer. The schools therefore need to raise tuition to get more money.

B-1 The following pairs of sentences are based on the lecture. Complete each paraphrase by filling in the blanks with appropriate words or phrases.

1   Running a college is getting to be too expensive, but there are a few ways to offset this without raising students' fees.

→   **Paraphrase** Even though maintaining a school ______________   ______________________,
     schools can still manage ____.

2   Professors and students should be looking at ourselves to improve our school.

→   **Paraphrase** The members of the school body, including ______________________________,
     should be able to ____.

3   Students performing better would help increase our school's ranking without us spending much money or raising tuition.

→   **Paraphrase** An inexpensive way to ____
     ____.

4   The universities will get free state-of-the-art facilities, which both students and faculty will be able to use.

→   **Paraphrase** The schools will be able to ____
     which can be accessed by ____.

5   And the corporations will know the students got an excellent education because they helped contribute to it.

→   **Paraphrase** Since the companies ____,
     they will ____.

B-2 Complete the following summary.

It actually is possible for universities to increase (1)______________________________ that they offer without having to raise students' tuition. First, both the (2)____________________________ can improve themselves. The faculty can teach and prepare for classes better, and the students can improve their performance as well. These actions should increase the school's (3)______________________________ ______________________ without a need for a tuition hike. Also, schools should strike agreements with corporations. The corporations can provide the schools with (4)______________________________. The schools in turn will produce well-educated students that the companies will then be able to (5)______________________________. This will also help schools avoid raising the cost of tuition.

Synthesizing & Organizing

A The following sentences are some important points from both the reading and the lecture. Combine each pair of sentences to create your own sentence using the given pattern.

1 **Reading** One ideal way to attract students is to ensure that the school provides them with an outstanding education.

   Lecture Professors could augment the quality of their lectures as well as develop better curriculums.

→ **Combine** The reading passage mentions that ___________________________________,

   so the professor responds by claiming that ___________________________________

   ___________________________________.

2 **Reading** Also, by increasing the school's academic rank, the school will attract both more students and better ones.

   Lecture And you, the students, could perform better both at school and after graduation.

→ **Combine** The writer claims that ___________________________________

   ___________________________________, which leads the professor to declare that

   ___________________________________.

3 **Reading** Unfortunately, many states are cutting general funding to schools, meaning that the schools must compensate for these lost funds in other ways.

   Lecture We should seek close ties with corporations.

→ **Combine** In response to the reading passage author's claim that ___________________________________

   ___________________________________, the professor responds by saying that

   ___________________________________.

4 **Reading** Most particularly hard hit are the funds for the general management of the university.

   Lecture First, we'll get free state-of-the-art facilities, which both students and faculty will be able to use.

→ **Combine** The writer claims that ___________________________________

   ___________________________________, so the lecturer states that ___________________________________

   ___________________________________.

B   Review the notes from the reading and the lecture. Complete the following chart with full sentences.

Introduction	1 The lecturer states that ____ ____ . 2 He then ____ ____ as to how they can do this.
Body 1	3 First, responding to the claim that ____ , the lecturer claims that ____ . 4 He also mentions that ____ ____ . 5 With a better academic rating, the school will ____ ____ .
Body 2	6 Also, since schools are seeing ____ , the professor urges ____ . 7 He claims ____ ____ . 8 These facilities will ____ ____ . 9 The companies will also ____ ____ .
Conclusion (Optional)	10 If a school follows the professor's suggestions, ______________________________________ ____ .

Writing & Checking

Nowadays, many universities are raising their students' tuition. In some cases, the raises are quite substantial. While many students are not pleased with these increases, there are some legitimate reasons for the hikes.

First, universities are constantly striving to upgrade their educational quality. Since fewer people are attending college these days, schools must fight for all the students they can get. One ideal way to attract students is to ensure that the school provides them with an outstanding education. Also, by increasing the school's academic rank, the school will attract both more students and better ones. Since it costs money to enhance the quality of education, the school's budget must increase. Therefore, tuition must also go up.

Second, many universities are finding themselves short of cash these days. This is particularly true of state universities, which often depend upon the state for the majority of their budgets. Unfortunately, many states are cutting general funding to schools. Most particularly hard hit are the funds for the general management of the university. While not necessarily a glamorous job, it is crucial to the well-being of the school. Without sufficient general management funds, many schools would be facing serious problems, so they need to compensate for the lost funds in other ways. It is therefore obvious why schools are increasing tuition every year.

Now listen to the lecture again. 15

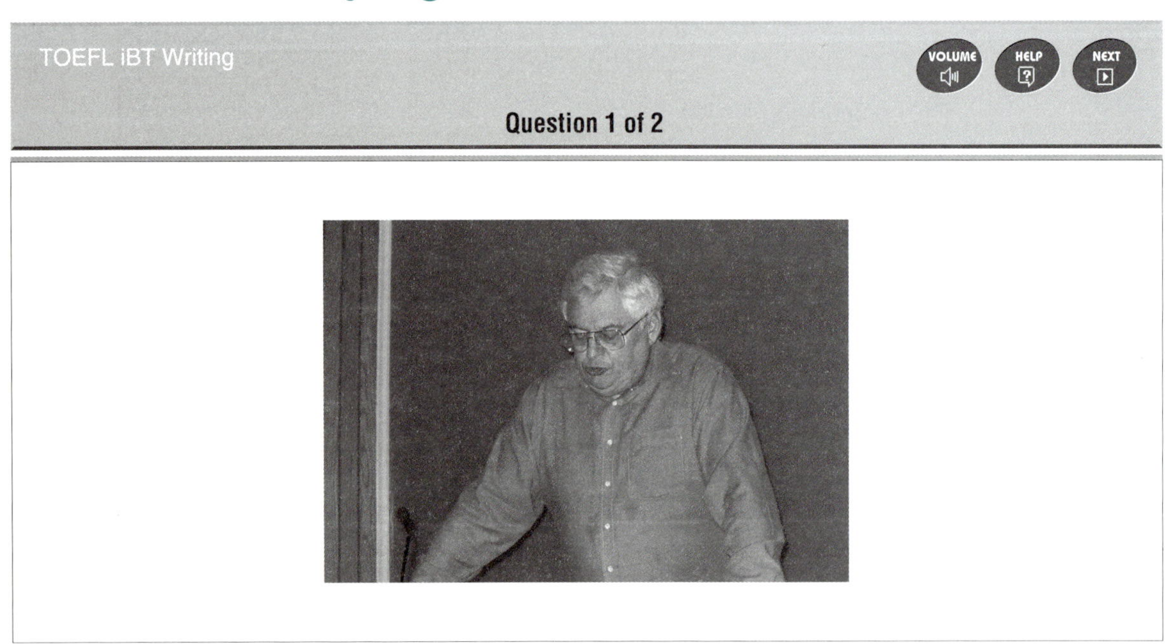

"""

A Summarize the points made in the lecture, being sure to specifically explain how they answer the problems raised in the reading passage.

B Check your response.

	Yes	No
1 Are all the important points from the lecture presented accurately?	☐	☐
2 Is the information from the lecture appropriately related to the reading?	☐	☐
3 Is the response well organized?	☐	☐
4 Are all the sentences grammatically correct?	☐	☐
5 Are all the words spelled correctly?	☐	☐
6 Are all the punctuation marks used correctly?	☐	☐

8 Environment

Note Taking & Outlining

A Read the following passage, and complete the note diagram.

Invasive species cause most of the worst problems in local ecosystems. The presence of a new species, particularly one at the top of the food chain, can destroy an ecosystem and cause numerous species to become extinct. One species that is causing numerous problems in America's waterways is the aquatic zebra mussel.

Native to Russia, the zebra mussel has recently invaded the Great Lakes and many other American lakes and rivers. The mussels attach themselves to the bottoms of boats, a convenient method that lets them travel easily. They also often attach themselves to water pipes. This action results in clogged pipes, some of which are used to bring drinking water to cities. The blocked pipes cost the cities huge amounts of money to unblock. Also, zebra mussels reproduce so rapidly that they often smother the spawning grounds of various fish and other mussels, thereby prohibiting their growth.

Additionally, zebra mussels in North America have very few natural enemies, meaning that it is difficult to eliminate them once they are established in a river or lake. Likewise, scientists have yet to discover an environmentally-safe way to kill the zebra mussels. These two facts help contribute to the extremely rapid expansion of the zebra mussel. Should this expansion not be stopped, zebra mussels will soon be causing problems in virtually all of the country's waterways.

invasive (a) aggressive; hostile

extinct (a) nonexistent; vanished

aquatic (a) of or relating to water

clog (v) to block

unblock (v) to clear out

smother (v) to suffocate; to cover entirely

spawning ground (phr) a place where a species reproduces

prohibit (v) to ban; to stop

eliminate (v) to remove; to get rid of

virtually (ad) almost; nearly

Invasive Zebra Mussels

1. **Have left Russia and invaded waterways in United States**
   - (1) _________________________ → costs lots of money to unblock
   - (2) _________________________ → smother spawning grounds of other species

2. **Are difficult to remove**
   - have few (3) _________________
   - no (4) _________________________ to kill them ⎤ → expand rapidly

B Listen to a lecture on the topic you just read about, and complete the note diagram. 🔊 16

estimate (v) to guess
mitigate (v) to ease; to lessen
procedure (n) a method; a way
implement (v) to utilize; to put into use
hitchhike (v) to ride along for free
sterilize (v) to purify; to disinfect; to sanitize
decontaminate (v) to clean; to purify
predator (n) a hunter
make an impact on (phr) to have an effect on
make a dent in (phr) to reduce

How to Get Rid of Zebra Mussels

1. Decontaminate ships better
- (1) _______________________________ with seawater → kills mussels
- check the entire ship b/c mussels can (2) _______________________________

2. Use predators to kill zebra mussels
- some (3) _______________________________ eat them → will get rid of mussels
- researchers need to increase predators' numbers
  → will start to (4) _______________________________

C Rewrite the main points from both notes as complete sentences.

Zebra Mussels		
Reading (Problems)		Listening (Solutions)
Zebra mussels have (1) _______________ _____________, where they clog water pipes and (2) _______________ of various fish and other mussels.	1	Before entering a waterway, ships' crews should (5) _______________ with saltwater, and they must (6) _______________ since mussels can survive for days out of water.
The zebra mussels have few (3) _______________ and there are no (4) _______________ _____________ to kill them, so scientists have not been able to reduce their numbers.	2	There are (7) _______________ that eat the mussels, so scientists must introduce them to the area and get their numbers to grow quickly so they can (8) _______________.

Paraphrasing & Summarizing

A-1 The following pairs of sentences are based on the reading. Complete each paraphrase by filling in the blanks with appropriate words or phrases.

1   The presence of a new species, particularly one at the top of the food chain, can destroy an ecosystem and cause numerous species to become extinct.

→ **Paraphrase** When a top predator appears in a new environment, ___________________

____.

2   Native to Russia, the zebra mussel has recently invaded the Great Lakes and many other American lakes and rivers.

→ **Paraphrase** While it comes from Russia, the zebra mussel ___________________

____.

3   Zebra mussels reproduce so rapidly that they often smother the spawning grounds of various fish and other mussels, thereby prohibiting their growth.

→ **Paraphrase** Since zebra mussels _______________________________________, they can

___________________________________, which keeps these species from growing larger in number.

4   Zebra mussels in North America have very few natural enemies, meaning that it is difficult to eliminate them once they are established in a river or lake.

→ **Paraphrase** In North America, the zebra mussel ___________________________________,

which makes it difficult to ____.

5   Should this expansion not be stopped, zebra mussels will soon be causing problems in virtually all of the country's waterways.

→ **Paraphrase** If zebra mussels continue to expand their territories, ___________________

____.

A-2 Complete the following summary.

When an invasive species moves into a new environment, it often causes problems for some native species, even causing them to (1)___________________________. This is the case for the zebra mussel. Coming from Russia, the mussel rode on boats to get to America. There, it (2)___________

___________________, which are expensive to unblock. Also, it reproduces so rapidly that it covers up (3)___________________________________ of other species, making these species reproduce more slowly. It is difficult to remove the mussels because they have few (4)___________________________ in North America. In addition, there is no (5)___________________________ to kill them. If the mussels are not killed, they will soon expand to all of America's waterways.

B-1 The following pairs of sentences are based on the lecture. Complete each paraphrase by filling in the blanks with appropriate words or phrases.

1   While the zebra mussel is causing problems, there are a couple of methods that could help mitigate the damage it's causing.

→ **Paraphrase** There are some ways to ____

____ .

2   Before a boat enters a lake or river system, the ship's ballast should be sterilized with seawater, which kills the mussels.

→ **Paraphrase** The crew needs to ____

____ .

3   Zebra mussels can survive out of water for several days, so the anchor chains and other parts out of water need to be decontaminated as well.

→ **Paraphrase** Zebra mussels do not always live in the water, so crews need to_______________

____ .

4   There are some species of birds and fish that eat zebra mussels.

→ **Paraphrase** ____

____ .

5   Researchers must discover a way quickly to increase the numbers of these species in the hope that they will start to make a dent in the number of mussels.

→ **Paraphrase** If scientists can ____

____________________________________ , these animals will be able to ____________________________ .

B-2 Complete the following summary.

While the zebra mussel has caused extremely expensive amounts of damage to (1)____________ _____________ , there are some ways to control their numbers. First, crew members on ships can do a couple of things. They can fill the ship's ballast (2)_____________________ since that will kill them. Also, they should check the entire ship for mussels because they can (3)___________________ _____________ for a few days. In addition, there are (4)_____________________ that will prey upon the zebra mussels. These should be introduced to the waterways. Finally, since there are not enough of these predators, people need to make sure they (5)_____________________ . These solutions can then reduce the number of zebra mussels.

Synthesizing & Organizing

A The following sentences are some important points from both the reading and the lecture. Combine each pair of sentences to create your own sentence using the given pattern.

1 **Reading** The mussels attach themselves to the bottoms of boats, a convenient method that lets them travel easily.

   Lecture Before a boat enters a lake or river system, the ship's ballast should be sterilized with seawater, which kills the mussels.

   → **Combine** The reading passage author writes that ________________________________

   ________________________________, so the professor responds by arguing that ____________

   ____.

2 **Reading** Also, zebra mussels reproduce so rapidly that they often smother the spawning grounds of various fish and other mussels, thereby prohibiting their growth.

   Lecture Zebra mussels can survive out of water for several days, so the anchor chains and other parts out of water need to be decontaminated as well.

   → **Combine** According to the professor, ____

   ________________________________, so that the mussels will ____________________

   ____, just like the reading passage described.

3 **Reading** Additionally, zebra mussels in North America have very few natural enemies, meaning that it is difficult to eliminate them once they are established in a river or lake.

   Lecture The natural predators of the zebra mussel should be introduced to the waterways.

   → **Combine** As a response to the reading passage claim that ____________________

   ________________________________, the professor mentions that ____________________

   ____.

4 **Reading** Likewise, scientists have yet to discover an environmentally-safe way to kill the zebra mussels.

   Lecture Researchers must discover a way quickly to increase the numbers of these natural predators in the hope that they will start to make a dent in the number of mussels.

   → **Combine** Because ____

   ________________________________, the professor declares that ____________________

   ____.

B Review the notes from the reading and the lecture. Complete the following chart with full sentences.

Introduction	1 The professor talks about different ways to __________________________ __________________________. 2 This is an invasive species from Russia that __________________________ __________________________. 3 The professor provides __________________________.
Body 1	4 First, he notes that __________________________ __________________________. 5 He mentions this because __________________________ __________________________. 6 Also, the professor notes that __________________________ __________________________. 7 This will keep the mussels from __________________________ __________________________.
Body 2	8 Second, the professor notes that __________________________ __________________________. 9 While the reading claims that __________________________ __________________________, the professor claims __________________________. 10 He also thinks __________________________ __________________________. 11 This will be beneficial because __________________________ __________________________.
Conclusion (Optional)	12 Although the zebra mussel is causing many problems, the professor seems confident that __________________________ __________________________.

Writing & Checking

Now read the passage again.

Invasive species cause most of the worst problems in local ecosystems. The presence of a new species, particularly one at the top of the food chain, can destroy an ecosystem and cause numerous species to become extinct. One species that is causing numerous problems in America's waterways is the aquatic zebra mussel.

Native to Russia, the zebra mussel has recently invaded the Great Lakes and many other American lakes and rivers. The mussels attach themselves to the bottoms of boats, a convenient method that lets them travel easily. They also often attach themselves to water pipes. This action results in clogged pipes, some of which are used to bring drinking water to cities. The blocked pipes cost the cities huge amounts of money to unblock. Also, zebra mussels reproduce so rapidly that they often smother the spawning grounds of various fish and other mussels, thereby prohibiting their growth.

Additionally, zebra mussels in North America have very few natural enemies, meaning that it is difficult to eliminate them once they are established in a river or lake. Likewise, scientists have yet to discover an environmentally-safe way to kill the zebra mussels. These two facts help contribute to the extremely rapid expansion of the zebra mussel. Should this expansion not be stopped, zebra mussels will soon be causing problems in virtually all of the country's waterways.

Now listen to the lecture again. 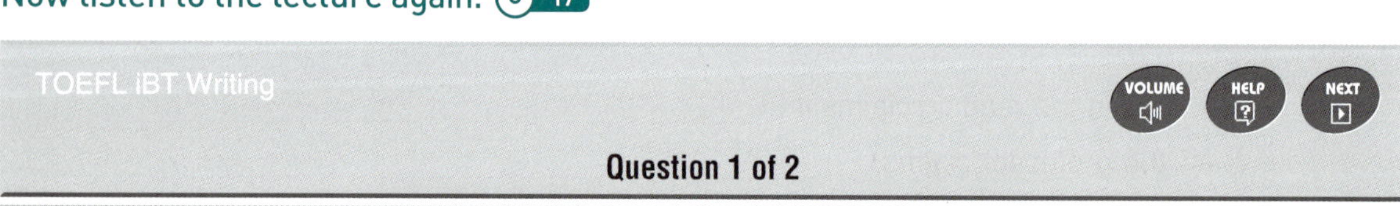

A Summarize the points made in the lecture, being sure to specifically explain how they answer the problems raised in the reading passage.

B Check your response.

		Yes	No
1	Are all the important points from the lecture presented accurately?	☐	☐
2	Is the information from the lecture appropriately related to the reading?	☐	☐
3	Is the response well organized?	☐	☐
4	Are all the sentences grammatically correct?	☐	☐
5	Are all the words spelled correctly?	☐	☐
6	Are all the punctuation marks used correctly?	☐	☐

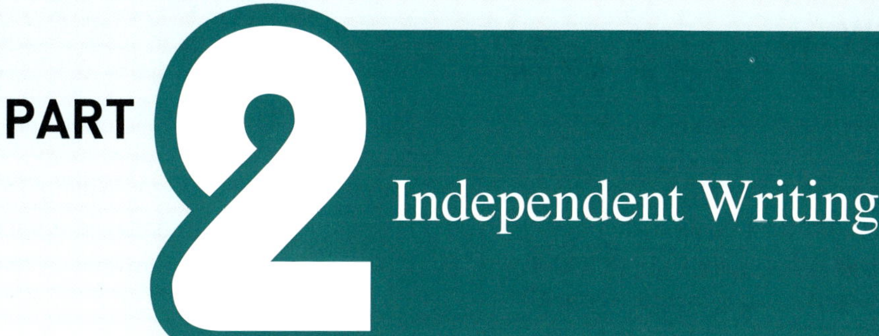

- **Chapter 3 Agree / Disagree**

- **Chapter 4 Preference**

Overview

■ Introduction

The second part of the Writing section of the TOEFL® iBT is the Independent Writing Task. In this task, you will be asked a question and then allowed 30 minutes to write an essay in response to the question. A typical essay will be about 300 words, though there is no maximum limit on the length of the essay.

Agree / Disagree

This is the predominant question type that has almost always occurred in the Independent Writing on the real TOEFL® iBT thus far. This question asks you to determine whether you agree or disagree with an issue and to support your position with appropriate reasons and examples.

Preference

This is a type of question that has occurred on the real TOEFL® iBT only a few times until now. This question mentions a topic and then asks you to state which of the two options you prefer and to support your choice with appropriate reasons and examples.

■ Question Types

1. Agree / Disagree

- Do you agree or disagree with the following statement?

[A sentence or sentences that present an issue]

Use specific reasons and examples to support your answer.

cf. This question type accounts for almost all the essay topics that have been asked on the TOEFL® iBT so far.

2. Preference

- Some people say X. Others believe Y. Which opinion do you agree with? Use specific reasons and examples to support your answer.

- Some people do X. Others do Y. Which… do you think is better? Use specific reasons and examples to support your opinion.

■ Useful Tips

1. Agree / Disagree

You should clearly state whether you agree or disagree with the given statement. Next, you should determine at least two main points which support your position. Then, you should provide specific reasons why the main points are valid as well as examples which support the main points.

2. Preference

You should clearly express which of the two options you feel more strongly about. Then, you should decide on at least two major points which support your choice. You should also provide reasons which support your main points. Finally, you should include specific examples which will bolster your main arguments.

■ Key Strategies

1. Understanding the Question
_ Read the question carefully, and make sure you understand exactly what it is asking.

_ Refer back to the question during your pre-writing and writing.

2. Brainstorming & Outlining
_ Brainstorm ideas on scratch paper before you begin writing.

_ Organize your main points in outline form.

_ Develop your outline into full sentences and paragraphs.

4. Writing the Thesis Statement & Topic Sentences
_ Make sure your thesis is clearly stated in your introductory paragraph.

_ Make sure your topic sentences support your thesis statement.

5. Writing the Details
_ Make sure your ideas are only about the original topic. Do not include details that are not relevant to the topic simply to make the essay longer.

_ Use the details to unify the essay and to give it coherence.

6. Completing & Checking Your Essay
_ Finish your writing with at least 5 minutes remaining in the task.

_ Reread your essay, and make any necessary revisions.

Sample iBT Question

Question Do you agree or disagree with the following statement?
People learn more from their peers than those older than them.
Use specific reasons and examples to support your answer.

Question 2 of 2

[Opening sentence] There is no question that our peers are a major influence on our lives. [Thesis statement] However, when it comes to learning valuable lessons about life, we learn much more from older people than our peers.

[Topic sentence 1] Unlike our peers, older people have a better understanding of life because they have already been through it, and we can benefit more from their seasoned knowledge. [General statement 1] Older people, not our peers, are in the enviable position of seeing the past with greater clarity, which can teach us important lessons. [Example 1] For example, I have learned more about the importance of a good education from my uncle than from my friends at school. Many of my friends rarely study and just use their time to have fun. However, my uncle has taught me that if I focus on studying instead of playing all the time, my life will be more fulfilling later on. [Closing sentence] Without his advice, I would not have such a mature perspective for someone my age.

[Topic sentence 2] Also, older people can steer us in the right direction and away from mistakes they have already made. [General statement 2] If we simply follow our peers, we will often experience similar pitfalls; however, we can avoid them if we listen and learn from our elders. [Example 2] For instance, when my brother tried out for the football team last year and did not make it, many of his peers told him to give up on the sport forever. But my father helped him realize that giving up on something was not the answer. So my brother practiced harder instead of abandoning the sport. This year, not only did he make the team, but he was also the captain. [Closing sentence] Ultimately, older people can help us make the right decisions when we face failure or adversary.

[Summary] In conclusion, people learn more from older people than their peers because they have more life experience, and they can give excellent, more mature advice. [Final comment] In this way, older people can be the biggest, most positive influence in our lives.

Chapter 3

Agree / Disagree

9 Living & Thinking

Understanding the Topic

Read the essay topic, and answer the following questions in words or phrases.

> Do you agree or disagree with the following statement?
>
> **Nowadays, people put too much emphasis on personal appearance and fashion.**
>
> Use specific reasons and examples to support your answer.

1 What is "too much emphasis on personal appearance and fashion"?

Being concerned with how one looks more than anything else

2 What are the advantages of putting a lot of emphasis on personal appearance and fashion?

Can help with career → get good job

Can increase self-esteem → gain confidence

3 What examples can you give about the advantages of putting emphasis on personal appearance and fashion?

Brother got competitive job because of his attention to his appearance

Brother was overweight and began to work out → became happier and more confident

4 What are the disadvantages of putting too much emphasis on personal appearance?

5 What examples can you give about placing too much emphasis on appearance?

Brainstorming

Based on your answers to the above questions, complete the brainstorming map.

3. ____________ ____________ ____________

e.g. exercise made brother happier & more confident

gain confidence in oneself

2. ____________ ____________ ____________

increase self-esteem

Disagree

Too much emphasis on personal appearance & fashion

1. ____________ ____________ ____________

good appearance → valuable

Agree

4. ____________ ____________ ____________

helps get good job

e.g. older brother got job because of his attention to his appearance

5. ____________ ____________ ____________

6. ____________ ____________ ____________

Outlining

Look at the brainstorming map, and complete your outline.

A Suggested Outline (Disagree)

1. **A good appearance is valuable.**
   - helps people get good jobs
   - e.g. boss told older brother he landed job because he took special care in how he looked

2. **Increases self-esteem**
   - people feel better about themselves when they look good
   - e.g. brother once overweight → now happier and more confident from daily exercise

B Your Outline (Agree)

1. _______________________________
   - _______________________________
   - e.g. _______________________________

2. _______________________________
   - _______________________________
   - e.g. _______________________________

Writing the Thesis Statement & Topic Sentences

Based on your outline above, express the main ideas in full sentences.

A Suggested Position (Disagree)

Introduction

Thesis statement It is crucial for people to pay close attention to their appearance.

Body

Topic sentence 1 Having a good appearance can be valuable to an individual when he is looking for a job.

Topic Sentence 2 If a person emphasizes his appearance, he can improve his self-esteem.

Conclusion

Summary It is good that people pay more attention to their appearance because it will help them secure better jobs and improve how they feel about themselves.

B Your Position (Agree)

Introduction

Thesis statement ______________________________

____

Body

Topic sentence 1 ______________________________

____

Topic sentence 2 ______________________________

____

Conclusion

Summary ______________________________

____

Writing the Details

Based on your outline, complete the essay with supporting details.

 Sample Essay (Disagree)

[Opening sentence] Our modern society is highly competitive, so people need to use every opportunity to get ahead in life. [Thesis statement] For this reason, it is crucial for people to pay close attention to their appearance. This includes both the way they look and the clothes they wear.

[Topic sentence 1] To begin with, having a good appearance can be valuable to an individual when he is looking for a job. [General statement 1] Many times, the way that a person looks and dresses can help him get hired. After all, an interviewer's first impression is often based upon how a person looks. So, if an individual ignores his appearance and fashion, he might not be successful during the interview process. [Example 1] My older brother had an experience just like this. A few months after he got his current job, his boss told my brother that he had been competing against a woman for the job. However, because my brother looked more professional, his boss decided to hire him, so my brother got the job. [Closing sentence 1] Taking special care of one's appearance can certainly help one's career. It certainly did for my brother.

[Topic sentence 2] Next, if a person emphasizes his appearance, he can improve his self-esteem. [General statement 2] Many people suffer from low esteem and a lack of self-confidence. However, people who have good bodies and wear fashionable clothes often feel better about themselves. Their appearance actually gives them more confidence. [Example 2] Again, my older brother is an excellent example. He was always overweight and very shy in middle school. He also had few friends and was not very popular. However, he started paying more attention to his appearance and began exercising in high school. As he started to slim up, he came out of his shell and almost immediately became a more confident, outgoing person. This change made him more popular at school too, so he started feeling better about himself. [Closing sentence 2] It seems clear to me that people are happier when they take care of their appearance and are confident in how they look.

[Summary] Ultimately, it is good that people pay more attention to their appearance because it will help them secure better jobs and improve how they feel about themselves. [Final comment] Taking special care of one's appearance and fashion is definitely a rewarding investment.

B Your Essay (Agree)

[Opening sentence] ____

____ [Thesis statement] ___________

____

[Topic sentence 1] ____

_________________________________ [General statement 1] _______________

____

[Example 1] ____

____

____

____

____

_________________________ [Closing sentence 1] _______________________

____

[Topic sentence 2] ____

_________________________________ [General statement 2] _______________

____

[Example 2] ____

____

____

____

____

_________________________ [Closing sentence 2] _______________________

____

[Summary] ____

____

[Final comment] ____

____

Completing & Checking Your Essay

A Read the following question, and write your own essay of at least 300 words. You have 30 minutes to plan, write, and revise your essay.

> Do you agree or disagree with the following statement?
>
> **People should spend money on things that last a long time, such as expensive pieces of jewelry, than spend money on short-term pleasures like vacations.**
>
> Use specific reasons and examples to support your answer.

B Check your essay.

Introduction

	Yes	No
Is the topic understood correctly?	☐	☐
Is there a clear thesis statement?	☐	☐

Body

Is there a topic sentence for each paragraph?	☐	☐
Are there clear and sufficient supporting details for the topic sentences?	☐	☐
Does each paragraph appropriately support the thesis statement?	☐	☐
Are there any redundant or irrelevant supporting details?	☐	☐
Are the ideas linked with appropriate transition words?	☐	☐

Conclusion

Is there a restatement of the thesis?	☐	☐
Does the conclusion sum up the main ideas of the essay properly?	☐	☐

Grammar & Vocabulary

Are all the sentences grammatically correct?	☐	☐
Are various sentence structures used?	☐	☐
Are various words and expressions used?	☐	☐
Are all the words spelled correctly?	☐	☐
Are the punctuation marks used correctly?	☐	☐

10 Culture & Leisure

Understanding the Topic

Read the essay topic, and answer the following questions in words or phrases.

> Do you agree or disagree with the following statement?
> **It is better to take a trip by oneself than to take a group tour with guidance.**
> Use specific reasons and examples to support your answer.

1 What is "to take a trip by oneself"?

To travel independently without the aid of a travel agent or tour guide

2 What are the advantages of taking a trip by oneself?

3 What examples can you give about the advantages of taking a trip by oneself?

4 What are the advantages of taking a group tour with guidance?

Everything planned → no stress; just enjoy the trip

Meet other travelers → form long-lasting friendships

5 What examples can you give about taking a group tour with guidance?

Family package tour to China → no worries about hotels, transportation, or sightseeing

Parents' honeymoon to Russia → met another couple & have been best friends ever since

Brainstorming

Based on your answers to the above questions, complete the brainstorming map.

3. __________
____
____

e.g. family package tour to China

no stress; just enjoy the trip

2. __________
____
____

everything planned out

Disagree

1. __________
____
____

Traveling alone is better than a group tour with guidance.

meet other travelers

Agree

4. __________
____
____

form long-lasting friendships

5. __________
____
____

e.g. my parents' honeymoon to Russia on a group tour

6. __________
____
____

Outlining

Look at the brainstorming map, and complete your outline.

A Suggested Outline (Disagree)

1. **Group tours plan everything for you.**
   - no stress or anxiety → just enjoy traveling
   - e.g. family package tour to China → easy b/c hotels, transportation, & lodging taken care of

2. **Meet other travelers**
   - form long-lasting friendships
   - e.g. my parents' honeymoon to Russia on a group tour → made good friends on trip

B Your Outline (Agree)

1. _______________________
   - _______________________
   - e.g. _______________________

2. _______________________
   - _______________________
   - e.g. _______________________

Writing the Thesis Statement & Topic Sentences

Based on your outline above, express the main ideas in full sentences.

A Suggested Position (Disagree)

Introduction

Thesis statement Taking a group tour is the best option for people considering a vacation.

Body

Topic sentence 1 Group tours plan travelers' entire itineraries.

Topic sentence 2 Group tours allow people to interact with one another while traveling.

Conclusion

Summary In conclusion, there is nothing better than a group tour when traveling. Group tours schedule everything on the trip, and they give individuals the opportunity to meet other individuals and form lasting friendships.

B Your Position (Agree)

Introduction

Thesis statement ____

____

Body

Topic sentence 1 ____

____

Topic sentence 2 ____

____

Conclusion

Summary ____

____

Writing the Details

Based on your outline, complete the essay with supporting details.

 Sample Essay (Disagree)

[Opening sentence] Many people are content to take trips by themselves and not use group or package tours. Unfortunately, they do not always have the best vacations. Instead, people should consider group tours. [Thesis statement] Taking a group tour is the best option for people considering a vacation.

[Topic sentence 1] First, group tours plan travelers' entire itineraries. [General statement 1] Because their trip has already been arranged, people do not have to worry about where they are going or how they are getting there. They can simply relax, enjoy their trip, and not get stressed out about anything. [Example 1] For example, my family once took a package tour to China. The travel agency arranged everything. It took care of the hotel reservations, transportation, and sightseeing. My family did not have to worry about anything. We just looked at the schedule the travel agency had provided and followed it. Thanks to the travel agency, we could just relax and enjoy our entire trip. This made things easier on my father since he did not have to worry every single minute about where we would go next. All in all, we had a great trip. [Closing sentence 1] Group tours take the anxiety of daily planning out of traveling and let travelers enjoy their vacations without any stress.

[Topic sentence 2] Another benefit of group tours is that they allow people to interact with one another while traveling. [General statement 2] Travelers are able to form tight friendships with people whom they otherwise would never have met because they are traveling together for a number of days. [Example 2] For instance, for their honeymoon, my parents went to Russia on a group tour. They met another couple on that trip, and everyone had a great time together. Even after many years, they remain very close friends and travel together from time to time. If my parents had traveled by themselves, they never would have met this couple, and they would have lost out on a good friendship. [Closing sentence 2] Group tours allow people to meet others on the same trip and help them form strong friendships, unlike traveling independently.

[Summary] In conclusion, there is nothing better than a group tour when traveling. Group tours schedule everything on the trip, and they give individuals the opportunity to meet other individuals and form lasting friendships. [Final comment] Group tours are the best way to travel when taking a trip.

B Your Essay (Agree)

[Opening sentence] ____

______________________________ [Thesis statement] _________________

____

[Topic sentence 1] ____

__________________________ [General statement 1] _________________

____

[Example 1] ____

____

____

____

____

______________________ [Closing sentence 1] _____________________

____

[Topic sentence 2] ____

__________________________ [General statement 2] _________________

____

[Example 2] ____

____

____

____

____

______________________ [Closing sentence 2] _____________________

____

[Summary] ____

____

[Final comment] ____

____

Completing & Checking Your Essay

A Read the following question, and write your own essay of at least 300 words. You have 30 minutes to plan, write, and revise your essay.

> Do you agree or disagree with the following statement?
>
> **Movies and television have more negative effects than positive effects on young people's behavior.**
>
> Use specific reasons and examples to support your answer.

B Check your essay.

Introduction

	Yes	No
Is the topic understood correctly?	☐	☐
Is there a clear thesis statement?	☐	☐

Body

	Yes	No
Is there a topic sentence for each paragraph?	☐	☐
Are there clear and sufficient supporting details for the topic sentences?	☐	☐
Does each paragraph appropriately support the thesis statement?	☐	☐
Are there any redundant or irrelevant supporting details?	☐	☐
Are the ideas linked with appropriate transition words?	☐	☐

Conclusion

	Yes	No
Is there a restatement of the thesis?	☐	☐
Does the conclusion sum up the main ideas of the essay properly?	☐	☐

Grammar & Vocabulary

	Yes	No
Are all the sentences grammatically correct?	☐	☐
Are various sentence structures used?	☐	☐
Are various words and expressions used?	☐	☐
Are all the words spelled correctly?	☐	☐
Are the punctuation marks used correctly?	☐	☐

11 School & Education I

Understanding the Topic

Read the essay topic, and answer the following questions in words or phrases.

> Do you agree or disagree with the following statement?
>
> **It is better to take the most difficult and challenging classes in university or at college even if it means that you probably will not get top grades (marks) in them.**
>
> Use specific reasons and examples to support your answer.

1. What are "difficult and challenging classes" at a university or college?

   Classes the student might not be familiar with and that involve a lot of work

2. What are the advantages of taking more difficult classes?

   More demanding professors → learn more & develop better study skills

   Set high goals → increase confidence and experience

3. What examples can you give about taking difficult and challenging classes?

   Difficult math class → learned more than ever before

   French class → gained confidence

4. What are the advantages of taking easier classes and getting high scores?

5. What examples can you give about taking a relatively easy class?

Brainstorming

Based on your answers to the above questions, complete the brainstorming map.

Central topic: **Take challenging classes in college; top scores aren't most important.**

Two branches: **Agree** and **Disagree**

Agree branch:
- e.g. math class
- more demanding professors
- learn more & develop better study skills
- benefit from setting higher goals
- increase confidence & experience
- e.g. French class

Disagree branch:
- 3. ______________ ______________ ______________
- 2. ______________ ______________ ______________
- 1. ______________ ______________ ______________
- 4. ______________ ______________ ______________
- 5. ______________ ______________ ______________
- 6. ______________ ______________ ______________

Outlining

Look at the brainstorming map, and complete your outline.

A Suggested Outline (Agree)

1. **Learn more and develop better study skills**
   - more demanding professors
   - e.g. took tough math class → learned more than before

2. **Benefit from setting higher goals**
   - increase confidence & experience
   - e.g. French class gave me confidence → more important than high grade

B Your Outline (Disagree)

1. _______________________________
   - _______________________________
   - e.g. _______________________________

2. _______________________________
   - _______________________________
   - e.g. _______________________________

Writing the Thesis Statement & Topic Sentences

Based on your outline above, express the main ideas in full sentences.

 **A** Suggested Position (Agree)

Introduction

Thesis statement Taking challenging and difficult classes is the best way for me to realize my full potential even if my grades are not top-notch.

Body

Topic sentence 1 I can learn more and develop better study skills if I take difficult and challenging classes.

Topic sentence 2 By setting higher goals for myself, I can achieve more as a student and individual than I would if I set low goals or none at all.

Conclusion

Summary Grades are not everything. It is better to take challenging classes because, as students, we will learn more and increase our confidence and experience.

B Your Position (Disagree)

Introduction

Thesis statement ____

____

Body

Topic sentence 1 ____

____

Topic sentence 2 ____

____

Conclusion

Summary ____

____

Writing the Details

Based on your outline, complete the essay with supporting details.

 Sample Essay (Agree)

[Opening sentence] Once many students enter college, they take the easiest classes available to maintain high GPAs. [Thesis statement] However, I believe that taking challenging and difficult classes is the best way for me to realize my full potential even if my grades are not top-notch.

[Topic sentence 1] First of all, I can learn more and develop better study skills if I take difficult and challenging classes. [General statement 1] In those classes, the professors will be much more demanding and expect the best from their students. [Example 1] For example, I once took a math class with a teacher who was infamous for being really tough. She definitely lived up to her reputation. I had loads of homework every night, and the class was a struggle at times. However, I got used to the heavy course load, and, while tough, the teacher was fair, and I learned more in that math class than in any other one I had ever taken. [Closing sentence 1] Taking challenging courses is definitely a good way to learn more.

[Topic sentence 2] Moreover, by setting higher goals for myself, I can achieve more as a student and individual than I would if I set low goals or none at all. [General statement 2] Completing tough courses regardless of my final grades will increase my confidence and experience. [Example 2] Last year, I enrolled in a French language course for the first time. I was nervous at first, and the course was demanding. But, in time, I developed a lot of confidence in this class. This year, I am continuing with French, and it is becoming much easier for me because of my experience. To me, it is the experience and confidence that counts, not getting a perfect grade. [Closing sentence 2] Taking harder courses at university will clearly outweigh the easy ones.

[Summary] Grades are not everything. It is better to take challenging classes because, as students, we will learn more and increase our confidence and experience. This will be more beneficial in the future than high grades from easy courses. [Final comment] Easy classes might produce top grades, but challenging ones prepare a student for life.

B Your Essay (Disagree)

[Opening sentence] ____

_________________________________ [Thesis statement] _______________

____

[Topic sentence 1] ____

_________________________ [General statement 1] _________________

____

[Example 1] ____

____

____

____

____

_________________ [Closing sentence 1] _________________________

____

[Topic sentence 2] ____

_________________________ [General statement 2] _________________

____

[Example 2] ____

____

____

____

____

_________________ [Closing sentence 2] _________________________

____

[Summary] ____

____

[Final comment] ____

____

Completing & Checking Your Essay

A Read the following question, and write your own essay of at least 300 words. You have 30 minutes to plan, write, and revise your essay.

> Do you agree or disagree with the following statement?
>
> **It is better to have a yearlong break before attending university.**
>
> Use specific reasons and examples to support your answer.

B Check your essay.

Introduction

	Yes	No
Is the topic understood correctly?	☐	☐
Is there a clear thesis statement?	☐	☐

Body

Is there a topic sentence for each paragraph?	☐	☐
Are there clear and sufficient supporting details for the topic sentences?	☐	☐
Does each paragraph appropriately support the thesis statement?	☐	☐
Are there any redundant or irrelevant supporting details?	☐	☐
Are the ideas linked with appropriate transition words?	☐	☐

Conclusion

Is there a restatement of the thesis?	☐	☐
Does the conclusion sum up the main ideas of the essay properly?	☐	☐

Grammar & Vocabulary

Are all the sentences grammatically correct?	☐	☐
Are various sentence structures used?	☐	☐
Are various words and expressions used?	☐	☐
Are all the words spelled correctly?	☐	☐
Are the punctuation marks used correctly?	☐	☐

12 School & Education II

Understanding the Topic

Read the essay topic, and answer the following questions in words or phrases.

Do you agree or disagree with the following statement?

A teacher's ability to relate well with his or her students is more important than the ability to give them knowledge.

Use specific reasons and examples to support your answer.

1   What is an "ability to relate well" with students?

An ability to understand and have friendly relationships with students

2   What are the advantages of a teacher's ability to relate well with his or her students?

Can get students' attention in class

Can command students' respect

3   What examples can you give about a teacher's ability to relate well with students?

Use PowerPoint presentations to get students' attention

Some teachers I respect → listen to my personal problems

4   What are the advantages of teachers giving students knowledge rather than relating well to them?

5   What examples can you give about the importance of a teacher's ability to give students knowledge?

Brainstorming

Based on your answers to the above questions, complete the brainstorming map.

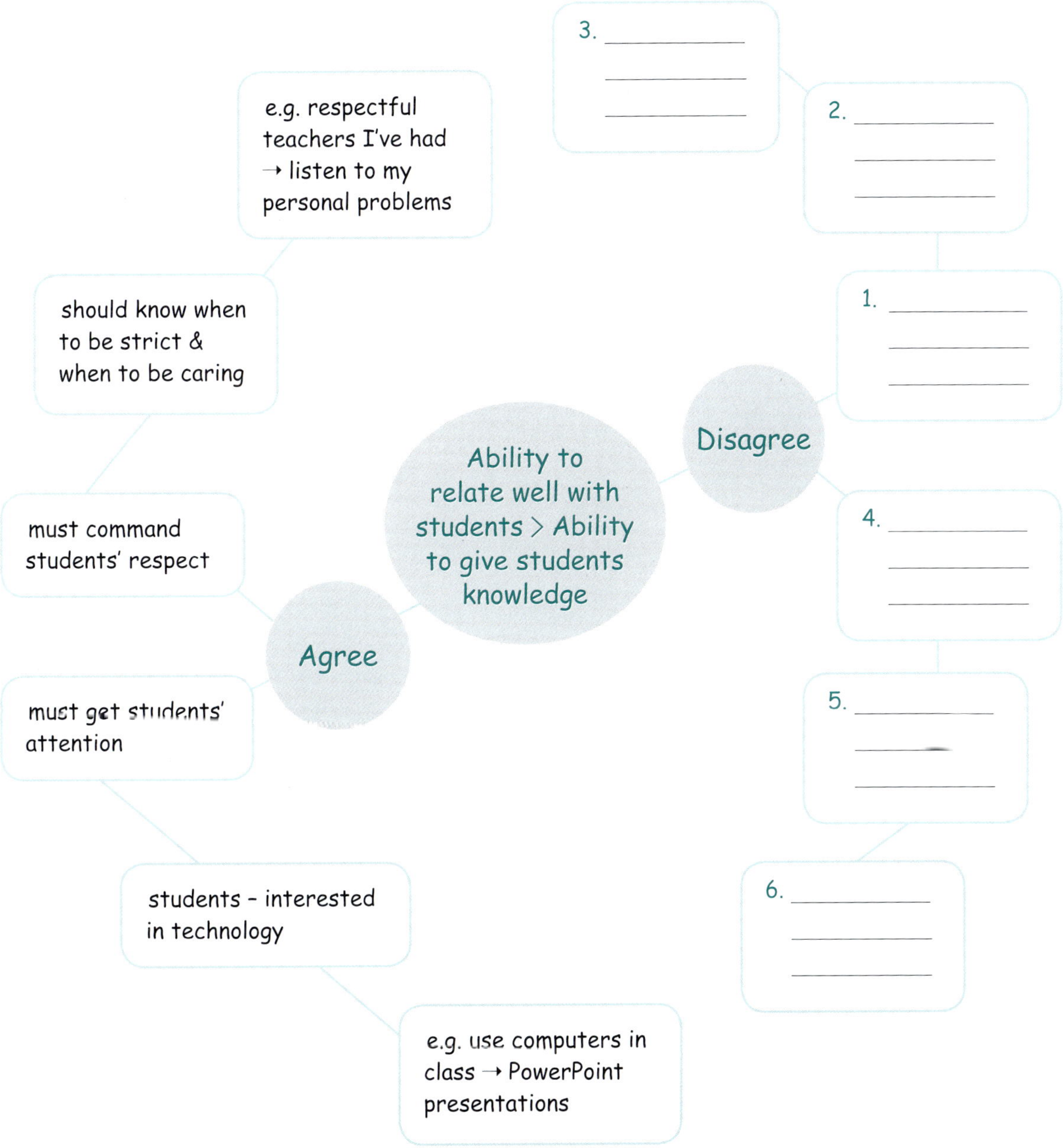

3. _______________
____
____

2. _______________
____
____

e.g. respectful
teachers I've had
→ listen to my
personal problems

1. _______________
____
____

should know when
to be strict &
when to be caring

Disagree

Ability to
relate well with
students > Ability
to give students
knowledge

4. _______________
____
____

must command
students' respect

Agree

5. _______________
____
____

must get students'
attention

6. _______________
____
____

students – interested
in technology

e.g. use computers in
class → PowerPoint
presentations

Outlining

Look at the brainstorming map, and complete your outline.

A Suggested Outline (Agree)

1. **Must be able to get their students' attention**
   - students are interested in technology
   - e.g. better to use PowerPoint instead of merely lecturing

2. **Need to be able to command students' respect**
   - should be strict but also know when to ease up on students
   - e.g. several respectful teachers → understand my personal problems and give some advice

B Your Outline (Disagree)

1. _______________________________
   - _______________________________
   - e.g. _______________________________

2. _______________________________
   - _______________________________
   - e.g. _______________________________

Writing the Thesis Statement & Topic Sentences

Based on your outline above, express the main ideas in full sentences.

 **A** Suggested Position **(Agree)**

Introduction

Thesis statement A teacher unable to relate to his or her students will never be able to get their attention and command their respect, which are two very important aspects of teaching.

Body

Topic sentence 1 Teachers have to know not only how to get their students' attention but also how to keep a hold of it in order to teach them.

Topic sentence 2 Teachers must be able to command the respect of their students in order to relate well to them.

Conclusion

Summary In my experience, my best teachers have been the ones who have been able to relate well to their students. By doing so, they could get their students' attention and command their respect.

B Your Position **(Disagree)**

Introduction

Thesis statement ____

____

Body

Topic sentence 1 ____

____

Topic sentence 2 ____

____

Conclusion

Summary ____

____

Writing the Details

Based on your outline, complete the essay with supporting details.

 Sample Essay (Agree)

[Opening sentence] Some people think a teacher's ability to give the students knowledge is one of the most important qualities of a teacher. [Thesis statement] In this day and age, however, a teacher unable to relate to his or her students will never be able to get their attention and command their respect, which are two very important aspects of teaching.

[Topic sentence 1] These days, teachers have to know not only how to get their students' attention but also how to keep a hold of it in order to teach them. [General statement 1] The world has changed very much in the past decade, and students these days are not interested in the same things they were into ten or twenty years ago. [Example 1] For example, we live in an age dominated by electronics, particularly computers. Most students my age know how to use all of the latest gadgets. Unfortunately, many teachers are technologically inept, so they have difficulty relating to students that way. Most of them never incorporate technology into their classes. Instead, they just lecture, which makes their classes boring. Some of them, however, use computers for things like PowerPoint presentations, which really helps to get most students' attention. [Closing sentence 1] Teachers that can relate to their students in areas like technology are definitely more able to keep their students' attention.

[Topic sentence 2] Teachers must also be able to command the respect of their students in order to relate well to them. [General statement 2] They must be strict in their classes yet should also know when their students, for whatever reason, are unable to study their best. [Example 2] For example, I have had several teachers who have been very strict and made their classes difficult. However, I always respected those teachers. The reason is that they knew when they were pushing the students too hard. When we were tired from having too many tests, they would not give us homework, or they would teach a fun lesson for us. Also, in the case of some teachers, I knew I could talk to them about any personal problems I had. I felt that these teachers would understand my problems and would therefore be able to give me some advice. [Closing sentence 2] Since these teachers could relate to their students so well, the students respected them more than they did other teachers.

[Summary] In my experience, my best teachers have been the ones who have been able to relate well to their students. By doing so, they could get their students' attention in class and command their respect. [Final comment] Teachers that cannot relate well to their students tend to have more difficulties with their students in class.

B Your Essay (Disagree)

[Opening sentence]

[Thesis statement]

[Topic sentence 1]

[General statement 1]

[Example 1]

[Closing sentence 1]

[Topic sentence 2]

[General statement 2]

[Example 2]

[Closing sentence 2]

[Summary]

[Final comment]

Completing & Checking Your Essay

A Read the following question, and write your own essay of at least 300 words. You have 30 minutes to plan, write, and revise your essay.

Do you agree or disagree with the following statement?

Parents make the best teachers.

Use specific reasons and examples to support your answer.

B Check your essay.

Introduction

	Yes	No
Is the topic understood correctly?	☐	☐
Is there a clear thesis statement?	☐	☐

Body

	Yes	No
Is there a topic sentence for each paragraph?	☐	☐
Are there clear and sufficient supporting details for the topic sentences?	☐	☐
Dose each paragraph appropriately support the thesis statement?	☐	☐
Are there any redundant or irrelevant supporting details?	☐	☐
Are the ideas linked with appropriate transition words?	☐	☐

Conclusion

	Yes	No
Is there a restatement of the thesis?	☐	☐
Does the conclusion sum up the main ideas of the essay properly?	☐	☐

Grammar & Vocabulary

	Yes	No
Are all the sentences grammatically correct?	☐	☐
Are various sentence structures used?	☐	☐
Are various words and expressions used?	☐	☐
Are all the words spelled correctly?	☐	☐
Are the punctuation marks used correctly?	☐	☐

$\boxed{13}$ Environment & Science

Understanding the Topic

Read the essay topic, and answer the following questions in words or phrases.

Do you agree or disagree with the following statement?

It is more important to use land for human needs such as farming, housing, and industry than to save it for endangered animals.

Use specific reasons and examples to support your answer.

1   What are "endangered animals"?

Animals whose populations are so small that they are in danger of becoming extinct

2   What are the advantages of using land for human needs?

Distribution of human populations → live more comfortably

Do not interfere with the extinction of animals → contribute to nature taking its course

3   What examples can you give about the importance of using land for human needs?

Overcrowded cities, such as Tokyo, Seoul, & New York → distribution of populations

Endangered animal preserves → interference in nature

4   What are the advantages of saving land for endangered animals?

5   What examples can you give about the importance of saving land for endangered animals?

Brainstorming

Based on your answers to the above questions, complete the brainstorming map.

3. ____________
____
____

e.g. endangered animal preserves → interference in nature

2. ____________
____
____

should not interfere with nature

1. ____________
____
____

Disagree

law of nature – species go extinct throughout history

Use land for human needs > Save land for endangered animals

4. ____________
____
____

Agree

humans need access to more land

5. ____________
____
____

huge populations → overcrowded cities

6. ____________
____
____

e.g. Tokyo, Seoul, & New York – over 10 million people

Outlining

Look at the brainstorming map, and complete your outline.

A Suggested Outline (Agree)

1. **The population of the planet is growing every year.**
   - overcrowded cities → people need new land to move to
   - e.g. Tokyo, Seoul, & New York

2. **It is natural for some animals to go extinct.**
   - should not interfere with nature
   - e.g. endangered animal preserves → interference in nature

B Your Outline (Disagree)

1. _______________________________
   - _______________________________
   - e.g. _______________________________

2. _______________________________
   - _______________________________
   - e.g. _______________________________

Writing the Thesis Statement & Topic Sentences

Based on your outline above, express the main ideas in full sentences.

 **A** Suggested Position (Agree)

Introduction

Thesis statement While it would be nice to set aside land for endangered animals, it is much more important to use all available land for humans.

Body

Topic sentence 1 Humans need to use all of the land they can gain access to.

Topic sentence 2 Animals have gone extinct on Earth during every period in which life has existed on the planet.

Conclusion

Summary While it is unfortunate that some endangered animals become extinct, people should be more concerned about taking care of humans and making sure that humans themselves survive.

B Your Position (Disagree)

Introduction

Thesis statement ______________________________________

____

Body

Topic sentence 1 ______________________________________

____

Topic sentence 2 ______________________________________

____

Conclusion

Summary ______________________________________

____

Writing the Details

Based on your outline, complete the essay with supporting details.

 Sample Essay (Agree)

[Opening sentence] The population of Earth continues to increase every year, so people require more and more land upon which to farm, build houses, and operate factories. [Thesis statement] While it would be nice to set aside land for endangered animals, it is much more important to use all available land for humans.

[Topic sentence 1] To begin with, humans need to use all of the land they can gain access to. [General statement 1] As the planet's population continues to grow, people need to move onto land that was previously occupied only by animals. [Example 1] In many countries, there are large numbers of cities with over a million people. In fact, some cities, like Tokyo, Seoul, and New York, have populations of over ten million. These cities are overcrowded, so many people need to move out of them and onto new lands. While they may be moving to lands that are inhabited by endangered animals, the welfare of humans is much more important than that of a few endangered animals. [Closing sentence 1] People have to take care of Earth's expanding population, and the best way to enable people to live more comfortably is to move onto lands inhabited by animals.

[Topic sentence 2] Also, animals have gone extinct on Earth during every period in which life has existed on the planet. [General statement 2] It is a fact of life that some species die out while others flourish. People should not interfere with the extinction of animals but should instead allow nature to take its course. [Example 2] As a matter of fact, when some countries establish biological preserves for endangered animals to live on, they are interfering with nature. Man is the dominant species on this planet, so it is inevitable that some animals will go extinct because of man. [Closing sentence 2] Keeping endangered animals alive on these preserves is merely refusing to allow nature to let some animals live while killing off others.

[Summary] While it is unfortunate that some endangered animals become extinct, people should be more concerned about taking care of humans and making sure that humans themselves survive. [Final comment] It is much more important to worry about human civilization than to worry about endangered animals.

B Your Essay (Disagree)

[Opening sentence] ____

____ [Thesis statement] ___________

____

[Topic sentence 1] ____

________________________________ [General statement 1] _______________

____

[Example 1] ____

____

____

____

____

________________________ [Closing sentence 1] __________________________

____

[Topic sentence 2] ____

________________________________ [General statement 2] _______________

____

[Example 2] ____

____

____

____

____

________________________ [Closing sentence 2] __________________________

____

[Summary] ____

____

[Final comment] ____

____

Completing & Checking Your Essay

A Read the following question, and write your own essay of at least 300 words. You have 30 minutes to plan, write, and revise your essay.

Do you agree or disagree with the following statement?

Renewable sources of energy (sun, water, wind) will soon replace fossil fuels (coal, gas, oil).

Use specific reasons and examples to support your answer.

B Check your essay.

	Yes	No
Introduction		
Is the topic understood correctly?	☐	☐
Is there a clear thesis statement?	☐	☐
Body		
Is there a topic sentence for each paragraph?	☐	☐
Are there clear and sufficient supporting details for the topic sentences?	☐	☐
Does each paragraph appropriately support the thesis statement?	☐	☐
Are there any redundant or irrelevant supporting details?	☐	☐
Are the ideas linked with appropriate transition words?	☐	☐
Conclusion		
Is there a restatement of the thesis?	☐	☐
Does the conclusion sum up the main ideas of the essay properly?	☐	☐
Grammar & Vocabulary		
Are all the sentences grammatically correct?	☐	☐
Are various sentence structures used?	☐	☐
Are various words and expressions used?	☐	☐
Are all the words spelled correctly?	☐	☐
Are the punctuation marks used correctly?	☐	☐

Chapter 4

Preference

14 Family & Society

Understanding the Topic

Read the essay topic, and answer the following questions in words or phrases.

> Some people think that the family is the most important influence on young adults. Other people think that friends are the most important influence on young adults. Which view do you agree with? Use specific reasons and examples to support your position.

1   What are "young adults"?

Individuals in their late teens to early twenties

2   How is the family the most important influence on young adults?

Parents' contribution to education → emotional & financial support

Offer good advice → more mature and more experienced than friends

3   What examples can you give about family influence?

Cousin's going to college → family completely financed so could focus on classes

Brother won money in science contest → Mom and Dad said to save for college

4   How are friends the most important influence on young adults?

5   What examples can you give about friends' influences?

Brainstorming

Based on your answers to the above questions, complete the brainstorming map.

e.g. cousin graduated from college

financial & emotional support

parents' contribution to education

offer sound advice in good and bad times

more mature & experienced

e.g. advise brother to save money, not waste

Family < Friends

Family > Friends

3. ___________ ___________ ___________

2. ___________ ___________ ___________

1. ___________ ___________ ___________

4. ___________ ___________ ___________

5. ___________ ___________ ___________

6. ___________ ___________ ___________

Outlining

Look at the brainstorming map, and complete your outline.

A Suggested Outline (Family > Friends)

1. **Parents contribute to education.**
   - university not possible without parents' financial support
   - e.g. cousin: financial support from her parents → first to graduate in her family

2. **Family gives sound advice.**
   - family members usually more mature & more experienced.
   - e.g. brother's science contest money → in the bank for college

B Your Outline (Family < Friends)

1. _______________________________
   - _______________________________
   - e.g. _______________________________

2. _______________________________
   - _______________________________
   - e.g. _______________________________

Writing the Thesis Statement & Topic Sentences

Based on your outline above, express the main ideas in full sentences.

 Suggested Opinion (Family > Friends)

Introduction

Thesis statement I believe that families have the most important influences on young adults.

Body

Topic sentence 1 Parents are the only ones who are able to contribute to a young person's educational goals.

Topic sentence 2 Families give sound advice during young adults' good and bad times.

Conclusion

Summary In conclusion, there is no question that young adults are positively influenced the most by their families because their families support their future education after high school and often provide better advice than their more youthful friends can.

B Your Opinion (Family < Friends)

Introduction

Thesis statement ____

____

Body

Topic sentence 1 ____

____

Topic sentence 2 ____

____

Conclusion

Summary ____

____

Writing the Details

Based on your outline, complete the essay with supporting details.

 Sample Essay (Family > Friends)

[Opening sentence] Young adults are very impressionable and are easily influenced in numerous ways, such as by their friends. [Thesis statement] Nevertheless, I believe that families have the most important influences on young adults because they contribute to young people's educational goals and give sound advice during good times and bad.

[Topic sentence 1] First of all, parents are the only ones who are able to contribute to a young person's educational goals. [General statement 1] Most young adults would not be able to attend university without their parents' financial support. [Example 1] For instance, my cousin was accepted to a high-ranking university, so his parents took out some personal loans, which allowed him to attend the school. Also, due to their support, he did not have to work, so he could focus exclusively on his studies. Ultimately, he became the first person in his family ever to graduate from university. [Closing sentence 1] Parents can therefore enable their children, who are young adults, to go to college.

[Topic sentence 2] Additionally, families give sound advice during young adults' good and bad times. [General statement 2] The reason is that many times parents and other older family members have been through a certain situation and are able to offer expert counsel, unlike the young person's friends, who are not as mature. [Example 2] For example, my older brother received a large sum of money from a science contest he entered and won in high school. Most of his friends told him to go out and buy a new cell phone and clothes. However, my mom and dad said that it might be better to save the money for college and put it in the bank. My dad pointed out that it will come in handy for him one day. My brother realized they were right. [Closing sentence 2] Nothing can replace the positive influence of the family on a young adult's life.

[Summary] In conclusion, there is no question that young adults are positively influenced the most by their families because their families support their future education after high school and often provide better advice than their more youthful friends can. [Final comment] Without their families, young adults would have much more difficult times navigating their ways through their lives.

B Your Essay (Family < Friends)

[Opening sentence] ____

____ [Thesis statement] __________

____

[Topic sentence 1] ____

________________________________ [General statement 1] ______________

____

[Example 1] ____

____

____

____

____

________________________ [Closing sentence 1] __________________

____

[Topic sentence 2] ____

________________________________ [General statement 2] ______________

____

[Example 2] ____

____

____

____

____

________________________ [Closing sentence 2] __________________

____

[Summary] ____

____

[Final comment] ____

____

Completing & Checking Your Essay

 Read the following question, and write your own essay of at least 300 words. You have 30 minutes to plan, write, and revise your essay.

> Some people prefer to spend time with one or two close friends. Others choose to spend time with a large number of friends. Which of these two ways of spending time do you think is better? Use specific reasons and examples to support your answer.

B **Check your essay.**

Introduction

	Yes	No
Is the topic understood correctly?	☐	☐
Is there a clear thesis statement?	☐	☐

Body

	Yes	No
Is there a topic sentence for each paragraph?	☐	☐
Are there clear and sufficient supporting details for the topic sentences?	☐	☐
Does each paragraph appropriately support the thesis statement?	☐	☐
Are there any redundant or irrelevant supporting details?	☐	☐
Are the ideas linked with appropriate transition words?	☐	☐

Conclusion

	Yes	No
Is there a restatement of the thesis?	☐	☐
Does the conclusion sum up the main ideas of the essay properly?	☐	☐

Grammar & Vocabulary

	Yes	No
Are all the sentences grammatically correct?	☐	☐
Are various sentence structures used?	☐	☐
Are various words and expressions used?	☐	☐
Are all the words spelled correctly?	☐	☐
Are the punctuation marks used correctly?	☐	☐

15 Environment & Technology

Understanding the Topic

Read the essay topic, and answer the following questions in words or phrases .

> Some people say that the Earth is being harmed (damaged) by human activity. Others believe that human activity makes the Earth a better place to live. Which opinion do you agree with? Use specific reasons and details to support your choice.

1   What is "human activity"?

Actions by companies, governments, or individuals

2   How is the Earth being harmed by human activity?

3   What examples can you give about human activity harming the Earth?

4   How is human activity making the Earth a better place to live?

Doctors donating time → poor people receive medical care & improve quality of lives

Some people do not use their cars as much → reduce greenhouse gases

5   What examples can you give about human activity benefiting the Earth?

Documentary on Doctors without Borders → help people in third-world countries

People taking public transportation in some cities → better air quality

Brainstorming

Based on your answers to the above questions, complete the brainstorming map.

3. __________
____
____

e.g. docu. on Doctors w/o Borders → healthier societies

third-world countries receive important medical care

2. __________
____
____

doctors donate time and skills

Human activity makes the Earth a better place.

1. __________
____
____

Human activity harms the Earth.

people use cars less

4. __________
____
____

reduces greenhouse gases

5. __________
____
____

e.g. people in cities use public transportation → better air quality

6. __________
____
____

Outlining

Look at the brainstorming map, and complete your outline.

A Suggested Outline (Human activity makes the Earth a better place.)

1. **Doctors donate time and skills.**
   - places in Africa and elsewhere receive vital medical care
   - e.g. entire societies in third-world countries benefit from Doctors without Borders

2. **People in certain cities use cars less.**
   - reduction in greenhouse gases
   - e.g. people using only public transportation in some cities → better air quality

B Your Outline (Human activity harms the Earth.)

1. _______________________________
   - _______________________________
   - e.g. _______________________________

2. _______________________________
   - _______________________________
   - e.g. _______________________________

Writing the Thesis Statement & Topic Sentences

Based on your outline above, express the main ideas in full sentences.

 **A** Suggested Opinion (Human activity makes the Earth a better place.)

Introduction

Thesis statement Human beings continue to do positive things which are beneficial to Earth and therefore make it a better place to live.

Body

Topic sentence 1 Doctors are donating their time to societies in third-world countries.

Topic sentence 2 People in many cities of the world are using their cars less and less these days.

Conclusion

Summary Ultimately, humans are doing many good things to make Earth a better place. Two of these actions are doctors donating their medical skills and people using their cars less. Doctors improve the health of people in needy societies, and the air quality has improved in places where people rely less on their own cars.

B Your Opinion (Human activity harms the Earth.)

Introduction

Thesis statement _______________________________

____

Body

Topic sentence 1 _______________________________

____

Topic sentence 2 _______________________________

____

Conclusion

Summary _______________________________

____

Writing the Details

Based on your outline, complete the essay with supporting details.

 Sample Essay (Human activity makes the Earth a better place.)

[Opening sentence] Something that I often see on the news is how Earth is being destroyed by people. [Thesis statement] However, human beings continue to do positive things which are beneficial to Earth and therefore make it a better place to live.

[Topic sentence 1] First, doctors are donating their time to societies in third-world countries. [General statement 1] Places in Africa are benefiting from their aid and becoming healthier regions to live in more than ever before. [Example 1] For example, there is an organization called Doctors without Borders. They donate their vacation time to traveling to needy regions of the world and offering the people living there free medical care. Those regions are benefiting on every level—not just a medical one—from the doctors' help. Through their assistance, the quality of life for people in these areas has greatly improved. [Closing sentence 1] Thanks to people in groups like Doctors without Borders, Earth has become a better place to live.

[Topic sentence 2] Furthermore, people in many cities of the world are using their cars less and less these days. [General statement 2] This helps eliminate harmful pollutants from the atmosphere and improves the quality of the environment. [Example 2] To give an example, people in certain cities have taken it upon themselves to rely less on their own cars and more on public transportation. In doing so, many citizens have reported vast improvements in the air quality of their cities. This proves that human activity can benefit Earth. [Closing sentence 2] If more people continue to make similar changes in their everyday behavior, Earth will continue to become a better place.

[Summary] Ultimately, humans are doing many good things to make Earth a better place. Two of these actions are doctors donating their medical skills and people using their cars less. Doctors improve the health of people in needy societies, and the air quality has improved in places where people rely less on their own cars. [Final comment] Actions by humans can improve the quality of Earth and life on it in many ways.

B Your Essay (Human activity harms the Earth.)

[Opening sentence] ____

___________________________________ [Thesis statement] _________

____

[Topic sentence 1] ____

_________________________________ [General statement 1] _________

____

[Example 1] ____

____

____

____

____

_________________________ [Closing sentence 1] _________________

____

[Topic sentence 2] ____

_________________________________ [General statement 2] _________

____

[Example 2] ____

____

____

____

____

_________________________ [Closing sentence 2] _________________

____

[Summary] ____

____

[Final comment] ____

____

Completing & Checking Your Essay

A Read the following question, and write your own essay of at least 300 words. You have 30 minutes to plan, write, and revise your essay.

> Some people say that the Internet provides us with a lot of valuable information. Others believe that too much information on the Net causes many problems. Which opinion do you agree with? Why or why not? Use specific reasons and examples to support your answer.

B Check your essay.

Introduction

	Yes	No
Is the topic understood correctly?	☐	☐
Is there a clear thesis statement?	☐	☐

Body

	Yes	No
Is there a topic sentence for each paragraph?	☐	☐
Are there clear and sufficient supporting details for the topic sentences?	☐	☐
Does each paragraph appropriately support the thesis statement?	☐	☐
Are there any redundant or irrelevant supporting details?	☐	☐
Are the ideas linked with appropriate transition words?	☐	☐

Conclusion

	Yes	No
Is there a restatement of the thesis?	☐	☐
Does the conclusion sum up the main ideas of the essay properly?	☐	☐

Grammar & Vocabulary

	Yes	No
Are all the sentences grammatically correct?	☐	☐
Are various sentence structures used?	☐	☐
Are various words and expressions used?	☐	☐
Are all the words spelled correctly?	☐	☐
Are the punctuation marks used correctly?	☐	☐

16 Business & Economy

Understanding the Topic

Read the essay topic, and answer the following questions in words or phrases.

> Some people prefer to work for a large company. Others prefer to work for a small company. Which would you prefer? Use specific reasons and details to support your choice.

1 What is a "small company / large company"?

A small company - one building or location & fewer than fifty workers

A large company - different locations & more than fifty workers

2 What are the benefits of working at a small company?

Job satisfaction → employees feel they play important roles at their companies

More flexibility → workers have high interest & energy levels

3 What examples can you give about the benefits of working at a small company?

Recent nationwide survey → over half of small company employees responded positively

TV documentary → various duties & more energy

4 What are the benefits of working at a large company?

5 What examples can you give about the benefits of working at a large company?

Brainstorming

Based on your answers to the above questions, complete the brainstorming map.

3. ___________ ___________ ___________

2. ___________ ___________ ___________

e.g. recent nationwide survey – more employee satisfaction

1. ___________ ___________ ___________

employees feel they play key roles at work

Work for a large company

job satisfaction

4. ___________ ___________ ___________

Work for a small company

5. ___________ ___________ ___________

more flexibility

can experience various duties

6. ___________ ___________ ___________

e.g. TV documentary: a variety of tasks → interest & energy levels ↑

Outlining

Look at the brainstorming map, and complete your outline.

 Suggested Outline (Small company $>$ Large company)

1. Greater job satisfaction
- employees feel they are making bigger contributions & they play key roles at their companies
  - e.g. recent nationwide survey $\rightarrow$ positive responses from over half of the small company employees

2. More flexibility
- workers perform a variety of duties $\rightarrow$ reduces burnout and boredom
- e.g. TV documentary $\rightarrow$ a variety of tasks keeps interest and energy levels high

 Your Outline (Small company $<$ Large company)

1. _______________________________

   - _______________________________

   - e.g. _______________________________

2. _______________________________

   - _______________________________

   - e.g. _______________________________

Writing the Thesis Statement & Topic Sentences

Based on your outline above, express the main ideas in full sentences.

A Suggested Opinion (Small company > Large company)

Introduction

Thesis statement While large companies might give bigger paychecks to their employees, small companies provide better working environments for their employees.

Body

Topic sentence 1 When it comes to job satisfaction, a large company simply cannot compete with a small company.

Topic sentence 2 Another important factor is that smaller companies also allow their employees flexibility, unlike large companies.

Conclusion

Summary In summation, small companies provide better work experiences for people because they are ultimately more satisfying and flexible than large companies.

B Your Opinion (Small company < Large company)

Introduction

Thesis statement ____

____

Body

Topic sentence 1 ____

____

Topic sentence 2 ____

____

Conclusion

Summary ____

____

Writing the Details

Based on your outline, complete the essay with supporting details.

 **A**   Sample Essay (Small company > Large company)

[Opening sentence] These days, it seems that many people want to work for large companies. In their minds, bigger is better. **[Thesis statement]** However, while large companies might give bigger paychecks to their employees, small companies provide better working environments for their employees.

[Topic sentence 1] One major advantage is job satisfaction. When it comes to job satisfaction, a large company simply cannot compete with a small company. **[General statement 1]** Because of its size, employees often feel that they are making a bigger contribution when they work at a small company as opposed to when they work at a large one. At a large company, workers often feel like they are simply anonymous individuals. **[Example 1]** In a recent nationwide survey, employees at both small and large companies were questioned about their overall job satisfaction. Over half of the small company employees responded positively, citing the fact that they believe they play key roles at their companies. In contrast, fewer than a third of the workers at large companies believed that their contributions were of importance. **[Closing sentence 1]** This clearly shows how employees at small companies feel more valued than employees at large companies.

[Topic sentence 2] Another important factor is that smaller companies also allow their employees flexibility, unlike large companies. **[General statement 2]** Employees at small companies often have various duties, which keep their interest and energy levels high. **[Example 2]** Last year, a TV documentary revealed that many employees at small companies perform multiple duties and, in turn, have higher energy levels than their large company counterparts. In short, the variety of duties lets workers at small companies maintain their interest in their jobs. Performing different jobs also helps reduce burnout and boredom, according to the program. Unfortunately, workers at large companies do not often get the opportunity to do a variety of tasks. **[Closing sentence 2]** Task flexibility enables employees at small companies to have excellent work environments.

[Summary] In summation, small companies provide better work experiences for people because they are ultimately more satisfying and flexible than large companies. **[Final comment]** People spend a large part of their adult lives at their jobs, and, by working at small companies, they can improve their levels of satisfaction with their work.

B Your Essay (Small company $<$ Large company)

[Opening sentence] ____

______________________________________ [Thesis statement] ______________

____

[Topic sentence 1] ____

______________________________ [General statement 1] ________________

____

[Example 1] ____

____

____

____

____

______________________ [Closing sentence 1] ____________________________

____

[Topic sentence 2] ____

______________________________ [General statement 2] ________________

____

[Example 2] ____

____

____

____

____

______________________ [Closing sentence 2] ____________________________

____

[Summary] ____

____

[Final comment] ____

____

Completing & Checking Your Essay

A Read the following question, and write your own essay of at least 300 words. You have 30 minutes to plan, write, and revise your essay.

> Some people think governments should spend as much money as possible exploring outer space (for example, traveling to the moon and to other planets). Other people disagree and think governments should spend this money on our basic needs on Earth. Which of these two opinions do you agree with? Use specific reasons and details to support your answer.

B Check your essay.

Introduction

	Yes	No
Is the topic understood correctly?	☐	☐
Is there a clear thesis statement?	☐	☐

Body

	Yes	No
Is there a topic sentence for each paragraph?	☐	☐
Are there clear and sufficient supporting details for the topic sentences?	☐	☐
Does each paragraph appropriately support the thesis statement?	☐	☐
Are there any redundant or irrelevant supporting details?	☐	☐
Are the ideas linked with appropriate transition words?	☐	☐

Conclusion

	Yes	No
Is there a restatement of the thesis?	☐	☐
Does the conclusion sum up the main ideas of the essay properly?	☐	☐

Grammar & Vocabulary

	Yes	No
Are all the sentences grammatically correct?	☐	☐
Are various sentence structures used?	☐	☐
Are various words and expressions used?	☐	☐
Are all the words spelled correctly?	☐	☐
Are the punctuation marks used correctly?	☐	☐

This part provides you with a list of essential essay topics reconstructed from the ones that have so far been asked on the TOEFL® iBT. By practicing writing your essays on these topics, you will effectively prepare yourself for the Independent Writing of the TOEFL® iBT.

Essential Essay Topics

Essential Essay Topics for Independent Writing

1   Do you agree or disagree with the following statement? University students should not be required to attend classes. Instead, they should be able to receive credits through a final test or paper. Use specific reasons and details to explain your answer.

2   Some people say that students learn the most important things in life inside the classroom. Others believe that they learn the most important lessons of life outside the classroom. Which opinion do you agree with? Why? Use specific reasons and examples to support your answer.

3   Do you agree or disagree with the following statement? Universities should give the same financial support to their students' sports and social activities as they give to their classes and libraries. Use specific reasons and examples to support your opinion.

4   Do you agree or disagree with the following statement? It is better for students to take classes for more than 11 months throughout the year. Use specific reasons and details to support your answer.

5   Do you agree or disagree with the following statement? Schools (universities, colleges, and high schools) should teach students about specific careers and jobs instead of general subjects. Use specific reasons and examples to support your answer.

6   Do you agree or disagree with the following statement? A teacher's ability to relate well with his or her students is more important than the ability to give them knowledge. Use specific reasons and examples to explain your answer.

7   Do you agree or disagree with the following statement? It is more important to learn general knowledge in various subjects than to learn specialized knowledge in one subject. Use specific reasons and examples to support your answer.

8   Do you agree or disagree with the following statement? It is more important for a teacher to help students gain self-confidence than to teach them specific knowledge. Use specific reasons and examples to support your answer.

9   Do you agree or disagree with the following statement? It is more important to give students prizes or awards for their efforts than for their achievements (successes or grades). Use specific reasons and details to support your answer.

10   Do you agree or disagree with the following statement? Classmates have more influences on a child's success in school than parents do. Use specific reasons and examples to support your answer.

11   Do you agree or disagree with the following statement? It is more important to learn knowledge from studying than to develop creativity. Use specific reasons and examples to support your answer.

12   Do you agree or disagree with the following statement? It is better to take the most difficult and challenging classes in university or at college even if it means that you probably will not get top grades (marks) in them. Use specific reasons and examples to support your answer.

13   Do you agree or disagree with the following statement? In high schools or colleges, it is more desirable for a group project to be evaluated the same regardless of the individual students' performances. Use specific reasons and examples to support your answer.

14   Do you agree or disagree with the following statement? It is more important to choose the subjects that you are interested in than the subjects you need to prepare for a job or a career. Use specific reasons and examples to support your answer.

15   Do you agree or disagree with the following statement? Grades (marks) can encourage students to learn. Use specific reasons and examples to support your answer.

16   Do you agree or disagree with the following statement? Teachers should give students homework every day. Use specific reasons and examples to support your answer.

17   Do you agree or disagree with the following statement? All teachers should be required to update their knowledge every five years. Use specific reasons and examples to support your answer.

18   Do you agree or disagree with the following statement? It is better to have a yearlong break before attending university. Use specific reasons and examples to support your answer.

19   Do you agree or disagree with the following statement? A university education is essential to success in life. Use specific reasons and examples to support your answer.

20   Do you agree or disagree with the following statement? It is more important to understand ideas and concepts than to learn facts. Use specific reasons and examples to support your answer.

21   Do you agree or disagree with the following statement? Parents make the best teachers. Use specific reasons and examples to support your answer.

22   Do you agree or disagree with the following statement? All universities should require students to take a science class even though their major has no relevance to this field. Use specific reasons and examples to support your answer.

23   Do you agree or disagree with the following statement? Twenty years from now, students will no longer use printed books. Use specific reasons and examples to support your answer.

B   Living & Thinking

1   Do you agree or disagree with the following statement? It is better to learn from co-workers and friends than to learn from teachers and supervisors. Use specific reasons and examples to support your answer.

2   Some people say that a person should make important decisions alone. Others believe that it is always better to ask others for advice. Which opinion do you agree with? Use specific reasons and examples to support your answer.

3   Do you agree or disagree with the following statement? The best way for a good future is to plan carefully when you are young. Use specific reasons and details to explain your answer.

4   Do you agree or disagree with the following statement? There are so many sources of news and information that it is difficult to know whom to believe and who is telling the truth. Use specific reasons and examples to support your answer.

5   Do you agree or disagree with the following statement? Nowadays, people put too much emphasis on personal appearances and fashion. Use specific reasons and examples to support your answer.

6   Do you agree or disagree with the following statement? Young people enjoy life more than older people do. Use specific reasons and examples to support your answer.

7   Do you agree or disagree with the following statement? To speak well is more important than to write well. Use specific reasons and examples to support your answer.

8   Do you agree or disagree with the following statement? Letting a friend make a mistake is better than saying or doing something that would destroy the friendship. Use specific reasons and examples to support your answer.

9   Do you agree or disagree with the following statement? It is more important to keep old friends than to make new friends. Use specific reasons and examples to support your answer.

10   Do you agree or disagree with the following statement? Observing or studying animals teaches us a lot about human nature. Use specific reasons and details to support your answer.

11   Do you agree or disagree with the following statement? Most people prefer having others make decisions for them. Use specific reasons and examples to support your answer.

12   Do you agree or disagree with the following statement? It is important to know about the events happening around the world that are not related to you. Use specific reasons and examples to support your answer.

13   Do you agree or disagree with the following statement? People should spend money on things that last a long time, such as an expensive piece of jewelry, and not spend money on short-term pleasures like vacations. Use specific reasons and examples to support your answer.

14   Do you agree or disagree with the following statement? People today spend too much time on personal enjoyment - the thing they like to do - rather than doing what they should do. Use specific reasons and examples to support your answer.

15   Do you agree or disagree with the following statement? The ability to cooperate well with others is more important today than in the past. Use specific reasons and examples to support your answer.

16   Do you agree or disagree with the following statement? Today, people do so many different things that they can only do a few things well. Use specific reasons and examples to support your answer.

17   Do you agree or disagree with the following statement? Because modern life is complex, young people should have the ability to plan and organize. Use specific reasons and details to support your answer.

18   Do you agree or disagree with the following statement? People must get their news from newspapers; television news doesn't provide enough information. Use specific reasons and details to support your answer.

19   Do you agree or disagree with the following statement? Getting advice from friends of an older age is more valuable than advice from friends your own age. Use specific reasons and details to support your answer.

20   Do you agree or disagree with the following statement? It is better to do one project first and then begin to do another than to do several projects at the same time. Use specific reasons and details to support your answer.

C   Family & Society

1   Do you agree or disagree with the following statement? The extended family (such as grandparents, cousins, aunts, and uncles) is less important now than it was in the past. Use specific reasons and examples to support your answer.

2   Do you agree or disagree with the following statement? It is more important to spend time at work than to spend time with family. Use specific reasons and details to support your answer.

3   Do you agree or disagree with the following statement? Young people do not give enough time to help their communities. Use specific reasons and details to support your answer.

4   Do you agree or disagree with the following statement? Living today is more comfortable and easier than when your grandparents were children. Use specific reasons and details to support your answer.

5   Do you agree or disagree with the following statement? Parents can no longer control
       what their children do; their behavior is more affected by television, movies, and other
       influences from outside the home. Use specific reasons and examples to support
       your answer.

D   Business & Economy

1   Do you agree or disagree with the following statement? Being happy with a job is
       more important than having a high salary. Use specific reasons and examples to
       support your answer.

2   Do you agree or disagree with the following statement? It is unrealistic for people to
       expect to work for the same company or employer for all of their lives. Use specific
       reasons and details to support your answer.

3   Do you agree or disagree with the following statement? It is better to work for a large
       company than for a small company. Use specific reasons and details to support your
       answer.

4   Do you agree or disagree with the following statement? Most advertisements make
       products seem much better than they really are. Use specific reasons and examples
       to support your answer.

5   Do you agree or disagree with the following statement? Getting a job in which you
       work with other people is better than getting a job in which you work alone. Use
       specific reasons and details to support your answer.

E   Culture & Leisure

1   Do you agree or disagree with the following statement? People today spend too
       much time paying attention to the personal lives of celebrities or famous people. Use
       specific reasons and examples to support your answer.

2   Do you agree or disagree with the following statement? It is better to take a trip by oneself than to take a group tour with guidance. Use specific reasons and examples to support your answer.

3   Do you agree or disagree with the following statement? It is better to watch serious movies that are designed to make you think than to watch movies that are primarily designed to amuse or entertain. Use specific reasons and examples to support your answer.

4   Do you agree or disagree with the following statement? Governments should spend more money supporting the arts than supporting athletics such as an Olympic team. Use specific reasons and examples to support your answer.

5   Do you agree or disagree with the following statement? Movies and television have more negative effects than positive effects on young people's behavior. Use specific reasons and examples to support your answer.

6   Do you agree or disagree with the following statement? The second reading of a book is more interesting than the first reading. Use specific reasons and examples to support your answer.

7   Do you agree or disagree with the following st atement? People learn more by watching television than by reading books. Use specific reasons and examples to support your answer.

8   Do you agree or disagree with the following statement? Twenty years from now, people will have more time for leisure activities. Use specific reasons and examples to support your answer.

9   Do you agree or disagree with the following statement? The purpose of television should be to educate, not to entertain. Use specific reasons and examples to support your answer.

F   Environment & Technology

1   Do you agree or disagree with the following statement? Renewable sources of energy (sun, water, wind) will soon replace fossil fuels (coal, gas, oil). Use specific reasons and examples to support your answer.

2   Do you agree or disagree with the following statement? It is more important to use land for human needs such as farming, housing, and industry than to save it for endangered animals. Use specific reasons and examples to support your answer.

3   Do you agree or disagree with the following statement? The most effective way for the government to conserve energy is to increase the price of gasoline and electricity. Use specific reasons and examples to support your answer.

4   Some people say that the Internet provides us with a lot of valuable information. Others believe that too much information on the Net causes many problems. Which opinion do you agree with? Why or why not? Use specific reasons and examples to support your answer.

5   Do you agree or disagree with the following statement? Twenty years from now, people will not use their cars as frequently as they do now. Use specific reasons and details to support your answer.

6   Do you agree or disagree with the following statement? People should not be allowed to use mobile (cell) phones when they use public transportation (e.g. buses, trains, and airplanes). Use specific reasons and details to support your answer.

This section measures your ability to use writing to communicate in an academic environment. There will be two writing tasks.

For the first writing task, you will read a passage and listen to a lecture and then answer a question based on what you have read and heard. For the second writing task, you will answer a question based on your own knowledge and experience.

Now, listen to the directions for the first writing task.

Actual Test 01  

Writing Based on Reading and Listening
Directions

For this task, you will have three minutes to read a passage about an academic topic. A clock at the top of the screen will show how much time you have to read. You may take notes while you read. You **will** be able to see the reading passage again when it is time for you to write. You may use your notes to help you answer the question.

You will then have **20 minutes** to write a response to a question that asks you about the relationship between the lecture you have heard and the reading passage. Try to answer the question as completely as possible using information from the reading passage and the lecture. The question does **not** ask you to express your personal opinion.

Typically, an effective response will be 150 to 225 words. Your response will be judged on the quality of your writing and on the completeness and accuracy of the content.

Now you will see the reading passage for 3 minutes. Remember that it will be available to you again while you are writing. Immediately after the reading time ends, the lecture will begin, so keep your headset on until the lecture has ended.

Reading

While the modern age has led to many improvements in people's lifestyles, one negative aspect has emerged. Namely, the cost of raising children in the United States has ballooned. In fact, raising a child costs more in America than in any other country on Earth.

According to a recent study, on average, parents must pay approximately $260,000 to feed, clothe, and educate their children from the day they are born until they graduate from university at approximately the age of twenty-one. For many families, the costs are even higher since they send their children to expensive private schools and universities, some of which charge over $40,000 a year for tuition and room and board. This number does not include travel or toys and other playthings, which can also be expensive.

Incredibly, rearing children in America requires about a third more money than in other Western countries like France and Spain. One reason for this is the limited socialism found in many European countries, where parents do not have to pay tuition for their children to attend schools. Also, while the standard of living is lower in these countries than in the U.S., prices are also cheaper, a big advantage that enables parents to save more money.

Finally, there is the matter of what parents spend their money on. Parents in most countries use the majority of money dedicated to their children on necessities like clothes and food. However, Americans typically spend money on items people from other countries would consider excessive. For example, American parents expend considerable amounts of money on private tutoring—in education, music, and athletics. Also, they pay extremely high amounts for health care for their children. Altogether, it makes bringing up American children very expensive.

Question

Directions: You have 20 minutes to plan and write your response. Your response will be judged on the basis of the quality of your writing and on how well your response presents the points in the lecture and their relationship to the reading passage. Typically, an effective response will be 150 to 225 words.

Question: Summarize the points made in the lecture, being sure to specifically explain how they answer the problems raised in the reading passage.

While the modern age has led to many improvements in people's lifestyles, one negative aspect has emerged. Namely, the cost of raising children in the United States has ballooned. In fact, raising a child costs more in America than in any other country on Earth.

According to a recent study, on average, parents must pay approximately $260,000 to feed, clothe, and educate their children from the day they are born until they graduate from university at approximately the age of twenty-one. For many families, the costs are even higher since they send their children to expensive private schools and universities, some of which charge over $40,000 a year for tuition and room and board. This number does not include travel or toys and other playthings, which can also be expensive.

Incredibly, rearing children in America requires about a third more money than in other Western countries like France and Spain. One reason for this is the limited socialism found in many European countries, where parents do not have to pay tuition for their children to attend schools. Also, while the standard of living is lower in these countries than in the U.S., prices are also cheaper, a big advantage that enables parents to save more money.

Finally, there is the matter of what parents spend their money on. Parents in most countries use the majority of money dedicated to their children on necessities like clothes and food. However, Americans typically spend money on items people from other countries would consider excessive. For example, American parents expend considerable amounts of money on private tutoring—in education, music, and athletics. Also, they pay extremely high amounts for health care for their children. Altogether, it makes bringing up American children very expensive.

Writing Based on Knowledge and Experience
Directions

For this task, you will write an essay in response to a question that asks you to state, explain, and support your opinion on an issue. You will have **30 minutes** to write your essay.

Typically, an effective essay will contain a minimum of 300 words. Your essay will be judged on the quality of your writing. This includes the development of your ideas, the organization of the content, and the quality and accuracy of the language you used to express ideas.

Click on **Continue** to go on.

Question

Copy   Cut   Paste

Directions: Read the question below. You have 30 minutes to plan, write, and revise your essay. Typically, an effective response will contain a minimum of 300 words.

Question:

Do you agree or disagree with the following statement?

Most advertisements make products seem much better than they really are.

Use specific reasons and examples to support your answer.

Actual Test 02 

Writing Based on Reading and Listening Directions

For this task, you will have three minutes to read a passage about an academic topic. A clock at the top of the screen will show how much time you have to read. You may take notes while you read. You **will** be able to see the reading passage again when it is time for you to write. You may use your notes to help you answer the question.

You will then have **20 minutes** to write a response to a question that asks you about the relationship between the lecture you have heard and the reading passage. Try to answer the question as completely as possible using information from the reading passage and the lecture. The question does **not** ask you to express your personal opinion.

Typically, an effective response will be 150 to 225 words. Your response will be judged on the quality of your writing and on the completeness and accuracy of the content.

Now you will see the reading passage for 3 minutes. Remember that it will be available to you again while you are writing. Immediately after the reading time ends, the lecture will begin, so keep your headset on until the lecture has ended.

Reading

One of the most controversial aspects of law enforcement these days are speed cameras. These are cameras that are installed at various places and then used to monitor the speeds of passing drivers. Equipped with radar detectors, they take pictures of speeders, which then results in violators being sent a speeding ticket that they must pay some time later. While many people dislike speed cameras, they are actually beneficial to society.

For one, they have made the roads safer. While there are sometimes signs that indicate that speed cameras are nearby, most of the time they are hidden from view. Therefore, if drivers feel or know that there is a speed camera in the vicinity, they often drive slower since the price of speeding tickets can be two hundred or more dollars. Slower speeds mean fewer accidents, so speed cameras are already helping protect people.

Second of all, because of speed cameras, police officers do not have to waste much of their time finding speeders. This frees the police to do the more important aspects of their job, like catching criminals and helping keep the public safe. In fact, thanks to the success of speed cameras, more and more are being installed, so, in the future, police officers may never have to issue any speeding tickets at all.

Finally, because speed cameras provide hard evidence that an individual was, in fact, speeding, fewer people are protesting their tickets in court. This decrease in complaints is starting to free up traffic courts, which are constantly backlogged with cases. So, instead of challenging their tickets, most violators, when they receive a picture of their transgression in the mail, simply write a check and pay their fine.

Question

Question 1 of 2

00:20:00

Directions: You have 20 minutes to plan and write your response. Your response will be judged on the basis of the quality of your writing and on how well your response presents the points in the lecture and their relationship to the reading passage. Typically, an effective response will be 150 to 225 words.

Question: Summarize the points made in the lecture you just heard, explaining how they cast doubt on specific points made in the reading passage.

One of the most controversial aspects of law enforcement these days are speed cameras. These are cameras that are installed at various places and then used to monitor the speeds of passing drivers. Equipped with radar detectors, they take pictures of speeders, which then results in violators being sent a speeding ticket that they must pay some time later. While many people dislike speed cameras, they are actually beneficial to society.

For one, they have made the roads safer. While there are sometimes signs that indicate that speed cameras are nearby, most of the time they are hidden from view. Therefore, if drivers feel or know that there is a speed camera in the vicinity, they often drive slower since the price of speeding tickets can be two hundred or more dollars. Slower speeds mean fewer accidents, so speed cameras are already helping protect people.

Second of all, because of speed cameras, police officers do not have to waste much of their time finding speeders. This frees the police to do the more important aspects of their job, like catching criminals and helping keep the public safe. In fact, thanks to the success of speed cameras, more and more are being installed, so, in the future, police officers may never have to issue any speeding tickets at all.

Finally, because speed cameras provide hard evidence that an individual was, in fact, speeding, fewer people are protesting their tickets in court. This decrease in complaints is starting to free up traffic courts, which are constantly backlogged with cases. So, instead of challenging their tickets, most violators, when they receive a picture of their transgression in the mail, simply write a check and pay their fine.

Writing Based on Knowledge and Experience
Directions

For this task, you will write an essay in response to a question that asks you to state, explain, and support your opinion on an issue. You will have **30 minutes** to write your essay.

Typically, an effective essay will contain a minimum of 300 words. Your essay will be judged on the quality of your writing. This includes the development of your ideas, the organization of the content, and the quality and accuracy of the language you used to express ideas.

Click on **Continue** to go on.

Question

Copy   Cut   Paste

Directions: Read the question below. You have 30 minutes to plan, write, and revise your essay. Typically, an effective response will contain a minimum of 300 words.

Question:

Some people say that students learn the most important things in life inside the classroom. Others believe that they learn the most important lessons of life outside the classroom.

Which opinion do you agree with? Why? Use specific reasons and examples to support your answer.

How to Master Skills for the TOEFL® iBT Writing

Writing

Intermediate

Answer Book

How to Master Skills for the TOEFL® iBT Writing

Writing

Intermediate

Answer Book

Contents

PART 1
Integrated Writing

Sample iBT Question

■ Reading

요즘 들어 교육에서 가장 논란이 되고 있는 화제 가운데 하나는 교사의 봉급을 지급하는 방법이다. 많은 사람들은 성과급으로 교사의 봉급을 지급하는 데 찬성한다. 다시 말해, 교사들은 얼마나 잘 가르치고 학생들이 얼마나 잘 해나가는지에 따라 봉급을 받게 된다. 이 제도는 여러 가지 이유에서 실행되어야 한다.

우선, 이 제도는 교사의 봉급을 정하는 아주 공평한 방법이다. 현재는 교사들이 우선적으로 연공 서열에 따라 봉급을 받는다. 교편을 잡은 지 오래 될수록 교사는 봉급을 더 많이 받는다. 하지만 이것은 공평하지 않다. 이제, 가장 실력 있는 교사들은 교사 생활을 한 지 그리 오래 되지 않았더라도 자신의 능력에 따라 더 많은 봉급을 받을 수 있다. 또한 무능한 교사들은 10년, 20년 교사직에 있었더라도 더 적은 월급을 받게 될 것이다.

두 번째로, 성과급을 지급할 경우 대부분의 교사들은 더욱 분발하게 된다. 실제로 교사들은 서로 경쟁을 시작하게 되고 이에 따라 학생들에게 제공하는 교육의 질이 향상될 것이다. 모든 교사들은 서로 경쟁할 때 발전한다. 마찬가지로, 교실에서 더 나은 수업을 하려다 보면 더 나은 교수법을 개발하기 시작할 것이다.

마지막으로, 교사들이 더 노력하고 일한다면 학생들도 많은 혜택을 누리게 될 것이다. 교사들이 더 나은 수업을 한다는 것은 학생들이 훨씬 더 잘 배울 수 있게 된다는 것을 의미한다. 또한 학생들 역시 교사들이 얼마나 열심히 가르치는지를 보면서 더 열심히 공부해야겠다는 생각을 하게 될 것이다.

확실히 성과급 제도는 교사나 학생 모두에게 여러 가지 장점이 있다. 모든 학교는 되도록 빨리 이 제도의 시행을 고려해 봐야 한다.

■ Listening

교사들에게 성과급 제도를 실시하는 것이 그럴 듯하게 들린다는 것은 압니다. 하지만 사실 이 제도에는 많은 단점이 있습니다. 여러분이 그 단점들에 관해 생각해 본 적이 없을지도 모르니 한번 짚어보도록 하겠습니다.

우선, 각 교사의 능력을 누가 평가할까요? 아마도 교장 선생님이 할 확률이 가장 크겠죠. 대다수 교장들은 정직하게 평가하겠지만 그렇지 않은 교장들도 있습니다. 우선, 교장이 여러 교사들을 관리하는 데 성과급 정책을 이용할 수도 있어요. 교사들은 교장이 정한 규칙을 따라야 하며 그렇지 않으면 감봉을 당할 수도 있죠. 또한, 교장이 여러 교사를 편애할 수도 있고 친한 사람의 월급을 올려주기 위해 실력 있는 교사를 무시할 수도 있습니다. 그런 일이 일어나서는 안 되죠.

또 다른 이유도 있습니다. 물론, 교사들이 더 열심히 노력하고 새로운 교수법과 전략을 개발하기 위해 노력할 거예요. 하지만 교사들은 아마도 효과적인 교수법을 동료와 공유하고 싶어하지 않을 겁니다. 결국, 그들은 다른 교사들보다 더 많은 봉급을 받고자 할 테니까요. 교육이란 이렇게 되어서는 안 됩니다. 교육은 지식을 나누는 것이지 감춰두는 것이 아닙니다. 또한 교사들 간의 협력도 줄어들게 될 것입니다. 이 모든 새로운 경쟁은 반드시 교사들 간에 경쟁 관계를 야기하게 되어 있습니다.

마지막으로, 이 제도는 학생들에게도 부정적인 영향을 미칠 수 있습니다. 성과급은 점수에 의해 결정되기 때문에 교사들이 공부를 안 하는 학생에게 낙제점이나 낮은 점수를 주려고 하지 않을 거예요. 아마도 성적 부풀리기가 수도 없이 생길 것입니다. 또한 일부 교사들은 유급시켜야 할 학생을 진급시키기도 할 거예요. 이런 일은 학생에게 해가 되며 일어나서는 안 되는 일입니다.

이렇듯이 성과급 제도는 많은 단점이 있습니다. 학교 측에서 이 제도를 실시하기 전에 충분히 검토를 해 보아야 할 것입니다.

Sample Answer

[도입문장] 읽기 지문은 교사들의 능력에 따른 봉급제를 찬성한다. [주제문] 하지만 교수는 성과급제가 좋지 않은 몇 가지 이유를 제시한다.

[반박 1] 우선, 교수는 십중팔구 교장이 각 교사를 평가하게 될 것이라고 말한다. 교수는 일부 교장들은 누가 가장 실력이 있고 누가 가장 실력이 형편없는지를 평가할 때 편견을 가질 수 있다고 주장한다. 그는 교장이 교사들로 하여금 교장 자신이 정한 규칙을 따르게 하고 그렇지 않으면 좋지 않은 점수를 줄 수도 있다고 말한다. [관련 진술 1] 실력 없는 교사는 봉급이 적고 실력 있는 교사는 봉급이 많기 때문에 일부 교장들이 봉급 결정에 있어 일부 교사를 편애할 수 있다는 점에 대해 교수는 우려를 표한다.

[관련 진술 2] 두 번째로, 교수는 교사들이 더욱 노력하고 더 나은 교수법을 개발할 수도 있다는 점을 인정한다. [반박 2] 하지만, 그는 교사들이 좋은 교수법을 다른 교사들과 공유하지 않을 것이라고 생각한다. 그는 모든 교사들이 서로 경쟁하게 될 것이라고 말한다. 또한 교사들 간에 경쟁 관계가 생겨 전반적인 교육의 질이 향상되지 않으리라고 믿는다.

[반박 3] 마지막으로, 교수는 교사들이 성적이 나쁜 학생들을 낙제시키지 않을지도 모른다고 생각한다. 또한 그는 교사들이 유급시켜야 할 학생들을 진급시켜서 학생들에게 피해를 줄지도 모른다고 생각한다. 따라서 많은 학생이 성과급제의 긍정적 혜택을 받지 못하게 될 것이다. [관련 진술 3] 이 점을 볼 때 교사들이 열심히 가르치는 모습을 보고 학생들이 더 열심히 공부하게 되리라는 본문의 주장은 옳지 않다.

Chapter 1　Casting Doubt

Unit 1　Technology

Note Taking & Outlining

A

개인 교통 수단 분야에서 가장 발전 가능성이 있는 것으로 스마트카를 들 수 있다. 스마트카는 선진 공학 또는 모종의 인공 지능을 장착한 컴퓨터를 활용한 차량을 말한다. 스마트카는 아직 완전한 개발 단계에 이르지는 못했지만 궁극적으로는 스마트카를 모는 모든 사람에게 도움을 줄 것이다.

스마트카의 장점 중 한 가지는 교통 흐름을 보다 원활하게 만든다는 것이다. 스마트카는 운전 중 해야 하는 일의 상당 부분을 해결할 수 있기 때문에 차를 탄 사람이 다른 일을 볼 수 있다. 스마트카는 대부분 스스로 운전을 하기 때문에 차량이 없는 최적의 경로와 그에 합당한 속도를 선택할 수 있다. 이로 인해 이동 시간이 훨씬 단축되고 교통 흐름도 지속적으로 원활하게 유지할 수 있다.

그뿐만 아니라, 스마트카는 유지비가 적게 든다. 스마트카는 거의 전적으로 컴퓨터에 의해 움직이기 때문에 수리를 해야 하는 사소한 문제가 발생하는 경우 컴퓨터가 이를 차주에게 알릴 수 있다. 그러면 차주는 과도한 비용이 들 정도로 문제가 커지기 전에 저렴한 비용으로 차를 수리할 수 있다.

 ¹traffic flow faster
²optimal routes
³maintenance costs
⁴minor problem

B

W: Let's move on to another piece of technology that we are sure to see in the future. I'm talking, of course, about smart cars. Now, don't get too thrilled about them. Yeah, it would be nice to have smart cars do all the driving for us, but they probably won't be as breathtaking as everyone anticipates. Here, let me explain for you.

To begin with, you've all seen movies with scenes of smart cars zipping around through traffic, right? Well, unfortunately, that probably won't be what will happen. It's a documented fact that, as automobile technology has improved, the amount of traffic has steadily increased. So while we may have cars do the driving for us, you can expect to sit in longer traffic jams. Just because they're smart cars doesn't mean that they'll be smart enough to get you out of a traffic jam.

Second of all, they are not going to be cheap to maintain. "Why?" you may ask. Well, most of the parts of a smart car will be custom-made. This means that, due to the manufacturing process, replacing the parts will be expensive. Sure, the labor bill may be cheap, but the bill for the parts is going to be astronomical in some cases. So think about those things before you get too excited about smart cars, okay?

W: 미래에 만나게 될 또 한 가지 기술로 넘어가 봅시다. 물론, 스마트카에 관한 이야기예요. 그렇다고 너무 흥분하지는 말길 바래요. 스마트

카가 우리를 대신해 운전을 다 해준다면 정말 멋질 겁니다. 하지만 여러분들이 기대하는 것만큼 그렇게 놀랍지는 않을 거예요. 그 이유를 설명해 드리죠.

우선, 여러분들은 영화에서 스마트카가 차들 사이를 씽씽 달리는 장면을 봤을 거예요. 하지만 안타깝게도 그런 일은 아마 없을 겁니다. 자동차 기술이 발달할수록 교통량이 점점 증가한다는 것은 입증된 사실입니다. 그래서 자동차가 사람들을 대신해 운전을 하게 되더라도 더 길어진 교통 정체 속에서 앉아 있어야 할 거예요. 스마트카라고 해서 교통 정체에서 빠져나올 수 있을 만큼 차가 똑똑하다는 얘기는 아니니까요.

두 번째로, 유지비가 만만치 않을 거예요. 왜냐고 묻는 학생이 있을지도 모르겠군요. 스마트카 부품의 대부분이 주문 생산이에요. 다시 말해, 제조 공정 때문에 부품 교환에 비용이 많이 든다는 얘기죠. 물론, 공임은 쌀지도 모르지만 어떤 경우에는 부품 교환 비용이 어마어마할 수도 있어요. 그래서 스마트카에 대해 흥분하기에 앞서 먼저 이런 문제들에 대해 생각해 보아야 합니다.

 ¹amount of traffic
²longer traffic jams
³custom-made parts
⁴astronomical amount of money

C

Reading (Main Points)

1 Smart cars will be able to select ¹the best routes and avoid highly traveled roads, which will decrease ²the amount of travel time for people.
2 Because computers will warn the owners of ³impending problems, they can fix the problems while they are ⁴still minor, which will not require a large amount of money.

Listening (Refutations)

1 Historically speaking, traffic always ⁵becomes worse with each technological development, therefore smart cars will still get stuck in ⁶traffic jams.
2 Since many of the parts are ⁷custom-made, they have to be manufactured specially, so the cost of replacing them will be ⁸much higher than normal.

Paraphrasing & Summarizing

A⁻¹ 

1 Smart cars operate by making use of sophisticated technology as well as computers that can think for themselves to some extent.
2 By doing the majority of the driving, a smart car will enable all the passengers, including the driver, to do other things.
3 The car will decide which way it will go by looking at

how many cars are on various roads and <u>checking the speed limits of the roads</u>.

4 The computers in a smart car will <u>let their owner know anytime there is a problem</u>, no matter how small it may be.

5 Because the owner can <u>fix the problem while it is still minor</u>, he will not have to suffer a major problem and therefore <u>have to pay lots of money to fix it</u>.

A-2

Smart cars are not completely developed yet, but they are going to be very important in the future. They will help drivers [1]<u>get to their destinations</u> much faster. They will do this by taking over the driving. This will allow the passengers and driver to do other things, and it will also ensure that the car takes [2]<u>the fastest route possible</u> by avoiding traffic. In addition, owners will not have to [3]<u>pay high maintenance fees</u>. The car's computers will monitor all possible problems, thereby enabling the owner [4]<u>to fix any problems</u> before they develop into something major. This will then save the owner a lot of money on [5]<u>repair costs</u>.

스마트카는 아직 완전히 개발되지는 않았지만 미래에 아주 중요한 역할을 하게 될 것이다. 스마트카는 운전자가 목적지에 훨씬 빨리 도착할 수 있게 해 줄 것이다. 스마트카는 운전자 대신 운전을 하기 때문에 이런 일이 가능하다. 탑승자와 운전자는 다른 일을 볼 수 있고 차는 교통 정체를 피해 가능한 가장 빠른 경로를 택할 수도 있다. 그뿐만 아니라, 차주는 비싼 유지비도 필요하지 않다. 자동차의 컴퓨터가 모든 발생 가능한 문제들을 파악하므로 차주는 문제가 커지기 전에 모든 문제를 해결할 수 있다. 이로 인해 차주는 수리 비용을 많이 절약하게 될 것이다.

B-1

1 Even though people would love to <u>let their cars handle the driving</u>, smart cars will probably not <u>live up to their expectations</u>.

2 It is well known that <u>traffic becomes worse as automobiles become more advanced</u>.

3 The artificial intelligence in smart cars will not be sufficient enough <u>to keep the cars from getting stuck in traffic</u>.

4 It is going to be expensive to <u>put the majority of new parts in smart cars</u> because of the way that <u>many of the parts must be made</u>.

5 Even though <u>it will not cost a lot to pay the mechanic</u> for his actual work, it will still be extremely expensive to <u>pay for the replacement parts</u>.

B-2

While most people are expecting great things from smart cars, they will probably not be quite as wonderful as people think they will be. Even though vehicular technology is constantly improving, traffic actually [1]<u>becomes worse</u> with every improvement. There will probably be more, not fewer, [2]<u>traffic jams</u>. So, while the cars will be driving themselves, making it easier on the owners, the trips will actually [3]<u>take longer</u>. Also, when the cars need to be maintained with [4]<u>replacement parts</u>, the owners will have to pay a lot of money. Since smart cars are custom-made, the parts are going to be expensive to replace, thereby requiring their owners to [5]<u>spend excessively</u>.

다수의 사람들은 스마트카에 대해 무엇인가 대단한 것을 기대하지만 스마트카는 사람들이 생각하는 것만큼 그렇게 대단하지 않을지도 모른다. 자동차 기술이 계속해서 발달하고 있긴 하지만 그런 발전이 있을 때마다 사실 교통 상황은 점점 악화된다. 그래서 교통이 원활해지는 게 아니라 교통 정체가 더 심해질지도 모른다. 그래서 자동차가 스스로 운전을 하는 동안 차주는 편해질지 모르지만 사실 이동 시간은 더 길어질 수도 있다. 또한 부품을 교환해야 하는 경우 엄청난 비용이 들 수도 있다. 스마트카는 주문 생산을 하기 때문에 부품 교환비가 만만치않아 차주는 엄청난 비용을 지불해야 할 것이다.

Synthesizing & Organizing

A

1 The reading passage claims that <u>smart cars will be able to choose the best routes to arrive at their destinations quickly</u>, but the speaker claims that <u>traffic is going to increase as the technology in cars improves</u>.

2 The author declares that <u>it will take less time to travel and that traffic will always be moving</u>, yet the professor states that <u>there will actually be longer traffic jams than before</u>.

3 In contrast to the statement in the reading claiming that <u>it will be cheap to maintain smart cars</u>, the professor asserts that <u>the manufacturing process involved in creating replacement parts ensures that maintenance costs will be high</u>.

4 Whereas the reading passage asserts that <u>owners will be able to repair their cars cheaply because the problems requiring fixing will be minor</u>, the lecturer declares that <u>the replacement parts themselves are going to cost an incredible amount of money</u>.

B

1 The reading passage and lecture both discuss <u>aspects of smart cars</u>.

2 However, the professor states that <u>smart cars will not be as great as people expect</u>.

3 She gives two reasons why <u>she believes they will</u>

not improve on current vehicles.

4 First, the professor asserts that smart cars will not resemble scenes in movies where they move rapidly through cities.

5 She states that, as automobile technology has improved, it has always created more traffic, not less.

6 This contradicts the reading passage, which affirms that smart cars will avoid traffic jams by controlling the routes they drive along.

7 Also, the lecture claims that future traffic jams involving smart cars will be bigger than they currently are.

8 Next, the lecturer mentions the maintenance costs of smart cars.

9 She declares that most smart car parts are custom-made, so they must be specially manufactured, making them incredibly expensive.

10 The reading, however, states that smart cars will tell their owners when they have minor problems, allowing them to be fixed rather cheaply.

11 However, the professor states that, while labor fees will not be expensive, any repair work involving spare parts will be.

12 In conclusion, the professor has a dim view of the future of smart cars, which directly contrasts the opinion of the author of the reading passage, who believes smart cars will be very beneficial.

1 지문과 강의 둘 다 스마트카의 여러 가지 측면에 관해 말한다.

2 하지만, 교수는 스마트카가 사람들이 기대하는 것만큼 대단하지는 않을 것이라고 한다.

3 교수는 스마트카가 현재의 자동차에서 진전이 없으리라고 보는 두 가지 이유를 말한다.

4 첫 번째로, 교수는 스마트카가 영화에 나오는 장면처럼 도시 사이를 질주하는 일은 없으리라고 주장한다.

5 그녀는 자동차 기술이 발전할수록 항상 교통량이 많아졌지 적어지는 일은 없었다고 말한다.

6 이것은 지문과 상반되는 내용으로, 지문에서는 스마트카가 운전 중에 경로를 제어해 교통 정체를 피할 수 있을 거라고 말한다.

7 또한, 강의에서는 스마트카까지 가세한 미래의 교통 체증이 현재보다 더 심해질 것이라고 주장한다.

8 다음으로, 교수는 스마트카의 유지비를 언급한다.

9 그녀는 스마트카가 주문 생산 방식이기 때문에 특별 제작을 해야 해서 엄청난 비용이 든다고 단언한다.

10 하지만 지문에서는 스마트카는 차주에게 문제가 커지지 않은 상태에서 알려줌으로써 저렴한 비용으로 수리가 가능하다고 말한다.

11 하지만, 교수는 공임은 비싸지 않지만 부품이 필요한 모든 수리는 비용이 만만치 않을 거라고 이야기한다.

12 결론적으로, 교수는 스마트카의 미래에 대해 어두운 견해를 갖고 있는데, 이것은 지문을 쓴 사람의 의견에 직접적으로 대치된다. 지

문의 저자는 스마트카가 대단히 유용하리라고 본다.

Unit 2 Environment I

Note Taking & Outlining

A

많은 환경론자들은 생태계에 새로운 종을 도입하는 것을 경계한다. 생태계는 깨지기 쉬워서 외래종을 새로운 지역에 도입할 경우 많은 문제를 일으키는 일이 자주 있다. 사실, 외래종이 새로운 생태계에 침입하면 흔히 여러 가지 부작용을 낳는다.

우선, 새로운 종의 도입은 여러 가지 면에서 지역 생태계를 파괴한다. 첫 번째로 외래종은 포식자가 되어 다른 토착종들을 잡아먹어서 멸종에 이르게 한다. 또 다른 방법은 그 지역의 소중한 먹이를 엄청나게 소비하는 것이다. 이러한 소비로 다른 동물들은 원래 먹던 것만큼 충분한 먹이를 섭취하지 못한다. 이로 인해 토착종의 수가 감소하게 된다.

비자생종이 해를 끼치는 또 다른 방법은 그 지역에 사는 사람에게 재정적 손실을 입히는 것이다. 한 가지 예로 미 남서부 지역의 메스킷콩을 들 수 있다. 이 식물은 물이 거의 없는 지역에서 잘 자란다. 그러나 이 식물은 토양에서 물을 다 흡수해 버리기 때문에 주변 지역의 목초가 충분히 성장하지 못하고 죽는다. 이로 인해 해당 지역의 목장주들은 동물 사료비 지출이 더 커지기 때문에 재정적 피해를 입는다. 그뿐만 아니라, 메스킷콩은 번식 속도가 빨라 농부들은 땅에서 이 나무를 제거하기 위해 많은 돈을 들여야 한다.

[1] eat native species
[2] enough food
[3] soak up all the water
[4] regenerate very easily

B

M: Why don't we discuss a few more invasive species before today's class ends? Now, although we've discussed a lot of harmful invasive species, please remember that they are not always detrimental to the local ecosystem. In fact, I could name a few that have actually been, well, beneficial. Don't believe me? Okay, listen to this.

Everyone knows that Kansas is famous for wheat and Texas is celebrated for cows. Well, they are both, uh, invasive species. And they haven't done any harm to the environment. For example, wheat has not caused the extinction of any local wildlife. It doesn't use up an excessive amount of resources like some invasive species do. And cows, of course, are not predators, so no animals have been killed by them while they graze.

Those are two examples of harmless invasive species. But how about invasive species that are, uh, beneficial?

Yeah, it sometimes happens. A perfect case is that of the cane toad, which was introduced for farmers down in Florida, among other places. Cane toads devour many harmful insects, so they keep the bug population down. Also, since the toads eat so many insects, farmers don't have to use any pesticides that could be dangerous to humans. So, cane toads are actually helpful to many people, showing that invasive species sometimes do have benefits.

M: 수업을 끝내기 전에 추가로 몇 가지 외래종에 대해 이야기해 봅시다. 앞서 공부한 내용이 여러 가지 해로운 외래종에 대해서였지만 외래종이라고 해서 지역 생태계에 늘 해롭기만 한 것은 아니라는 사실을 기억하기 바랍니다. 사실, 실제적으로 유익한 몇 가지 외래종의 예를 들 수도 있어요. 못 믿겠다고요? 좋아요, 잘 듣기 바래요.

캔자스는 밀로 유명하고 텍사스는 소로 유명하다는 것은 누구나 잘 알고 있을 거예요. 하지만 이 두 가지 다 외래종이에요. 이 종들은 해당 환경에 아무런 해도 끼치지 않았어요. 예를 들어, 해당 지역의 야생생물 가운데 밀 때문에 멸종한 종은 없습니다. 밀은 일부 외래종처럼 과도한 양의 자원을 소비하지도 않습니다. 물론, 소는 포식동물이 아니라서 풀을 뜯는 동안 어떠한 동물도 잡아먹지 않았죠.

이 두 가지는 무해한 외래종의 예입니다. 그런데 유익한 외래종은 어떻게 해서 가능할까요? 이런 현상은 실제로 일어납니다. 아주 좋은 예가 여러 다른 지역 가운데 특히 남부 플로리다 지역 농부들을 위해 도입된 수수두꺼비입니다. 수수두꺼비는 많은 해충을 닥치는 대로 잡아먹기 때문에 해충의 수를 줄일 수 있습니다. 또한 수수두꺼비는 많은 해충을 잡아먹기 때문에 농부들은 인간에게 해를 끼칠 수도 있는 살충제를 전혀 사용하지 않아도 됩니다. 그래서 수수두꺼비는 사실 많은 이들에게 유익한데, 이는 외래종이 때로는 유익하기도 하다는 것을 보여줍니다.

 wheat
²cows
³cane toad
⁴pesticides

C

Reading (Main Points)

1   Invasive species can ¹harm the ecosystem by killing all the native species or ²eating their food supply.
2   Some nonnative species like ³the mesquite tree can cause ⁴financial damage because of its killing of local plant life or the cost of paying for its removal.

Listening (Refutations)

1   Many invasive species, like ⁵wheat and cows, do not have any negative effects on their new ecosystems because they do not ⁶kill any of the local plant or animal life.
2   Some invasive species, like ⁷the cane toad, which kills bugs and keeps farmers from ⁸having to use

pesticides that can be harmful to humans, can actually be helpful to people.

Paraphrasing & Summarizing

A-1

1   When nonnative species go to a new place, they can often cause many problems because most local environments can be disrupted easily.
2   Some nonnative species hunt and kill native species, occasionally to the point of wiping them out entirely.
3   Some native species have to eat less than their normal diet because invasive species are devouring all of their food.
4   Some invasive species are detrimental because they cause locals to lose money.
5   It is expensive for farmers to have mesquite trees eliminated from a plot of land since they grow back fast.

A-2

Because ecosystems can easily be disrupted, most environmentalists do not want animal or plant species introduced to a new area. For example, invasive species might act as predators and kill all of a local species. Or they might simply eat ³other animals' food sources, which will cause these animals to starve to death. Other invasive species cause ⁴significant financial damage. An example of this is the mesquite tree. This tree kills all the local grass, so farmers need to purchase more food for their animals. The trees are also hard to ⁵eliminate from the land, so farmers have to spend a lot of money paying for their removal.

생태계는 쉽게 파괴되기 때문에 대부분의 환경론자들은 동물종이나 식물종을 새로운 지역에 도입하기를 원하지 않는다. 예를 들어, 외래종은 포식자의 역할을 해 일정 지역의 한 종을 멸종시키기도 한다. 그런가 하면 다른 동물의 식량원을 먹어 치우는 경우도 있는데, 이렇게 되면 이 동물들은 굶어 죽게 된다. 다른 외래종은 심각한 재정적 피해를 입히기도 한다. 이것의 한 예가 메스큇 나무이다. 이 나무는 해당 지역의 초목을 전부 죽게 만들기 때문에 농부들은 가축이 먹을 사료 구입에 더 많은 돈을 쓰게 된다. 이 나무는 또한 땅에서 제거하기가 쉽지 않기 때문에 농부들은 이 식물을 제거하는 데 많은 비용을 써야 한다.

B-1

1   While many invasive species damage their new environments, this is not always the case.
2   It is well known that many farmers grow wheat in Kansas and many ranchers raise cows in Texas.

3   Cows are harmless creatures that <u>do not do
    anything to other animals while they are out in the
    fields</u>.
4   The cane toad in Florida, one of the places the
    animal was introduced, <u>has actually helped the local
    environment</u>.
5   Because cane toads <u>eliminate many insects</u>, there
    is no need to <u>fill the environment with potentially
    harmful pesticides</u>.

B-2

Many people believe that all invasive species harm
their new environments, but that is not necessarily true.
Some nonnative plants and animals do not [1]<u>damage
their local ecosystems</u>. Two examples of this are
[2]<u>Kansas wheat and Texas cows</u>. The wheat has never
killed another local species. Likewise, the cows simply
graze in their fields and do not harm others. Also, some
invasive species can actually [3]<u>benefit their new homes.</u>
[4]<u>The cane toad in Florida</u> is one such example. It kills
many insects that eat farmers' crops. Also, its presence
means that farmers do not have to resort to using [5]<u>any
harmful pesticides</u> on their crops. In this case, the cane
toad has truly improved the local environment.

많은 사람들은 외래종은 전부 새로운 환경에 해를 입힌다고 생각한다.
하지만 반드시 그렇지만은 않다. 어떤 비자생종 식물이나 동물은 지역
생태계에 해를 입히지 않는다. 이것의 두 가지 예가 캔자스 밀과 텍사스
소이다. 밀이 다른 지역 종을 멸종시킨 경우는 한 번도 없었다. 마찬가
지로, 소 역시 풀밭에서 풀을 뜯기만 하지 다른 동물에게 피해를 입히지
는 않는다. 그뿐만 아니라, 일부 외래종은 실제로 새로운 환경에 도움을
주는 경우도 있다. 플로리다의 수수두꺼비가 그러한 예이다. 이 두꺼비
는 농부가 재배한 농작물을 먹어 치우는 해충을 잡아먹는다. 또한 수수
두꺼비가 있으면 농작물에 유해한 살충제를 사용하지 않아도 된다. 이
경우에는 사실 수수두꺼비로 인해 지역 환경이 개선되었다.

Synthesizing & Organizing

A

1   The reading declares that <u>nonnative species may
    become predators and hunt native species to
    extinction</u>, but the professor claims that <u>the growing
    of wheat, which is a nonnative species, has not
    resulted in any species becoming extinct</u>.
2   While the author of the reading passage claims
    that <u>many invasive species can damage their local
    environments by eating a significant amount of a
    food source</u>, the lecturer states that <u>cows are not
    dangerous to their new environments because they
    have never harmed any other species</u>.

3   In opposition to the claim that <u>mesquite trees kill the
    local grass so farmers have to pay more for feed</u>,
    the professor asserts that <u>some invasive species,
    like the cane toad, are beneficial because they eat
    lots of harmful insects</u>.
4   Contrasting the reading's assertion that <u>eliminating
    mesquite trees is expensive to farmers</u>, the
    professor believes that <u>cane toads are helpful
    to humans because the land does not require
    potentially harmful pesticides since the animals eat
    insects</u>.

B

1   The reading passage and lecture both talk about
    <u>invasive species</u>, but they disagree as to <u>the effects
    on their new environments</u>.
2   The professor believes that <u>invasive species have
    no effect on their environment or are beneficial</u>.
3   However, the reading passage believes <u>they are
    harmful</u>.
4   The lecturer first states that <u>many invasive species,
    like Kansas wheat and Texas cows, do not negatively
    affect the environment</u>.
5   He claims that <u>neither one of them has caused the
    extinction of any species</u>.
6   The reading, however, disagrees and claims that
    <u>many nonnative species are predators, so they hunt
    some animals to extinction</u>.
7   Also, they sometimes eat all of an area's food
    supply, which <u>causes local animals to die of
    starvation</u>.
8   The professor also asserts that <u>some invasive
    species can be beneficial to their new environment</u>.
9   He cites the example of <u>the cane toad in Florida</u>.
10 He claims that <u>cane toads eat insects, so they keep
    the bug population down and allow farmers not to
    use dangerous insecticides</u>.
11 However, the reading claims that <u>some invasive
    species, like the mesquite tree, cause financial harm
    to farmers</u>.
12 The reading states that <u>since mesquite trees kill
    grass, farmers must pay more for animal feed</u>.
13 It is also expensive to <u>remove them from the land</u>.
14 Clearly, <u>the two passages disagree with one another
    with regards to the value of invasive species</u>.

1   지문과 강의는 모두 외래종에 대해 다루지만 새 환경에 미치는 영
    향에 대해서는 견해를 달리 한다.
2   교수는 외래종이 환경에 영향을 미치지 않거나 유익하다고 생각한다.
3   하지만, 지문에서는 외래종이 유해하다고 본다.
4   강의자는 처음에 캔자스 밀이나 텍사스 소와 같이 많은 외래종이

환경에 부정적 영향을 미치지 않는다고 말한다.

5 그는 두 경우 다 어떠한 종도 멸종시키지 않았다고 주장한다.

6 하지만, 지문은 견해가 달라 많은 비자생종이 천적 역할을 하며 일부 동물을 사냥해 멸종에 이르게도 한다고 주장한다.

7 게다가, 때로는 한 지역의 식량원을 전부 먹어 치워 그 지역 동물이 굶어 죽게 만들기도 한다.

8 교수는 또한 일부 외래종은 새 환경에 도움을 줄 수 있다고 주장한다.

9 그는 플로리다의 수수두꺼비를 예로 든다.

10 그는 수수두꺼비는 해충을 잡아먹기 때문에 해충의 수를 감소시켜 농부들이 살충제를 사용하지 않게끔 한다고 주장한다.

11 하지만, 지문에서는 메스킷 나무와 같은 일부 외래종이 농부들에게 재정적 피해를 입힐 수도 있다고 주장한다.

12 지문에서는 메스킷 나무가 초목을 죽이기 때문에 농부는 사료값을 더 많이 지출해야 한다고 말한다.

13 그뿐만 아니라, 토지에서 메스킷 나무를 제거하는 데도 비용이 많이 든다.

14 확실히, 두 내용은 외래종의 가치와 관련해 서로 견해를 달리 한다.

Unit 3 Sociopolitics

Note Taking & Outlining

A

미국 정치에서 논란이 되는 문제는 휘발유세를 인상할 것인가 말 것인가 하는 문제이다. 많은 이들은 휘발유세를 인상하면 경제가 살아날 것이라고 믿기 때문에 이를 지지한다. 하지만 휘발유세를 올리면 분명히 미국 경제에 부정적 영향을 미칠 것이기 때문에 이는 잘못된 생각이다.

우선, 휘발유세를 올리는 것은 경제에 도움이 되지 않는다. 많은 사람들이 자동차를 이용해 출근을 한다. 정부가 휘발유세를 몇 퍼센트 올리면 사람들의 통근 비용이 증가한다. 많은 경우, 사람들은 이러한 추가 비용을 감당할 능력이 없다. 그뿐만 아니라, 사람들이 휘발유 값에 더 많은 비용을 지출할 경우 다른 제품 구매에 돈을 덜 쓰게 된다. 미국 경제는 소비자의 소비에 의해 움직이기 때문에 소비의 감소는 경제에 심각한 피해를 입힌다.

두 번째로, 휘발유세를 올리면 저소득층에 피해가 간다. 자연히, 휘발유세 인상으로 휘발유 값이 올라가는데. 이 사람들은 휘발유세를 낼 만한 돈이 없다. 게다가, 저소득층의 많은 사람들이 대중교통이 없는 지역에 거주하기 때문에 외출을 하거나 직장에 나가는 것조차 어려워질 수 있다. 기껏해야, 재정적 궁핍만 가중될 뿐이다.

¹people's finances
²the overall economy
³more expensive
⁴public transportation

B

M: While we're on the topic of taxes, let's discuss another touchy issue. I'm referring, of course, to the gasoline tax. I must say that I'm strongly in favor of raising the gas tax for a number of reasons. Allow me to explain a couple of them.

One argument people always like to use against the gas tax is that it will disrupt the economy. Well, I disagree. For one thing, our economy is way too complex for just one factor to hurt the economy. A raise in percentage points in the gas tax wouldn't in any way dramatically harm our economy. Also, there are many other factors that are already doing tremendous economic damage. Health care expenses and fixing the nation's infrastructure are just two of these.

Also, let's think about how people with low incomes would be affected. Yes, the gas tax would take money that they can't afford to spend out of their pockets. However, all it takes is a little creativity to solve this problem. For example, the government could give tax breaks to people whose incomes are below a certain level. This would, in a sense, give them a rebate on the gas tax. Or the government could also allow people with lower incomes to pay less money when they go to fill up their cars.

M: 세금 문제를 다루는 김에 또 다른 까다로운 문제에 대해서 이야기해 봅시다. 물론, 휘발유세에 대한 이야기입니다. 나는 여러 가지 이유로 휘발유세 인상에 찬성합니다.

사람들이 휘발유세에 반대하는 이유로 항상 언급하는 것이 휘발유세가 경제를 와해시키리라는 것입니다. 글쎄요, 내 생각은 다릅니다. 우선, 미국 경제는 단 한 가지 요소가 경제에 피해를 줄 수 없을 정도로 복잡한 구조로 되어 있습니다. 휘발유세를 몇 퍼센트 인상한다고 해서 경제에 절대로 심각한 피해가 가지 않습니다. 또한, 이미 경제에 엄청난 피해를 입히고 있는 많은 다른 요소들이 있습니다. 보건의료비 지출과 국가의 인프라 정비가 이에 해당되는 두 가지 예입니다.

또한, 저소득층에게 미치는 영향에 대해서도 생각해 봅시다. 그래요. 휘발유세는 저소득층의 주머니에서 쓸 수 있는 돈을 빼내 갈 것입니다. 하지만 이 문제를 해결하는 데는 약간의 창의성만 있으면 됩니다. 예를 들어, 정부는 소득이 일정 수준 이하인 사람들에게는 세제 감면 혜택을 주면 됩니다. 어떤 의미에서 이것은 세금 환급이라고도 할 수 있겠죠. 아니면 정부가 저소득층에게는 휘발유 구매 시 저가 적용 정책을 쓸 수도 있습니다.

¹very complex
²health care
³tax breaks
⁴gas stations

Reading (Main Points)

1. Increasing the gasoline tax would be bad for America because it would increase the prices of [1]people's daily commutes and also [2]reduce spending, which would harm the economy.
2. Raising the gasoline tax would harm people with low incomes since they would not be able to [3]afford gas and do not have access to good [4]public transportation.

Listening (Refutations)

1. A rise in the gasoline tax would not hurt the economy since [5]the economy is too big to be affected by it and also because there are other problems like [6]health care and infrastructure that are causing economic damage.
2. While a gasoline tax would hurt people with low incomes, the government could [7]give them tax breaks or [8]charge them less for gasoline at gas stations.

Paraphrasing & Summarizing

1. People who think increasing the gasoline tax would not hurt the economy are wrong.
2. If the gas tax increases, it will make getting to work and home more expensive for everyone.
3. More spending on gas will cause people to buy fewer other items.
4. People who do not make much money would not be able to afford gas if the gasoline tax goes up.
5. Those with low salaries who live in areas without buses or subways will not have enough money to get to work or drive to other places.

Although some people believe the government should increase the gasoline tax, it would actually [1]harm the economy. First, many people use their cars to drive to work. Raising the gas tax would make these trips [2]more expensive. And then people would spend less money [3]buying other products. The American economy needs people to buy things, or else it will start getting bad. Also, a high gasoline tax would be bad for people who [4]earn low salaries. They might not even be able to afford to [5]drive to work. Since they cannot take public transportation, it would be difficult for them to get around.

몇몇 사람들은 정부가 휘발유세를 인상해야 한다고 생각하지만 그것은 실제로 경제에 피해를 입힐 것이다. 우선, 많은 사람들이 자동차로 통근을 한다. 휘발유세를 인상할 경우 통근에 드는 비용이 비싸질 것이다. 그러면 사람들은 다른 제품 구매를 줄일 것이다. 미국 경제는 소비자가 제품을 구매해 줘야 하는데, 그렇지 않을 경우 경제는 엉망이 될 것이다. 게다가, 높은 휘발유세는 저소득층에게도 피해를 입힐 것이다. 자동차로 직장에 출근하기조차 어려워지고 대중교통이 없기 때문에 돌아다니기도 어려워질 것이다.

1. In my view, there are many reasons why the gasoline tax should be raised.
2. Due to the complexity of the economy, one factor alone cannot cause it to decline.
3. Many other things, such as the costs of medical expenses and repairing roads and bridges, are already harming the economy.
4. The government could lower taxes on people who make less than a certain amount of money.
5. It might be possible to charge poor people less money at gas stations.

B-2

The professor fully supports [1]increasing the gasoline tax for a couple of different reasons. First, he does not agree with arguments that a higher gas tax would harm the economy. Since the American economy is so [2]big and complex, it would be impossible for an increased gas tax to damage it. Likewise, issues like [3]health care and repairing infrastructure are already causing lots of damage to the economy. Second, while people with [4]low incomes would be hurt by an increased tax, there are ways to avoid this pain. The government could give them [5]tax breaks to compensate them for the increase in taxes. Or they could simply pay less when they go to fill up their cars.

교수는 두 가지 이유로 휘발유세 인상을 전적으로 지지한다. 첫 번째로는, 세금을 인상하면 경제에 피해가 가리라는 주장에 동의하지 않는다. 미국 경제는 규모가 대단히 크고 복잡하기 때문에 세금 인상이 영향을 미친다는 것이 불가능하다. 마찬가지로, 보건의료비나 인프라 정비와 같은 문제들은 이미 경제에 엄청난 피해를 주고 있다. 두 번째로, 저소득층이 세금 인상의 영향을 받긴 하겠지만 이 문제를 해결할 여러 가지 방법이 있다. 정부가 세금 인상에 대한 보상으로 세제 혜택을 줄 수도 있다. 아니면 휘발유 구매 시 저가 정책을 쓸 수도 있다.

Synthesizing & Organizing

A

1 The reading passage declares that increasing the gasoline tax would cause people to pay more money to get to work and home, but the professor claims that the gas tax would not hurt the American economy due to its complexity.

2 The reading claims that people spending more money on gas will purchase fewer other products, yet the professor claims that there are more pressing issues to the economy, such as health care expenses and fixing the country's infrastructure.

3 In response to the claim that poor people do not have enough money to pay a more expensive gas tax, the professor states that people with low incomes could be offered tax breaks by the government.

4 While the reading asserts that, due to a lack of public transportation, poor people would not be able to get to work if the gas tax goes up, the lecturer maintains that these individuals could be allowed to pay lower rates for gasoline at gas stations.

B

1 The professor firmly disagrees with the reading passage, which states that increasing the gasoline tax would harm the economy.

2 Instead, the professor feels that this would not have a negative effect on the economy.

3 To begin with, the reading passage declares that an increase in the gasoline tax would make people's commutes cost more.

4 The author also mentions that people would therefore spend less money.

5 Since the American economy needs people to spend money to remain strong, it would start to go into decline.

6 However, the professor believes the gas tax could not harm the economy since it is too complex to be affected by one tax.

7 Plus, a gas tax's effects cannot compare to health care costs and the repair of the country's infrastructure, which are already damaging the current economy.

8 The reading also states that people with low incomes will not be able to afford gas and may not be able to go to work or anywhere else.

9 The professor mentions that the government could simply give people tax breaks.

10 He also thinks that people with low incomes could pay less when they go to gas stations.

11 The professor and the reading passage are definitely in disagreement over the gasoline tax, and both provide a couple of reasons in defense of their arguments.

1 교수는 휘발유세 인상이 경제에 피해를 입힌다는 지문 내용에 전적으로 반대한다.

2 대신에, 교수는 이것이 경제에 부정적인 영향을 미치지 않으리라고 본다.

3 우선, 지문에서는 휘발유세 인상이 사람들의 통근비를 인상시킬 것이라고 주장한다.

4 또 저자는 이로 인해 사람들의 소비가 줄 것이라고 말한다.

5 미국 경제가 강하게 유지되려면 소비자가 소비를 해야 하기 때문에 그것은 경기 하락을 유발할 것이다.

6 하지만, 교수는 미국 경제가 너무 복잡한 구조를 가지고 있어 한 가지 세금에 의해 영향을 받지 않으므로 휘발유세가 미국 경제에 피해를 입히지는 않는다고 생각한다.

7 또한, 휘발유세의 효과는 이미 현 경제에 피해를 입히고 있는 보건 의료비나 인프라 정비에 드는 비용과는 비교가 되지 않는다.

8 지문에서는 또한 저소득층이 휘발유 값을 낼 능력이 안 되어 직장이나 다른 어떤 곳에도 갈 수 없을 것이라고 말한다.

9 교수는 정부가 이들에게 세제 혜택을 줄 수 있다고 말한다.

10 그는 또한 소득이 낮은 사람들이 휘발유 구매 시 저가 정책을 쓸 수도 있다고 생각한다.

11 교수와 지문은 휘발유세에 대해 완전히 상반된 견해를 보이며 둘 다 각자의 주장에 대해 두 가지 이유를 제시한다.

Unit 4 Environment II

Note Taking & Outlining

A

산불의 위험 때문에 일부 공원 산림 감시원들은 숲을 보호하는 새로운 방법을 장려하기 시작했다. 이 방법은 입화라고 한다. 그들은 실제로 숲에 불을 놓아 다양한 종류의 나무와 다른 식물들을 태운다. 안타깝게도, 입화는 여러 가지 이유에서 효과적인 방법이 아니다.

첫 번째로, 산불은 통제가 지극히 어렵다. 공원 산림 감시원은 대단한 주의를 기울인다고 하지만 입화가 통제를 벗어나는 일은 얼마든지 가능하다. 몇몇 경우에 실제로 이런 일이 발생하기도 했다. 산림 감시원이 불을 통제할 수 없기 때문에 정상적인 산불이 발생했을 때보다 훨씬 큰 피해를 입혔다. 사실, 산불은 예측이 불가능하다. 산림 감시원들은 한 지역만 태우고 싶어하지만 산불의 예측 불가능성 때문에 다른 지역을 더 태우기도 한다.

그뿐만 아니라, 입화는 비용도 만만치 않다. 산불을 놓고 통제하는 데 많은 비용이 든다. 이 과정에는 수많은 사람들과 장비가 필요하기 때문에 인건비와 장비 비용을 지불해야 한다. 더욱이, 산불이 통제 불가능하게 번지기 시작하면 제어하는 데 훨씬 많은 비용이 든다. 모든 것을 고려해볼 때, 입화는 많은 단점이 있어 실행하지 말아야 한다.

[1]regular forest fires
[2]unpredictable
[3]people and equipment
[4]burning uncontrollably

B

M: We all know that forest fires can cause lots of damage to the environment. Remember that one we had last year? Well, the forest is just now starting to recover. However, some environmentalists actually believe that starting forest fires is effective. Imagine that! *[chuckles]* It's called prescribed burning, and here are its advantages.

First, unlike a regular forest fire, which often burns uncontrollably, prescribed burning can be handled. Park rangers are able to manage exactly where the fire burns and even what plants and trees it burns down. There are many different prescribed burning experts and programs, so park rangers make sure to consult them before they commence with the burning. Even if the fire starts burning unpredictably, they have methods to ensure that the fire does not get out of their control and burn the wrong places.

Second, there are always fires in forests. They actually help rejuvenate the forests. However, natural forest fires can cause up to ten times the damage prescribed burning does. Not only that, but natural forest fires can also get into human settlements, burn down houses, and even kill people. By using prescribed burning, authorities can control exactly what gets burned while keeping the fire on a small scale. So they can help the forest recover yet prevent it from entirely burning down.

M: 우리 모두는 산불이 환경에 막대한 피해를 줄 수 있다는 것을 알고 있습니다. 지난해에 있었던 산불 기억하시죠? 숲은 이제 막 회복하기 시작했습니다. 하지만, 실제로 일부 환경론자들은 산불을 놓는 것이 효과적이라고 생각합니다. 한번 상상해 보세요. *[웃음]* 이것을 입화라고 하는데, 여기에는 여러 가지 이점이 있습니다.

우선, 종종 제어가 불가능한 정상적인 산불과는 달리 입화는 제어가 가능합니다. 공원 산림 감시원은 정확히 어디에 산불을 놓을지, 어떤 식물과 나무를 태울지를 알 수 있습니다. 많은 다양한 입화 전문가들과 프로그램이 있기 때문에 공원 산림 감시원은 입화에 앞서 조언을 들을 수 있습니다. 불이 예측 불가능하게 타기 시작했다고 하더라도 그들은 산불이 통제를 벗어나 다른 지역을 태우지 않도록 하는 방법이 있습니다.

두 번째로, 숲에는 항상 산불이 발생합니다. 산불은 실제로 숲을 회생시키는 역할을 합니다. 하지만 자연적인 산불은 입화에 비해 최고 10배까지 피해를 입히기도 합니다. 그뿐만 아니라, 자연적인 산불은 인간의 주

거지까지 번져 주택을 태우고 인명 피해를 입히기도 합니다. 입화를 이용하면 적은 규모에서 정확히 무엇을 태울지를 제어할 수 있습니다. 그래서 숲을 회복시키면서도 완전히 태우는 것을 막을 수 있습니다.

[1]where fires burn
[2]get out of control
[3]ten times
[4]a small scale

C

Reading (Main Points)

1 Some prescribed burning fires may get [1]out of control, which makes them burn more land than was planned and makes them [2]too unpredictable to control.

2 Prescribed burning is not cheap because [3]people's salaries and equipment costs must be paid, and it becomes [4]even more expensive if the fire starts to burn out of control.

Listening (Refutations)

1 [5]Park rangers consult experts to make sure that their fires don't burn out of control, and, if the fires [6]become unpredictable, they have ways to make sure the fires do not become very bad.

2 Prescribed burning can cause much less damage than [7]natural fires and can help a forest [8]rejuvenate by burning only a small part of it.

Paraphrasing & Summarizing

A-1

1 There are a lot of reasons why prescribed burning does not really help.

2 Despite the fact that park rangers claim they are careful, a prescribed burning can still suddenly get out of their control.

3 Sometimes unpredictable forest fires burn other areas of the forest that the park rangers did not intend to burn.

4 Initiating and controlling a forest fire can be expensive.

5 It can become more expensive to gain back control of a fire once it starts to get out of control.

A-2

Prescribed burning is the practice of starting forest fires [1]on purpose and controlling them so that they burn a small area of the forest. This method, however, has some disadvantages. The first disadvantage is that the fires can sometimes ²get out of control. Fires are hard to control, and some prescribed burnings have actually gotten out of control and burned unintended places. In fact, rangers sometimes wind up ³burning other places because they cannot control the fires. The second disadvantage is the cost involved. Paying ⁴people's salaries and equipment costs is expensive. Also, when the fires get out of control, it costs a lot of money to ⁵get them back under control.

입화는 고의로 산불을 놓아서 적은 면적의 숲을 태울 수 있도록 산불을 통제하는 방법을 말한다. 하지만, 이 방법은 몇 가지 단점이 있다. 첫 번째 단점은 불이 때로는 통제를 벗어난다는 것이다. 불은 통제하기가 어려운데, 일부 입화는 실제로 통제를 벗어나 의도치 않은 지역을 태우기도 했다. 사실, 공원 산림 감시원들은 불을 통제하지 못해 다른 지역을 태운 경우도 있었다. 두 번째 단점은 비용과 관련한 것이다. 인건비와 장비 사용에 드는 비용은 만만치가 않다. 그뿐만 아니라, 산불이 통제를 벗어나면 다시 제어하는 데 엄청난 돈이 든다.

B-1

1   According to certain environmentalists, prescribed burning actually works.
2   Park rangers can control prescribed burnings so well that they know which areas will burn and which plants and trees will get burned down.
3   Rangers know various methods to regain control of a fire if it should start burning unpredictably and go into the wrong parts of the forest.
4   Prescribed burnings are ten times less damaging than forest fires.
5   Prescribed burning enables rangers to control the parts of the forest that get burned while not allowing the fire to form on a large scale.

B-2

The professor claims that prescribed burning actually has a number of positive benefits. The first one he cites is that ¹park rangers are able to control these prescribed burnings. Because they consult with experts, they know exactly how ²to manage these forest fires. Also, if there is a case where the fire starts to get out of their control, they know a number of different ³methods to regain control. Second of all, the professor claims that natural forest fires ⁴cause ten times the damage that prescribed burnings do. Also, natural fires often damage homes and kill people. However, prescribed burnings can take place on ⁵a small scale, burn down unwanted areas, and help the forest to rejuvenate.

교수는 입화에 실제로 여러 가지 긍정적 효과가 있다고 주장한다. 그가 말한 첫 번째 효과는 이러한 입화를 공원 산림 감시원이 통제할 수 있다는 것이다. 전문가들과 상의하기 때문에 이러한 산불을 정확히 어떻게

통제할지 안다. 또한 산불이 통제를 벗어난다고 하더라도 산불을 잡는 여러 가지 방법을 알고 있다. 두 번째로, 교수는 자연적인 산불은 입화에 비해 10배나 되는 피해를 줄 수 있다고 주장한다. 그뿐만 아니라, 자연적인 산불은 종종 주택과 인명 피해를 가져온다. 하지만, 입화는 작은 규모로 발생해, 불필요한 지역을 태우고, 숲의 회생을 돕는다.

Synthesizing & Organizing

1   In contrast to the reading passage's claim that prescribed burnings often get out of control, the professor insists that park rangers can determine exactly where the fire will burn and also which plants and trees it will burn.
2   The author of the reading passage writes that prescribed burnings might burn places that rangers had not intended, yet the lecturer states that rangers can counter the unpredictable nature of forest fires by using methods to ensure that the fires do not get out of control.
3   The author of the writing declares that a prescribed burning costs a lot of money; however, the professor counters that claim by stating that forest fires can be much more dangerous and can burn homes and kill people.
4   The reading passage states that uncontrollably burning fires are expensive to get back into control, but the lecturer insists that these fires can be controlled by the authorities and burn on a small scale.

B

1   The lecturer claims that prescribed burnings are beneficial to forests, yet the reading passage declares the opposite.
2   The professor gives several reasons to counter the arguments in the reading passage.
3   First, in contrast to the claim that prescribed burnings can get out of control, the professor says that park rangers can keep these fires under control.
4   He also claims that rangers consult experts, so they know what they are doing.
5   Also, the professor states that rangers have methods to control unpredictable fires.
6   This is countered by the reading assertion that fires are so unpredictable that they can burn unintended sections of forest.
7   Second, the lecturer declares that natural forest fires can be ten times as dangerous as prescribed burnings and can even kill people.

8 Meanwhile, the reading says that <u>prescribed burnings are too expensive</u>.

9 The reading also states that <u>it costs a lot of money to get a fire back under control</u>.

10 However, the professor mentions that <u>these fires happen on a small scale, thus they are able to be controlled and can also help rejuvenate the forest</u>.

11 The professor and reading clearly disagree with one another with regards to <u>the usefulness of prescribed burning</u>.

1 강의자는 입화가 여러 가지 면에서 숲에 유익하다고 주장하지만 지문은 반대 내용을 담고 있다.

2 교수는 지문의 주장을 반박하기 위해 몇 가지 이유를 든다.

3 첫 번째로, 입화가 통제를 벗어날 수 있다는 주장에 반대해서 교수는 공원 산림 감시원이 이러한 산불을 통제할 수 있다고 말한다.

4 그는 또한 산림 감시원들은 전문가의 조언을 받기 때문에 자신들이 어떤 일을 하는지 안다고 주장한다.

5 또한, 교수는 산림 감시원은 예상치 못했던 산불을 통제하는 여러 가지 방법이 있다고 말한다.

6 지문에서는 산불은 너무도 예측 불가능해서 의도치 않았던 지역을 태울 수도 있다고 주장해 이를 반박한다.

7 두 번째로, 교수는 자연적인 산불은 입화에 비해 10배나 위험할 수 있으며 심지어 인명 피해를 가져올 수도 있다고 말한다.

8 한편, 지문에서는 입화가 비용이 너무 많이 든다고 말한다.

9 지문에서는 또한 불을 다시 잡는 데 많은 비용이 든다고 말한다.

10 하지만, 교수는 이러한 산불은 작은 규모로 일어나며 통제가 가능하고 숲을 회생시키는 역할도 한다고 말한다.

11 교수와 지문은 입화의 유용성에 대해 서로 확실히 상반된 견해를 보인다.

Unit 5 Education

Note Taking & Outlining

요즘 들어, 많은 학교와 연구 기관들이 점점 더 교육용 비디오와 DVD에 의존한다. 일부 순수주의자들은 책을 사용하는 쪽을 더 선호해 이러한 경향에 극렬히 반대하지만 시각 자료에 의존하는 것은 사실 바람직한 일이다.

무엇보다도, 교육 자료란 듣는 이들이 관심을 기울이지 않는다면 아무런 도움이 되지 않는다. 21세기는 비주얼 시대이다. 학생들은 책을 읽는 것보다 비디오나 DVD를 시청하는 것에 더 익숙하다. 교사가 시각 자료를 사용하면 학생들의 관심을 끌기가 더 쉽다. 또한, 비디오나 DVD는 그래픽이나 컴퓨터 애니메이션을 사용해 어려운 과정이나 생각을 더 쉽게 설명할 수 있다. 이러한 특성 때문에 어려운 주제도 훨씬 이해가 쉬워지는데, 이는 학생들이 교육을 심화시키는 데 확실히 도움을 주는 장점이다.

또한, 비디오와 DVD는 책보다 훨씬 저렴하다. 많은 시청각 자료는 10

달러 이내지만 책값은 이것의 2, 3배나 된다. 많은 학생들이 빠듯한 예산으로 생활하기 때문에 이러한 경제적 혜택은 상당한 도움이 된다. 그뿐만 아니라, 많은 학교들이 같은 책을 3, 40권 이상 구입해야 하는 반면 비디오나 DVD는 하나씩만 구입하면 된다. 학교 측은 시청각 자료를 구매함으로써 엄청난 비용을 절약해 다른 중요한 자료를 구입하는 데 쓸 수 있다.

[1]watching visual aids
[2]graphics and animation
[3]tight budgets
[4]purchase just one copy

W: I know many of you prefer watching educational DVDs to reading books. However, I must inform you that books are still much better than watching visual aids. Allow me to educate you as to why.

First, videos are limited by time. You can only impart so much information in a one- or two-hour video. Therefore, the video is likely to be incomplete and not contain all the necessary information. You don't have this issue with books. A 500-page book is filled with much more information than a two-hour DVD. In addition, visual materials are often designed more for entertainment than education. This means they are often highly simplified. You often can't explain difficult topics on videos. Again, books don't suffer from this problem.

Second of all, visual aids really aren't cheaper than books. Don't believe me? Okay, well, tapes and disks of movies are often rather cheap, but this isn't the case for educational materials. They are almost always very pricey, costing between fifty to one hundred dollars a copy. These prices make them much more expensive than most books. Also, even if you own an educational DVD, you still have to purchase the DVD player and television set, which aren't cheap. And, when they break down, as is often the case, they're expensive to repair and also cause annoying delays.

W: 여러분 가운데 다수가 책을 읽기보다는 교육용 DVD 시청을 더 좋아한다는 걸 압니다. 하지만, 시청각 자료를 이용하는 것보다 책이 훨씬 더 낫다는 것을 알려주고 싶네요. 그 이유를 말씀 드리죠.

우선, 비디오는 시간 제약이 있어요. 한 시간 또는 두 시간짜리 비디오는 너무나 많은 정보를 담고 있습니다. 그래서 비디오는 불완전하거나 필요한 모든 정보가 다 담겨 있지 않은 경우가 많아요. 책의 경우는 이런 문제가 없습니다. 500쪽짜리 책에는 2시간짜리 비디오보다 훨씬 많은 정보가 담겨 있습니다. 그뿐만 아니라, 시청각 자료는 교육보다는 오락을 위해 만들어지는 경우가 많아요. 다시 말해, 비디오는 대단히 단순화되어 있는 경우가 많습니다. 어려운 주제에 대해 비디오로 설명할 수는 없어요. 다시 한 번, 책은 이런 문제가 없습니다.

두 번째로, 시청각 자료는 사실 책에 비해 저렴하지 않습니다. 못 믿겠다고요? 좋아요, 그렇다면, 영화 테이프나 디스크는 저렴한 경우가 많지만 교육용 자료의 경우는 그렇지가 않아요. 편당 50에서 100달러 정도로 거의 예외 없이 가격이 매우 비싼 편입니다. 이로 인해 시청각 자료들은 대개 책보다 훨씬 비싸죠. 그뿐만 아니라, 교육용 DVD를 보려면 DVD 플레이어와 TV가 있어야 하는데, 이는 결코 저렴하지 않습니다. 그리고 흔히 있는 경우지만 고장이 나면 수리비도 많이 들고 시간이 지체되는 불편이 생길 수도 있습니다.

¹time restrictions
²often simplified
³educational materials
⁴repairs and delays

Reading (Main Points)

1 Educational visual aids can both ¹get the attention of students and ²explain difficult topics by using computer graphics or animation.

2 Visual aids are ³cheaper than books, which can be helpful to students on tight budgets, and schools only need ⁴one copy, so they can spend their money on other necessities.

Listening (Refutations)

1 Visual aids often provide limited information due to ⁵time constraints, and they often rely upon ⁶simplified explanations.

2 Educational visual aids can be ⁷much more expensive than books and also require expensive DVD players and TVs, equipment that can sometimes ⁸break down.

Paraphrasing & Summarizing

1 Despite the fact that some traditionalists are opposed to visual aids, they are actually beneficial to use.

2 Teachers can get students to pay attention if they show them DVDs or videotapes.

3 Since they use graphics and animation, visual aids can help students understand even difficult explanations.

4 The price of books may be two or three times higher than that of DVDs or videotapes.

5 Because schools will save a lot of money by purchasing visual aids, they can use the money to buy other things that they may need.

The use of ¹visual materials like DVDs and videotapes is something positive even though some people oppose them. The first reason given is that most students are used to watching videos instead of reading books. Therefore, the teachers can ²get their attention more easily. Also, these visual aids can make difficult concepts ³simple to understand by using graphics and animation. Second of all, the price of visual aids is much lower than that of books. This is good for students ⁴on tight budgets and for schools since the schools can buy just one DVD or tape and use the leftover money for ⁵other purchases.

DVD나 비디오테이프와 같은 시청각 자료를 사용하는 것에 반대하는 사람들이 있긴 해도 이것은 바람직한 일이다. 위에서 언급한 첫 번째 이유는 대다수 학생들이 책을 읽는 것보다는 비디오를 보는 것에 더 익숙하다는 것이다. 그래서 교사들은 더욱 쉽게 관심을 끌 수 있다. 또한, 이러한 시청각 자료들은 그래픽이나 애니메이션을 사용해 어려운 개념을 이해하기 쉽게 만들기도 한다. 두 번째로, 시청각 자료는 책보다 가격이 훨씬 저렴하다. 이것은 예산이 빠듯한 학생들에게 유익하며 학교도 DVD나 비디오를 하나씩만 사고 여분의 돈을 다른 것을 구매하는 데 사용할 수 있기 때문에 학교측에도 도움이 된다.

1 It is preferable to read a book than to watch a DVD or video.

2 Visual materials may not contain all the information that they should.

3 Entertaining, not educating, is the purpose of most visual materials.

4 Educational visual materials are more expensive than DVDs and videotapes of movies.

5 Without purchasing an expensive DVD player and TV, you cannot watch a DVD.

The professor feels that ¹reading books is a much preferable alternative to watching visual materials like DVDs and videotapes. First, she states that visual materials often provide ²incomplete information because they have to be so short. Books, on the other hand, hold much more information. Also, visual materials tend to simplify things since they are more interested in ³entertaining people instead of educating them. Also, the professor says that books are actually cheaper than DVDs and videotapes. The reason is that ⁴educational visual aids can be much more expensive than movies. Also, a person with a DVD needs to purchase ⁵a DVD player and a TV, which will cost more money to keep up.

교수는 DVD나 비디오테이프와 같은 시청각 자료를 보는 것보다 책을 읽는 것이 훨씬 나은 방법이라고 생각한다. 우선, 그녀는 시청각 자료는 너무나 길이가 짧아서 불완전한 정보가 담겨 있는 경우가 흔하다고 말한다. 그런 반면, 책에는 훨씬 많은 정보가 담겨 있다. 또한, 시청각 자료는 교육보다는 오락에 더 관심을 두기 때문에 다루는 내용을 단순화하는 경향이 있다. 또한, 교수는 책이 DVD나 비디오테이프에 비해 훨씬 저렴하다고 말한다. 그 이유는 교육용 시청각 자료가 영화보다 훨씬 비싸다는 것이다. 또한, DVD를 보려면 DVD 플레이어와 TV가 있어야 하는데, 유지비가 더 많이 든다.

Synthesizing & Organizing

A

1 The author of the reading declares that visual aids will enable teachers to capture their students' attention; however, the professor counters by saying that videos tend to be incomplete, thereby providing insufficient information.

2 The reading mentions that visual materials can take difficult processes and explain them easily with graphics or computer animation, yet the professor believes these materials are designed to entertain, not to educate, people.

3 In contrast to the reading, which states that books are two or three times more expensive than DVDs or videotapes, the professor claims that educational visual aids are never cheaper than books.

4 While the reading passage mentions that schools can save a lot of money by purchasing visual materials, the professor states that it is not possible to watch a DVD without an expensive DVD player and TV set.

B

1 The lecturer declares that visual materials are not particularly good.

2 This is in direct contrast to the reading passage, which claims DVDs and videotapes have many benefits.

3 First, the lecturer states that visual materials are often incomplete while books are not.

4 She says that videos are only a couple of hours long, so they cannot include all of the necessary information that a 500-page book can.

5 The author of the reading, meanwhile, claims that in this visual age, students prefer watching visual materials, which capture their attention.

6 Also, the reading states that they can make difficult topics easy through graphics and animation.

7 The professor, however, says that visual materials simplify explanations while books do not.

8 Second of all, the lecturer declares visual materials are more expensive than books. The reading, however, claims the opposite.

9 Also, the lecturer says that educational DVDs and videotapes can be fifty to one hundred dollars, yet the reading claims they are two or three times cheaper than books.

10 The reading further says that schools can save money by purchasing visual materials.

11 But the lecturer states that people still need to purchase expensive and unreliable DVD players and TVs.

12 The professor and reading passage stand on opposite sides of the debate over the usefulness of visual materials.

1 강의자는 시청각 자료가 특별히 유익하지는 않다고 주장한다.

2 이것은 지문의 내용과 직접적으로 대치되는데, 지문에서는 DVD와 비디오테이프가 많은 장점이 있다고 주장한다.

3 우선, 교수는 시청각 자료는 책에 비해 불완전한 경우가 많다고 말한다.

4 그녀는 비디오는 두 시간 길이에 불과하기 때문에 500쪽짜리 책이 가진 필요한 정보를 모두 담을 수가 없다고 말한다.

5 한편, 지문의 저자는 이 비주얼 시대에 학생들은 관심을 끄는 시청각 자료를 선호한다고 주장한다.

6 또한, 지문은 시청각 자료가 그래픽이나 애니메이션을 이용해 어려운 주제를 쉽게 만들 수 있다고 말한다.

7 하지만, 교수는 시청각 자료가 책에 비해 설명이 너무 단순하다고 말한다.

8 두 번째로, 강의자는 시청각 자료는 책보다 비싸다고 주장한다. 하지만, 지문에서는 반대의 견해를 보인다.

9 또한, 강의자는 교육용 DVD나 비디오테이프는 가격이 50에서 100달러 정도라고 말하지만, 지문에서는 그것들이 책에 비해 2, 3배는 저렴하다고 주장한다.

10 더 나아가 지문에서는 시청각 자료 구매를 통해 학교측이 비용을 절약할 수 있다고 말한다.

11 그러나 교수는 시청각 자료를 이용하기 위해서는 값도 비싸고 신뢰할 수도 없는 DVD 플레이어나 TV를 사야 한다고 말한다.

12 교수와 지문은 시청각 자료의 유용성에 관한 논쟁에서 정반대의 입장에 서 있다.

Unit 6 Business

Note Taking & Outlining

A

최근 들어 기업들에서는 상당 수의 직원들이 60대가 되어서 퇴직하는 대신 조기 퇴직을 택해 50대에 직장을 떠난다. 몇 건의 연구를 진행한 결과 기업들은 직원들의 이런 갑작스러운 조기 퇴직의 물결에 대한 두 가지 이유를 발견했다.

우선, 50대의 많은 직원들이 같은 고용주 밑에서 수 년 혹은 수십 년 동안 같은 업무를 해 왔다. 그 결과 같은 업무를 반복하는 과정에서 지치게 된다. 더욱이, 매일 반복되는 일과는 더 이상 도전의 가치를 느끼지 못하게 하고 그 대신 말할 수 없이 권태롭게 느껴진다.

두 번째로는, 나이 든 직원 가운데 많은 이들이 사내의 젊은 직원들과 스스로를 비교한다. 이런 비교를 하게 되면 보통은 바람직한 결과를 얻지 못한다. 나이가 많은 직원들은 젊은 직원과 보조를 맞출 수가 없다. 그래서 나이 든 직원들은 젊은 동료들에 비해 스스로 성취도가 낮다고 생각한다. 그뿐만 아니라, 나이 든 직원들은 자신들이 회사의 짐이 되며 과거만큼 도움이 되지 못하는 것처럼 느끼게 된다. 이러한 자책감 때문에 회사를 떠나 조기 퇴직을 하게 된다.

[1] burned out
[2] daily routines
[3] accomplish less work
[4] burdens on their companies

B

W: Now, I'd like to continue talking about how society underutilizes its elderly population. As people live longer and longer, it seems like such a waste for people in their fifties simply to retire and do nothing but play golf or go fishing. So let me give you a couple of suggestions.

Of course, many elderly people don't want full-time jobs. However, a large number would be willing to work part-time. This way of working would accomplish a couple of things. First, they wouldn't have to come in every day. This would keep the elderly from getting too worn out to do their jobs. Remember that the elderly have less energy. Also, letting them work part-time would keep their minds fresh, which means that they wouldn't become bored with their work.

Here's another idea. I know all of you young people think that you know everything, but your experiences are nothing compared to those of a fifty- or sixty-year-

old person. Companies need to do their best to utilize the skills that their older employees have. For example, they could give them a wider range of duties instead of making them repeat the same tasks over and over. And the companies could consult with their elderly employees more often. This effort would not only make them feel wanted but would also draw upon their many years of experience working at the company.

W: 사회에서 얼마나 노년층 인구를 잘 활용하지 못하고 있는지 계속해서 얘기해 보겠습니다. 인간의 수명이 점점 길어지면서 50대가 은퇴해서 단지 골프를 치거나 낚시를 간다는 것은 대단한 낭비처럼 보입니다. 그래서 몇 가지 제안을 해 보겠습니다.

물론, 많은 노년층 인구는 전일제 일자리를 원하지 않습니다. 그러나 많은 사람들이 시간제 근무는 하고 싶어 합니다. 이렇게 근무를 하게 되면 몇 가지 장점이 있습니다. 우선, 매일 출근을 하지 않아도 됩니다. 이는 나이 든 사람들이 너무 지쳐 일을 하지 못하게 되는 상황을 막을 수 있습니다. 노년층은 젊은 사람들보다 힘이 없다는 점을 잊지 말아야 합니다. 또한, 시간제 근무를 하게 되면 그들의 마음이 새로워져 업무에 대해 지겹다는 생각도 하지 않게 됩니다.

또 다른 방법도 있습니다. 젊은 여러분들은 자신들이 모든 것을 다 알고 있다고 생각한다는 것을 압니다. 하지만 여러분이 가진 경험은 50대나 60대나 가진 경험에 비할 때 아무 것도 아닙니다. 기업들은 나이 든 직원들이 가진 기술을 최대한 활용해야 합니다. 예를 들어, 동일한 작업을 계속 반복하게 하는 대신 다양한 업무를 할당할 수도 있습니다. 그리고 기업은 나이 든 직원들과 더 자주 상담할 수도 있습니다. 이러한 노력을 통해 노년층은 자신들이 필요하다고 느낄 뿐만 아니라 그 회사에서 일한 수년 간의 경험을 활용할 수 있을 것입니다.

[1] get worn out
[2] become bored
[3] a wider range of duties
[4] feel wanted

C

Reading (Problems)

1　Employees at the same jobs for many years become [1] burned out and also [2] bored by doing the same tasks again and again.
2　Older employees believe that they [3] accomplish less than younger employees and therefore feel they are [4] burdens on their companies.

Listening (Solutions)

1　It is recommended that companies hire elderly employees on [5] a part-time basis to keep them from becoming too [6] worn out and to keep them interested in their work.
2　Companies need to utilize [7] older employees' experiences by giving them various tasks and also

[8]consulting them on a more regular basis.

Paraphrasing & Summarizing

A-1

1   Nowadays, it has come to companies' attention that a great number of their elderly employees are quitting their jobs before they reach retirement age.

2   A large number of older workers have remained employed by their companies and made to do the same tasks for considerably long periods of time.

3   Doing the same jobs repeatedly makes older workers simply get tired of the monotony of their jobs.

4   Elderly employees are often measuring themselves against employees younger than they are.

5   The elderly have trouble keeping up with younger workers, which gives them the feeling that they are not as productive as these younger employees.

A-2

Companies have long wondered why many of their workers began [1]retiring in their fifties as opposed to their sixties, and now they have a couple of reasons as to why. First, many elderly employees [2]become bored after doing the same jobs day after day for very long periods of time. They simply quit because they cannot handle the boredom of their work. Second, elderly workers recognize that they are [3]being outworked by younger employees, which causes their opinions of their value to the company to decline. Realizing they are not [4]as productive as they could be and that they are [5]weighing down their employers with their presence, they simply quit their jobs.

기업들은 왜 많은 직원들이 60대가 아닌 50대에 퇴직을 하기 시작하는지 궁금해했는데, 몇 가지 이유가 밝혀졌다. 우선, 나이 든 많은 직원들이 매우 긴 기간 동안 매일매일 같은 업무를 반복하다 보니 권태를 느낀다. 그들은 단지 업무에서 오는 권태로움을 주체하지 못해서 직장을 그만둔다. 두 번째로, 나이 든 직원들은 젊은 직원들이 훨씬 더 많은 업무를 처리한다는 것을 깨닫게 되는데, 이로 인해 회사에서 그들의 가치에 대한 평가가 낮아진다. 그들은 과거에 비해 생산성이 떨어지고 자신들의 존재가 기업주에게 짐이 된다는 것을 깨닫고는 일을 그만두게 된다.

B-1

1   Let me carry on with some examples as to how we fail to help the elderly reach their full potential as workers.

2   Lots of older people would consider working only a few hours a week.

3   By only working part-time, the elderly would not tax their brains and could remain interested in their work.

4   Many people in their teens and twenties are arrogant know-it-alls, but their knowledge pales in comparison to those more than twice their age.

5   The effects of being consulted would be to make the older employees feel that they belong and also to make use of the stores of knowledge that have built up by their long years or employment.

B-2

The professor believes that it is pointless for people in their fifties to retire and not work anymore, so she provides some suggestions to get people to [1]stop retiring so early. She thinks that instead of working full-time, elderly people should be allowed to [2]work part-time. This measure would keep the employees [3]fresh and eager to do their jobs. Also, companies should try to involve their elderly employees in more activities and ask them for [4]their opinions on various things. This effort would give elderly workers the confidence they require and, at the same time, also help their companies by having them rely upon people with [5]many years of experience.

교수는 50대가 퇴직해서 더 이상 일을 하지 않는 것은 무의미하다고 생각해서 사람들이 그렇게 일찍 퇴직하는 것을 막기 위한 몇 가지 안을 내놓는다. 그녀는 나이 든 직원들이 전일제 근무를 하는 대신 시간제 근무를 할 수 있어야 한다고 생각한다. 이 조치로 인해 직원들은 마음이 새로워지고 일을 하고 싶은 의욕을 느낄 수 있다. 또한, 기업은 나이 든 직원이 보다 많은 활동을 하게 해야 하며 여러 가지 일들에 대해 의견을 구해야 한다. 이러한 노력을 통해 나이 든 직원들은 그들이 필요로 하는 자신감을 얻을 수 있으며, 동시에 수년 간의 경험으로 회사에 도움을 줄 수도 있다.

Synthesizing & Organizing

A

1   The author of the reading passage claims that elderly employees get exhausted when they keep doing the same jobs repeatedly, so the professor suggests having elderly employees work merely on a part-time basis.

2   The problem in the reading is that elderly employees are no longer challenged by their daily routines but are instead bored with them, so the professor suggests that part-time work would help keep their minds fresh while also keeping the employees interested in doing their jobs.

3   In the reading, the author suggests that older

employees cannot work as much as younger employees, thus making them less productive; however, the professor suggests <u>giving them a wider range of duties and not having them repeat tasks all the time</u>.

4   The author of the reading passage mentions that <u>older workers feel that they are burdens on their companies because they do not contribute much</u>, so the lecturer mentions that <u>companies could consult them on a more regular basis</u>.

B

1   The reading passage mentions a couple of reasons as to <u>why elderly employees are retiring in their fifties before they are required to do so</u>.

2   The professor provides a couple of solutions for <u>the problems that were mentioned in the reading passage</u>.

3   The first problem the reading mentions is that <u>employees often retire after getting burned out and bored from repeatedly doing the same work</u>.

4   So the professor believes <u>companies should allow elderly employees to work part-time, which will preserve their interest in their jobs</u>.

5   Also, working part-time will keep the elderly from <u>being bored at work and will keep their minds fresh</u>.

6   Another problem leading to early retirement is that <u>elderly employees compare themselves with younger employees and notice that they do less work and are burdening their companies</u>.

7   Therefore, the professor suggests that <u>companies could give their elderly employees many different tasks to do</u>.

8   Additionally, companies could consult elderly employees <u>on a more regular basis and draw upon their many years of experience</u>.

9   By doing so, companies could make their older employees feel as though <u>they are contributing more</u>.

10   In conclusion, <u>while the reading passage mentions a couple of important problems, the professor provides two methods that should effectively neutralize these problems and enable the elderly to contribute to their employers while not obligating them to take early retirement</u>.

1   지문은 나이 든 직원들이 50대에 조기 퇴직을 하는 두어 가지 이유를 언급한다.

2   교수는 지문에서 언급된 문제에 대한 두 가지 해결 방안을 제시한다.

3   지문에서 언급한 첫 번째 문제는 직원들이 동일한 업무를 반복하다

보니 지치고 권태를 느껴서 퇴직을 하는 일이 잦다는 것이다.

4   그래서 교수는 기업이 나이 든 직원들에게 시간제 근무를 시켜서 업무에 대한 흥미를 잃지 않게 해야 한다고 생각한다.

5   또한, 나이 든 직원들이 시간제 근무를 하게 되면 권태로움을 느끼지 않고 마음이 새로워지게 된다.

6   조기 퇴직을 유발하는 또 다른 문제는 나이 든 직원들이 자신을 젊은 직원들과 비교해서 그들에 비해 업무량이 적고 회사에 짐이 된다고 생각하는 것이다.

7   그래서 교수는 기업이 나이 든 직원들에게 여러 가지 다양한 업무를 맡겨야 한다고 제안한다.

8   그뿐만 아니라, 기업은 보다 정기적으로 나이 든 직원들과 상담하여 그들이 가진 수년 간의 경험을 활용할 수 있다.

9   그렇게 함으로써 기업은 나이 든 직원들로 하여금 그들의 기여도가 더 크다는 것을 느끼게 할 수 있다.

10   결론적으로, 지문은 중요한 두 가지 문제를 언급하지만 교수는 이러한 문제를 효과적으로 해결하고 나이 든 직원들이 스스로에게 조기 퇴직을 강요하지 않으면서도 회사에 더 기여할 수 있는 두 가지 방안을 제안한다.

Unit 7 Education

Note Taking & Outlining

A

요즘 들어 많은 대학에서 등록금을 인상하고 있다. 어떤 경우에는 등록금 인상분이 상당한 액수에 이르기도 한다. 많은 학생들이 이러한 인상에 불만을 표시하지만 이렇게 할 수 밖에 없는 몇 가지 합리적인 이유가 있다.

우선, 대학은 교육의 질을 업그레이드하기 위해 끊임없이 노력한다. 요즘에는 대학을 다니는 사람의 수가 줄어들어 학교는 더 많은 학생을 유치하기 위해 분투해야 한다. 학생들을 끌어들이는 한 가지 이상적인 방법은 반드시 훌륭한 교육을 제공하는 것이다. 학교의 학문적 위상을 높이면 보다 많은 학생, 보다 나은 학생을 유치할 수 있다. 교육의 질을 높이기 위해서는 비용이 들기 때문에 학교 예산을 늘릴 수밖에 없다. 따라서, 등록금 역시 올라가게 된다.

두 번째로, 요즘 많은 대학들은 재정이 부족하다. 이는 특히 주립대의 경우가 심한데, 주립대는 종종 대학 예산의 대부분을 주에 의존하고 있다. 하지만 안타깝게도, 많은 주들이 학교에 대한 지원을 줄이고 있다. 가장 타격을 받는 부분은 대학의 일반 행정을 위한 지원금이다. 일반 행정이 꼭 매력적인 일이라고 할 수는 없지만 대학 복지에 중요하다. 일반 행정을 위한 충분한 지원이 없으면 많은 학교들은 심각한 문제에 직면할 것이며 다른 방법으로 줄어든 기금을 보충하려 할 것이다. 그래서 대학은 해마다 등록금을 인상하게 된다.

[1] quality education
[2] school's academic rank
[3] state universities
[4] general management

B

M: I'm sure many of you just got your tuition bills, and I know that most of you weren't pleased. Tuition went up by 5% this year for the fifth year in a row. Running a college is getting to be too expensive, but there are a few ways to offset this without raising your fees.

Everyone wants to improve our school's quality. But, you know, money isn't totally necessary to do this. For example, we should be looking at ourselves to improve our school. Take professors, for example. We could augment the quality of our lectures as well as develop better curriculums. And you, the students, could perform better both at school and after graduation. That would help increase our school's ranking without us spending much money or raising tuition.

Here's another idea, especially for engineering or science-heavy schools like ours. We should seek close ties with corporations. Why should we do this? Well, both of us will benefit. First, we'll get free state-of-the-art facilities, which both students and faculty will be able to use. And second, the corporation will get the inside track on recruiting our students to work for them once they graduate. And the corporations will know the students got an excellent education because they helped contribute to it. It's a win-win situation for both parties.

M: 여러분 가운데 다수가 얼마 전에 등록금 고지서를 받고는 불만이 있을 거라 생각합니다. 등록금은 5년 연속으로 5%씩 올랐습니다. 대학 경영에는 점점 더 많은 비용이 들지만 등록금을 인상하지 않고 이를 해결할 수 있는 방법이 몇 가지가 있습니다.

누구라도 학교의 질이 향상되기를 바랍니다. 하지만 여러분도 알다시피, 돈만 이런 결과를 이뤄낼 수 있는 것은 아닙니다. 예를 들어, 학교를 향상시키기 위해 스스로를 살펴볼 수도 있습니다. 교수들을 예로 들어 봅시다. 우리는 더 나은 교과과정을 개발하거나 강의 수준을 향상시킬 수도 있습니다. 그리고 학생들이 학창 시절이나 졸업 후에 더 좋은 성과를 내는 것도 한 방법입니다. 이렇게 되면 비용을 많이 들이거나 등록금을 인상하지 않고도 학교의 위상을 높일 수 있습니다.

또 다른 방법으로는, 우리 대학처럼 특히 공학이나 과학 분야가 전문인 학교에 해당되는 한 가지 방법이 있습니다. 기업과 긴밀한 관계를 맺는 방법입니다. 왜 그래야 할까요? 양쪽 다에게 혜택이 가기 때문입니다. 우선, 우리 입장에서는 무료로 최신 시설을 이용할 수 있는데, 학생과 임직원 모두 이 시설을 사용할 수 있습니다. 두 번째로, 기업은 학생들이 일단 졸업하면 자기 회사를 위해 일할 학생 모집을 위한 유리한 입장에 서게 됩니다. 그리고 기업은 학생들이 훌륭한 교육을 받는 데 기여했으므로 학생들이 좋은 교육을 받았다는 것까지 알 수 있습니다. 이것은 양쪽 모두에게 도움이 되는 일입니다.

[1]better curriculums

[2]increase performance
[3]free facilities
[4]recruit new employees

C

Reading (Problems)

1 Schools need more money to improve [1]the quality of education and increase the school's [2]academic ranking if they want to attract more and better students.
2 Schools are getting [3]their general budgets cut as well as seeing less funding go to their general management, so they have to make up for this loss with [4]higher tuition.

Listening (Solutions)

1 In order to improve the school, professors can improve [5]curriculums and lecturing while students can do better both in the classroom and [6]after graduation.
2 Schools should increase [7]their ties with corporations so that they may receive free, exceptional facilities while the corporations will be able to [8]recruit the students who learned with those facilities.

Paraphrasing & Summarizing

1 The large raises in tuition upset a lot of students even though schools have some good reasons for increasing the price of school.
2 Schools have to be more competitive in recruiting new students since not as many students are going to school as there used to be.
3 Good students will be more interested in attending a school that has a high academic ranking.
4 Because states are contributing less money to universities, the schools need to raise the necessary money by using other methods.
5 The department that runs the school is fairly unremarkable, but, without it, the school would encounter many problems.

Even though students at universities are not pleased about [1]tuition increases, the schools have some good reasons for doing so. First, they have to improve themselves academically to [2]attract more students, especially since fewer students are going to college nowadays. This requires money. So does raising the school's [3]academic ranking, which will in turn attract better students to the school. Also, a lot of schools receive funding from [4]various states. However, they are receiving less funding nowadays. Also, [5]the general management departments at these schools need enough money to run properly, or else the school will suffer. The schools therefore need to raise tuition to get more money.

대학생들은 등록금 인상을 달가워하지 않겠지만 학교측이 그럴 수밖에 없는 몇 가지 그럴 듯한 이유가 있다. 우선, 요즘 들어 대학에 진학하는 학생 수가 점점 감소하고 있기 때문에 더 많은 학생을 유치하기 위해서는 학문적인 향상이 필요하다. 그러기 위해서는 돈이 필요하다. 학교의 순위를 높이기 위해서도 돈이 필요한데, 학교의 순위가 높아지면 더 나은 학생들을 유치할 수 있다. 또한, 많은 학교들이 여러 주의 지원을 받는다. 하지만, 요즘 들어 이 지원금이 줄고 있다. 또한, 이들 학교의 일반 행정부는 학교의 원활한 운영을 위해 충분한 돈이 필요한데, 그렇지 못할 경우 문제가 발생한다. 그래서 학교는 더 많은 기금을 마련하기 위해 등록금을 인상할 수밖에 없다.

B-1

1   Even though maintaining a school costs more every year, schools can still manage not to increase the price of tuition.
2   The members of the school body, including both students and faculty, should be able to make the school better by their own actions.
3   An inexpensive way to improve the school that does not require a tuition hike is for the students themselves to do better.
4   The schools will be able to receive outstanding new facilities which can be accessed by everyone attending and working at the school.
5   Since the companies were somewhat responsible for the students' educations, they will be aware of the high quality of education that the students have received.

B-2

It actually is possible for universities to increase [1]the quality of education that they offer without having to raise students' tuition. First, both the [2]faculty and students can improve themselves. The faculty can teach and prepare for classes better, and the students can improve their performance as well. These actions should increase the school's [3]academic ranking without a need for a tuition hike. Also, schools should strike agreements with corporations. The corporations can provide the schools with [4]excellent free facilities. The schools in turn will produce well-educated students that the companies will then be able to [5]recruit much more

easily. This will also help schools avoid raising the cost of tuition.

대학이 등록금을 인상하지 않고도 실제로 교육의 질을 높일 수 있다. 우선, 교직원과 학생들이 스스로를 향상시키는 것이다. 교직원들은 더 나은 강의와 준비를 하고 학생들은 더 열심히 학업에 임해야 한다. 이러한 실행을 통해 등록금을 인상하지 않고도 학교의 수준을 높일 수 있다. 또한, 학교들은 기업과 협력해야 한다. 기업은 학교 측에 훌륭한 무료 시설을 제공할 수 있다. 그렇게 되면 학교는 우수한 인재를 배출해 내고 기업은 훨씬 쉽게 직원을 채용할 수 있다. 이렇게 되면 학교측은 등록금 인상을 피할 수 있다.

Synthesizing & Organizing

A

1   The reading passage mentions that universities can attract students by giving them an excellent education, so the professor responds by claiming that professors can improve the quality of their lectures while also preparing for class better.
2   The writer claims that an improvement in the school's academic ranking will cause more and better students to attend, which leads the professor to declare that the students can do a better job when attending school and after graduating.
3   In response to the reading passage author's claim that cuts in the general funding of schools makes them have to look for funds elsewhere, the professor responds by saying that schools should make closer ties with corporations.
4   The writer claims that general management funds are disappearing, so the lecturer states that schools could get state-of-the-art facilities for free from various companies.

B

1   The lecturer states that schools do not have to raise tuition to improve the quality of education they provide for their students.
2   He then gives a couple of explanations as to how they can do this.
3   First, responding to the claim that schools need money to improve their academic ranking, the lecturer claims that the professors can do a better job of teaching and preparing for class.
4   He also mentions that the students can affect the school's academic rating in a positive manner. They can study harder and get better jobs.
5   With a better academic rating, the school will then be able to attract better students without having to raise tuition at all.

6   Also, since schools are seeing <u>their budgets cut by the state</u>, the professor urges <u>closer ties to businesses</u>.

7   He claims <u>the businesses can supply free facilities for the students to use</u>.

8   These facilities will <u>also offset budget losses to the university's general management funds</u>.

9   The companies will also <u>benefit by getting to hire competent workers when the students graduate</u>.

10 If a school follows the professor's suggestions, <u>he believes it will not have to increase its tuition</u>.

1   강의자는 학교측이 학생들에게 제공하는 교육의 질을 향상시키기 위해 등록금을 올릴 필요는 없다고 말한다.

2   그는 그 해결 방법에 관해 두 가지 설명을 한다.

3   우선, 학교의 순위를 높이기 위해 학교는 돈이 필요하다는 주장에 대해 강의자는 교수들이 강의와 수업 준비를 잘할 수 있다고 말한다.

4   그는 또한 학생들도 긍정적인 방법으로 학교의 학문적 평가에 영향을 미칠 수 있다고 말한다. 공부도 더 열심히 하고 더 나은 직장을 구할 수 있다.

5   학문적 위상이 높아지면 학교는 등록금을 전혀 인상시키지 않고도 더 나은 학생들을 유치할 수 있다.

6   또한, 주로부터 받는 지원금이 줄어들기 때문에 교수는 기업체와 더욱 긴밀한 유대 관계를 가져야 한다고 주장한다.

7   그는 기업은 학생들이 사용할 수 있는 무료 시설을 제공해 줄 수 있다고 주장한다.

8   이러한 시설들은 학교의 일반 행정 기금에 대한 예산 삭감을 상쇄시켜 줄 것이다.

9   기업 역시 학생들이 졸업을 하게 되면 유능한 직원을 채용함으로써 혜택을 받는다.

10 학교측이 교수의 제안을 받아들인다면 등록금을 인상하지 않아도 될 것이라고 교수는 생각한다.

Unit 8 Environment

Note Taking & Outlining

외래종은 지역 생태계에 일어나는 최악의 문제 가운데 대다수의 원인이 된다. 특히 먹이사슬의 가장 윗부분에 있는 새로운 종의 출현은 한 생태계를 파괴하고 수많은 종을 멸종시키기도 한다. 미국의 수로에서 가장 많은 문제를 일으키는 종 가운데 하나가 얼룩무늬홍합이다.

러시아 자생종인 얼룩무늬홍합은 최근에 5대호와 미국의 많은 다른 호수와 강을 침범했다. 얼룩무늬홍합은 선박의 바닥에 붙어 아주 쉽게 이동을 한다. 또한 송수관에 몸을 붙이기도 한다. 이렇게 되면 관이 막히게 되는데, 이러한 관 중의 일부는 도시로 식수를 운반하는 데 사용된다. 또한 얼룩무늬홍합은 대단히 번식 속도가 빨라 종종 다양한 어류와 다른 홍합류의 산란 장소를 완전히 덮어 다른 종이 자라지 못하게 만든다.

그뿐만 아니라, 북미 지역의 얼룩무늬홍합은 천적이 거의 없기 때문에 일단 강이나 호수에 자리를 잡으면 제거하기가 쉽지 않다. 게다가, 과학자들은 얼룩무늬홍합을 죽일 수 있는 환경친화적인 방법을 아직도 찾지 못했다. 이러한 두 가지 사실 때문에 얼룩무늬홍합은 극도로 빨리 증식하고 있다. 만약 이러한 증식을 막지 못한다면 얼룩무늬홍합은 얼마 지나지 않아 미국 전역의 수로에서 문제가 될 것이다.

[1]clog water pipes
[2]reproduce very rapidly
[3]natural enemies
[4]environmentally-safe way

B

W: Yes, the zebra mussel is one of the worst invasive species to hit America. Scientists estimate it has cost billions of dollars in damages. While it's causing problems, there are a couple of methods that could help mitigate the damage it's causing. Let me explain.

One, everyone knows zebra mussels moved from Russia to America by traveling on boats. Well, there must be better decontamination procedures implemented to kill any mussels found hitchhiking on boats. Before a boat enters a lake or river system, the ship's ballast should be sterilized with seawater, which kills the mussels. And the entire ship needs to be checked. Zebra mussels can survive out of water for several days, so the anchor chains and other parts out of water need to be decontaminated as well.

Two, there are some species of birds and fish that eat zebra mussels. For example, some ducks feed on them. Likewise, croakers, carp, and sturgeon are also their natural predators. These species should be introduced to the waterways. Unfortunately, there are not enough of these birds and fish to make an impact on the mussels' numbers. Researchers must discover a way quickly to increase the numbers of these species in the hope that they will start to make a dent in the number of mussels. This effort will help control their expansion.

W: 그래요, 얼룩무늬홍합은 미국에 침입한 외래종 가운데 최악의 경우에 속합니다. 과학자들은 얼룩무늬홍합이 수십 억 달러의 피해를 입혔다고 추정하고 있습니다. 얼룩무늬홍합이 문제를 일으키고는 있지만 그 문제를 완화시킬 수 있는 두 가지 방법이 있습니다.

먼저, 누구나 알고 있듯이 얼룩무늬홍합은 선박을 타고 러시아에서 미국으로 이동했습니다. 선박에 무임승차를 하는 얼룩무늬홍합을 전부 죽일 수 있는 더 나은 소독 방법이 분명 있을 거예요. 선박이 호수나 강으로 진입하기 전에 선박의 바닥짐을 해수로 소독해 얼룩무늬홍합을 죽이는 것입니다. 선박 전체를 확인해야 합니다. 얼룩무늬홍합은 물 밖에서도 며칠씩 생존할 수 있기 때문에 닻줄이나 물 밖으로 나온 다른 부분도 역시 소독을 해야 합니다.

두 번째로, 얼룩무늬홍합을 잡아먹는 조류와 어류가 있습니다. 예를 들어, 어떤 오리들은 얼룩무늬홍합을 잡아 먹습니다. 마찬가지로, 동갈민어, 잉어, 철갑상어 역시 얼룩무늬홍합의 천적입니다. 이러한 종들을 수로에 도입해야 합니다. 안타까운 것은 이러한 조류와 어류가 얼룩무늬홍합의 수에 영향을 미칠 만큼 많지가 않다는 것입니다. 연구자들은 이 종들이 얼룩무늬홍합의 수를 감소시킬 수 있다는 바람으로 이러한 종의 수를 단시간에 증가시킬 수 있는 방법을 찾아내야만 합니다. 이러한 노력이 얼룩무늬홍합의 증식을 억제하는 데 도움이 될 것입니다.

[1]sterilize ships' ballast
[2]survive out of water
[3]birds and fish
[4]reduce the number of mussels

Reading (Problems)

1   Zebra mussels have [1]invaded America's waterways, where they clog water pipes and [2]smother the spawning grounds of various fish and other mussels.
2   The zebra mussels have few [3]natural enemies, and there are no [4]environmentally-safe methods to kill them, so scientists have not been able to reduce their numbers.

Listening (Solutions)

1   Before entering a waterway, ships' crews should [5]sterilize their ballast with saltwater, and they must [6]check the entire ship since mussels can survive for days out of water.
2   There are [7]birds and fish that eat the mussels, so scientists must introduce them to the area and get their numbers to grow quickly so they can [8]start reducing the mussel population.

Paraphrasing & Summarizing

1   When a top predator appears in a new environment, it can wreak havoc on an ecosystem and completely wipe out many species.
2   While it comes from Russia, the zebra mussel now lives in American waterways like the Great Lakes.
3   Since zebra mussels have a high rate of reproduction, they can overrun the spawning grounds of other species, which keeps these species from growing larger in number.
4   In North America, the zebra mussel does not have many predators, which makes it difficult to find a natural solution to remove them from waterways.

5   If zebra mussels continue to expand their territories, all of America's lakes and river systems will have problems with them.

When an invasive species moves into a new environment, it often causes problems for some native species, even causing them to [1]go extinct. This is the case for the zebra mussel. Coming from Russia, the mussel rode on boats to get to America. There, it [2]clogs pipes, which are expensive to unblock. Also, it reproduces so rapidly that it covers up [3]the spawning grounds of other species, making these species reproduce more slowly. It is difficult to remove the mussels because they have few [4]natural predators in North America. In addition, there is no [5]environmentally-safe way to kill them. If the mussels are not killed, they will soon expand to all of America's waterways.

외래종이 새로운 환경에 들어오면 일부 자생종에게 문제를 유발해 때로는 멸종에 이르게 한다. 얼룩무늬홍합도 이 경우에 속한다. 러시아산인 얼룩무늬홍합은 선박을 타고 미국으로 왔다. 그래서 송수관을 막히게 만드는데, 관을 다시 뚫는 데는 비용이 많이 든다. 또한 번식 속도가 빨라 다른 종의 산란 장소를 뒤덮어 이러한 종들의 번식 속도가 느려지게 만든다. 얼룩무늬홍합은 천적이 거의 없어 제거하기도 쉽지 않다. 그뿐만 아니라, 얼룩무늬홍합을 제거할 환경 친화적인 방법도 없다. 얼룩무늬홍합을 제거하지 않는다면 얼마 지나지 않아 미국의 모든 수로를 침범할 것이다.

1   There are some ways to solve the problems the zebra mussel is causing.
2   The crew needs to sterilize the ship's ballast with saltwater to kill the mussels prior to entering any waterway.
3   Zebra mussels do not always live in the water, so crews need to search for them in every part of the ship that has touched water in order to eliminate them all.
4   Some animals and fish hunt zebra mussels.
5   If scientists can get the predators of the zebra mussel to reproduce quickly, these animals will be able to reduce the number of mussels.

While the zebra mussel has caused extremely expensive amounts of damage to [1]America's waterways, there are some ways to control their numbers. First, crew members on ships can do a couple of things. They can fill the ship's ballast [2]with seawater since that will kill them. Also, they should check the entire ship for mussels because they can [3]survive out of water for a few days. In addition, there are [4]some predators that will prey upon the zebra mussels. These should be introduced to the waterways. Finally, since there are not enough of these predators, people need to make sure they [5]reproduce rapidly. These solutions can then reduce the number of zebra mussels.

얼룩무늬홍합이 미국의 수로에 막대한 양의 피해를 입혔지만, 얼룩무늬홍합의 수를 줄일 수 있는 몇 가지 방법이 있다. 우선, 배의 선원들이 두 가지 조치를 취할 수 있다. 해수가 얼룩무늬홍합을 죽이기 때문에 선박의 바닥짐을 해수로 채울 수 있다. 또한, 얼룩무늬홍합은 물 밖에서도 며칠 동안 생존이 가능하기 때문에 얼룩무늬홍합이 없는지 선박 전체를 조사한다. 그뿐만 아니라, 얼룩무늬홍합을 잡아먹는 일부 천적이 존재한다. 이 종들을 수로에 도입해야 한다. 마지막으로, 이러한 천적의 수가 충분하지 않기 때문에 이들의 번식 속도를 빠르게 만들어야 한다. 이러한 해결책들이 얼룩무늬홍합의 수를 줄일 수 있을 것이다.

Synthesizing & Organizing

A

1 The reading passage author writes that the mussels can travel easily since they attach themselves to the bottoms of boats, so the professor responds by arguing that the ship's ballast should be filled with seawater to kill them.
2 According to the professor, the entire boat should be decontaminated, even the parts out of water, so that the mussels will not be able to survive and harm the spawning grounds of other species, just like the reading passage described.
3 As a response to the reading passage claim that there are few natural predators in North America which can remove zebra mussels, the professor mentions that people should introduce some of the zebra mussel's natural predators to the waterways.
4 Because there is no environmentally-safe way to kill zebra mussels, the professor declares that researchers need to increase the number of predators so that these animals can start reducing the number of zebra mussels.

B

1 The professor talks about different ways to reduce the number of zebra mussels from America's waterways.
2 This is an invasive species from Russia that is causing many problems in America's rivers.
3 The professor provides a couple of solutions to this infestation problem.
4 First, he notes that all ships entering waterways should be sterilized with seawater, which kills the mussels.
5 He mentions this because mussels often hitch rides on the bottoms of ships.
6 Also, the professor notes that the mussels can survive out of water for days, so crew members should sterilize the entire ship.
7 This will keep the mussels from getting into the waterways and clogging up all the pipes.
8 Second, the professor notes that some bird and fish species prey on the zebra mussel.
9 While the reading claims that it has few natural predators, the professor claims they could be introduced.
10 He also thinks scientists should try to increase the numbers of these predators so that they can eat more mussels.
11 This will be beneficial because scientists know of no environmentally-safe way to kill the mussels.
12 Although the zebra mussel is causing many problems, the professor seems confident that his ideas will help to eliminate them.

1 교수는 미국의 수로에서 얼룩무늬홍합의 수를 줄일 수 있는 여러 가지 방법에 대해서 말한다.
2 이 얼룩무늬홍합은 러시아에서 온 외래종으로 미국의 강에 많은 문제를 야기한다.
3 교수는 이 침입 문제에 대한 두 가지 해결방안을 제시한다.
4 첫 번째로, 그는 수로에 진입하는 모든 선박을 해수로 소독해 얼룩무늬홍합을 죽여야 한다고 지적한다.
5 그는 얼룩무늬홍합이 선박의 바닥에 붙어서 이동을 하기 때문에 이런 언급을 한다.
6 또한, 교수는 얼룩무늬홍합이 며칠 동안 물 밖에서도 살 수 있기 때문에 선원들이 선박 전체를 소독해야 한다고 말한다.
7 이렇게 하면 얼룩무늬홍합이 수로에 들어와 모든 관들을 막는 것을 예방할 수 있다.
8 두 번째로, 교수는 일부 조류와 어류가 얼룩무늬홍합을 삽아 먹는다고 지적한다.
9 지문에서는 천적이 거의 없다고 말하지만 교수는 천적을 도입할 수 있다고 말한다.
10 또한 그는 과학자들이 이러한 천적이 더 많은 얼룩무늬홍합을 잡아먹을 수 있도록 천적의 수를 늘리기 위해 노력해야 한다고 생각한다.
11 과학자들이 얼룩무늬홍합을 죽일 수 있는 다른 환경 친화적인 방법을 알지 못하기 때문에 이 방법은 유익할 것이다.
12 얼룩무늬홍합이 많은 문제를 일으키고는 있지만 교수는 이러한 방법이 얼룩무늬홍합을 제거하는 데 도움이 되리라 확신한다.

PART 2
Independent Writing

Sample iBT Question

Sample Answer

[도입문] 친구 집단이 우리의 삶에 가장 큰 영향을 미친다는 것은 의심의 여지가 없다. [논제 진술] 하지만, 인생의 소중한 가르침과 관련해서는 친구들보다는 연장자에게서 더 많은 것을 배우게 된다.

[주제문 1] 친구들과는 달리 연장자들은 경험을 통해 인생을 더 잘 이해하고 있기 때문에 그들의 노련한 지식으로부터 많은 도움을 받을 수 있다. [일반 진술 1] 친구는 그렇지 않지만 연장자들은 과거를 더욱 명확하게 볼 수 있는 부러운 위치에 있기에 그들은 우리에게 소중한 교훈을 가르쳐 줄 수 있다. [예 1] 예를 들어, 학창 시절에 나는 왜 교육을 잘 받아야 하는가에 대해 친구보다 삼촌에게서 더 많은 것을 배웠다. 친구들은 대개 공부를 거의 하지 않고 노는 데 시간을 썼다. 하지만, 삼촌은 항상 놀지만 말고 공부에 집중할 경우 나중에 인생이 훨씬 보람찰 것이라고 가르쳐 주셨다. [종결문 1] 삼촌의 충고가 없었더라면 나는 또래의 친구들에 비해 그토록 성숙한 시각을 가지지 못했을 것이다.

[주제문 2] 또한, 연장자들은 나를 올바른 방향으로 이끌어주고 그들이 이미 저지른 실수를 반복하지 않게 해 준다. [일반 진술 2] 만약 친구 말만 듣는다면 비슷한 실수를 종종 하게 될 것이다. 하지만, 연장자의 말을 듣고 따름으로써 실수를 피할 수 있다. [예 2] 예를 들어, 작년에 우리 형이 축구팀에 들려고 했으나 실패했을 때 친구들은 축구를 아예 그만두라고 했다. 하지만 아버지는 그만두는 것만이 능사가 아니라는 것을 형이 깨닫게 해 주셨다. 그래서 형은 축구를 그만두는 대신 더 열심히 연습했다. 올해 형은 축구팀에 들었을 뿐만 아니라 주장이 되기까지 했다. [종결문 2] 결국, 연장자들은 우리가 실패나 역경과 마주쳤을 때 올바른 결정을 내리도록 도와준다.

[요약] 결론적으로, 연장자들은 인생 경험도 많고 탁월하면서도 더 성숙한 충고를 해 줄 수 있기 때문에 사람들은 친구보다는 연장자에게서 더 많이 배운다. [최종 논평] 이렇게 연장자들은 우리의 삶에 가장 중요하면서도 긍정적인 영향을 준다.

Chapter 3 Agree / Disagree

Unit 9 Living & Thinking

Understanding the Topic

4 Young people think looks are everything → become too superficial /
Cosmetic surgery business booming → waste of money

5 Students judging one another only by appearance / A story about a mom who wasted her child's college money for plastic surgery for herself

Brainstorming

1 young people - looks & fashion = everything
2 become too superficial
3 e.g. students judge one another by looks, not personality or character
4 cosmetic surgery booming
5 waste of money
6 e.g. story about mom who spent child's university savings on plastic

Outlining

1 Cosmetic surgery business is booming.
   – individuals waste money on improving appearance
   – e.g. read an article about a mom who spent her child's university money on plastic surgery for herself
2 Young people think looks and clothes are everything.
   – become superficial and narrow-minded
   – e.g. groups at school include others because of how they look, not for their true character

Writing the Thesis Statement & Topic Sentences

Thesis statement People place too much emphasis on appearance and fashion.

Topic sentence 1 Judging from the increase in cosmetic surgery recently, it is obvious that some people consider their appearance to be more important than anything else.

Topic sentence 2 Many young people believe that how a person looks is the most important quality in an individual.

Summary In conclusion, the increase in cosmetic surgery and the weight young people put on appearances and fashion show how individuals in general place too much importance on how they look.

Writing the Details

A

[도입문] 현대 사회는 대단히 경쟁적이어서 사람들이 성공하기 위해서는 모든 기회를 이용해야 한다. **[논제 진술]** 이런 이유에서 외모에 특별히 신경을 써야 한다. 외모에는 어떻게 보이는가와 어떻게 입는가가 해당된다.

[주제문 1] 우선, 직장 생활을 하는 데 깔끔한 외모를 갖는 것은 개인에게 매우 중요하다. **[일반 진술 1]** 많은 경우, 어떻게 보이고 어떻게 입느냐가 직업을 구하는 데 도움이 된다. 결국, 면접관이 받는 첫인상은 그 사람의 외모에 의존하는 경우가 흔하다. 그래서 외관이나 옷차림에 신경을 쓰지 않을 경우 면접에 떨어질 수도 있다. **[예 1]** 내 형은 이런 경험을 한 적이 있다. 지금 하고 있는 일을 구한 지 몇 달 뒤에 상사가 형에게 그 자리를 두고 형과 다른 여자가 경합했었다고 말해 주었다. 하지만 형이 더 전문가다워 보였기 때문에 형을 고용하기로 결정했고 형이 그 자리를 갖게 된 것이다. **[종결문 1]** 자신의 외모를 잘 관리하는 것은 직장 생활에도 확실히 도움이 된다. 내 형의 경우에는 확실히 그랬다.

[주제문 2] 다음으로, 외모에 신경을 쓰면 자신감이 커진다. **[일반 진술 2]** 많은 사람들은 자부심과 자신감이 부족하다. 하지만 몸이 좋고 패션 감각이 있는 사람들은 종종 더 자신감을 갖는다. 사실상 외모가 더 큰 자신감을 주는 것이다. **[예 2]** 다시 한번, 내 형이 좋은 예가 될 것이다. 형은 중학교 시절 항상 비만이었고 수줍음을 많이 탔다. 친구도 거의 없었고 인기도 많지 않았다. 하지만 고등학교에 가자 외모에 좀 더 신경을 쓰고 운동을 시작했다. 살이 빠지기 시작하자 껍질을 깨고 나와 즉시 자신감도 생기고 성격도 외향적으로 바뀌었다. 이러한 변화로 인해 학교에서도 인기가 많아졌고 자신에 대해서도 자신감을 갖기 시작했다. **[종결문 2]** 사람들이 외모에 대해 신경을 쓰고 외모에 자신감을 가질 때 더 행복해지는 것 같다.

[요약] 결국, 외모에 신경을 쓰면 더 나은 직장을 구할 수도 있고 자신감도 생기기 때문에 외모에 더 많이 신경을 쓰는 것이 바람직하다. **[최종 논평]** 외모와 옷에 특별히 신경을 쓰는 것은 확실히 그럴 만한 가치가 있는 투자이다.

B

[Opening sentence] Today, more than ever, many people seem obsessed with how they look. **[Thesis statement]** Unfortunately, a large number of people place too much emphasis on their personal appearance and fashion.

[Topic sentence 1] One example of this is the amount of cosmetic surgery many people are having these days. Judging from the increase in cosmetic surgery recently, it is obvious that some people consider their appearance to be more important than anything else. **[General statement 1]** Because of their infatuation with how they look, they waste their money, which they could spend on more important things, and have cosmetic surgery instead. **[Example 1]** For example, a magazine article reported on a mother who became addicted to cosmetic surgery and was obsessed with improving her appearance. Eventually, she ended up spending her daughter's entire college savings to satisfy her vanity. Because of this mother's actions, her daughter will have difficulty attending college in the future. Sadly, this is not an isolated case, as many more people are wasting money to have surgery. **[Closing sentence 1]** In these instances, cosmetic surgery can have serious negative financial side effects on people and their families.

[Topic sentence 2] Also, many young people believe that how a person looks is the most important quality in an individual. **[General statement 2]** This mentality can make people become very superficial and narrow-minded, characteristics they will keep for the rest of their lives. **[Example 2]** Many students tend to value and accept others into their circle of friends for the sole reasons of how good they look and how fashionable they are. Because of this tendency, many students ignore the true personalities of their classmates and focus upon whether or not they look good. As these students grow older, they will continue to judge people based on their appearance rather than on their character, which may create later conflicts or problems. **[Closing sentence 2]** Undeniably, these days, young people focus too much on a person's outside, that is, his or her looks, and not enough on the person's inside, which is his or her personality.

[Summary] In conclusion, the increase in cosmetic surgery and the weight young people put on appearances and fashion show how individuals in general place too much importance on how they look. These two factors can have negative consequences for people, however. **[Final comment]** People should be concerned about their entire being, not just what they show on the outside.

[도입문] 오늘날은 어느 때보다도, 많은 사람들이 외모에 사로잡혀 있는 것 같다. **[논제 진술]** 안타깝게도, 많은 사람들이 외모와 옷에 너무 많은 가치를 둔다.

[주제문 1] 한 가지 예가 요즘 사람들이 많이 하는 성형 수술이다. 최근 성형 수술이 증가하는 것으로 볼 때, 어떤 사람들은 외모를 가장 중요하게 여기는 게 분명하다. **[일반 진술 1]** 외모에 사로잡힌 나머지 그들은 더 중요한 일에 쓸 수도 있는 돈을 낭비해가며 성형 수술을 받는다. **[예 1]** 예를 들어, 어떤 잡지에 성형 수술에 중독되어 외모를 가꾸는 것에만 사로잡힌 어머니에 대한 기사가 실렸다. 결국에 그 어머니는 자신의 허영심을 채우려고 딸의 대학 학자금을 몽땅 써버리고 말았다. 이 어머니의 행동 때문에 딸은 나중에 대학 진학이 어려울 것이다. 슬프게도, 이것은 예외적인 경우가 아닌데, 더 많은 사람들이 성형 수술을 받는 데 돈을 낭비하고 있기 때문이다. **[종결문 1]** 이러한 경우에, 성형 수술은 본인과 그 가족에게 심각한 재정적 피해를 입힐 수 있다.

[주제문 2] 또한, 많은 젊은이들이 한 개인에게 있어 가장 중요한 것이 외모라고 믿는다. [일반 진술 2] 이러한 생각 때문에 사람들은 매우 피상적이거나 편협해져서 평생 그런 성격으로 살아가게 된다. [예 2] 많은 학생들은 얼마나 잘 생겼고 얼마나 옷을 잘 입는가 하는 단순한 이유로 다른 사람을 평가하고 친구로 받아들이는 경향이 있다. 이러한 경향 때문에 많은 학생들이 급우의 진정한 개성은 신경도 쓰지 않고 외모가 멋진가에만 관심을 쏟는다. 이러한 학생들은 나이가 들면서 성격보다는 외모에 기초해 사람을 평가하게 되고, 이로 인해 나중에 갈등이나 문제가 생기기도 한다. [종결문 2] 확실히, 요즘 젊은이들은 사람의 겉모습 즉 외모에만 너무 많은 가치를 두고, 내면 즉 성격에는 별로 가치를 두지 않는다.

[요약] 결론적으로, 성형 수술의 증가와 젊은이들이 외모나 옷에 두는 가치를 보면 일반 사람들이 겉모습을 얼마나 중요하게 생각하는지 알 수 있다. 하지만, 이 두 가지 요소는 부정적인 결과를 낳을 수 있다. [최종 논평] 사람들은 밖으로 보이는 것만이 아닌 전체적인 인간에 신경을 써야 한다.

Completing & Checking Your Essay

A

Agree

Some people like to spend their hard-earned money on short-term pleasures such as summer vacations. However, I think it is better to spend money on things like expensive jewelry, which will last a long time, because these items will give people enjoyment for years and years and will also be solid investments for people's retirements.

Short-term pleasures are exactly that: short term. Purchasing expensive items is better because of their longevity. That is, people will have opportunities to enjoy them for a much longer period than, for instance, a one- or two-week vacation. For example, when they were younger, my grandparents saved their money and bought a small country home. For years, they vacationed there in the summer. However, that was not their only intention. They planned for it to remain in the family for as long as possible so that future generations could also enjoy it. In this sense, it is desirable that people buy more expensive items which will last a long time because they will be able to enjoy them for a much greater period of time.

Also, purchasing things that last a long time could allow people to retire earlier. If they use their money wisely by investing in valuable items, they will be able to gain large returns on them and enjoy their lives for longer periods after retiring. Furthermore, they will not have to work as long as people who do not purchase long-lasting, valuable items that increase in value. For example, my uncle always invested his money in diamonds instead of

spending it on short-term pleasures such as trips, and, thanks to the money he earned from his investments, he was able to retire at the age of fifty. In the long run, investing clearly outweighs spending.

In conclusion, I firmly believe that people should spend their money on long-lasting items because they will enjoy them for a longer period of time and possibly even be able to retire earlier than they had expected if they have invested wisely. While trips and other short-lived pleasures may be fun, they are not really good uses of a person's money.

어떤 사람들은 힘들게 번 돈을 여름 휴가 같은 단기간의 즐거움을 위해 쓰기를 좋아한다. 하지만, 나는 오래 가는 값비싼 보석과 같은 것들에 돈을 쓰는 게 더 낫다고 생각한다. 왜냐하면 이러한 것들은 오랫동안 사람들에게 기쁨을 주고 은퇴를 위한 든든한 투자가 될 수도 있기 때문이다.

단기간의 즐거움은 말 그대로 단기일 뿐이다. 값비싼 물품을 구입하는 것이 오래간다는 점에서 더 낫다. 다시 말해서, 사람들은 가령 고가의 휴가 여행보다는 값비싼 물품을 훨씬 오랫동안 즐길 수 있다. 예를 들어, 우리 할아버지 할머니는 젊었을 때 돈을 저축해서 시골에 작은 별장을 사셨다. 여러 해 동안 여름이면 그곳에서 휴가를 보내셨다. 하지만, 그분들의 의도는 그것만이 아니었다. 그분들은 다음 세대들도 즐길 수 있도록 별장을 되도록 오래 가족의 소유로 남기고 싶어하셨다. 이런 의미에서, 오래 가는 고가의 품목을 선택하는 것이 훨씬 긴 시간 동안 즐길 수 있기 때문에 바람직하다.

또한, 오래 가는 물건을 구입하면 은퇴를 더 일찍 할 수 있다. 돈을 고가의 물건에 투자해 현명하게 쓴다면 그로 인해 꽤 괜찮은 수익을 올리고 은퇴를 해서도 더 오랜 시간 동안 인생을 즐길 수 있다. 더욱이, 오래 가는 귀중한 물건을 구입하지 않은 사람만큼 오랫동안 일하지 않아도 된다. 예를 들어, 나의 삼촌은 언제나 여행 같은 단기간의 즐거움 대신 다이아몬드에 돈을 투자했고 거기에서 얻은 돈 덕분에 50살에 은퇴하실 수 있었다. 결국, 확실히 투자가 소비보다 낫다.

요약하자면, 나는 더 오랫동안 즐길 수 있고, 지혜롭게 투자한다면 예상보다 더 일찍 은퇴를 할 수도 있기 때문에 사람들이 오래 가는 물건에 돈을 써야 한다고 굳게 믿는다. 여행과 다른 단기적인 즐거움은 재미는 있을지 모르나 돈을 정말로 요령 있게 쓰는 방법은 아니다.

Disagree

While some people say it is best to spend money on long-lasting items such as jewelry, I totally disagree with their opinion. Purchasing expensive items leaves people with not enough money for them to enjoy other pleasures in their lives.

First of all, long-lasting items such as jewelry require people to spend large sums of money. If someone invests in these items, that person may not have enough money to buy anything else. Furthermore, things that last a long time are usually put away for safekeeping and are never really enjoyed by their owners. For example, a friend of my father's sometimes spent much of his salary on expensive necklaces and earrings for his wife. Of course, she was happy, but she never wore them for fear of losing them. Also, they could never buy other nice things for themselves because he spent all of his money on buying her jewelry. Spending money on long-lasting things only ties up people's money and reduces the quality of their lives.

Also, individuals who buy long-lasting items will miss out on enjoying their lives by doing things like traveling. Once they spend all of their money on expensive items such as jewelry, they will have nothing left to do the things they want to do, like, for example, see the world. This situation is very sad because life is short, and no one knows what the future will bring. People should spend money for their current enjoyment rather than save it for the distant future. For instance, my great uncle always invested his money in old books instead of taking his family on vacations and spending time with them. Because of this, his family never had the opportunity to travel together and make wonderful memories that would last for years. Instead of spending money on long-lasting things, people should instead spend their money on fun-filled trips with friends or family.

In conclusion, people who spend money on long-lasting, expensive items like jewelry limit their ability to buy other things for themselves and deprive themselves of the opportunity to travel and truly enjoy life. People should spend their money on fun things and not worry about the fact that they are short-term pleasures because you never know what the future will bring.

어떤 사람들은 보석 같이 오래가는 물건에 돈을 써야 한다고 말하지만 나는 그 의견에 전적으로 반대한다. 값비싼 물건을 구매하면 삶의 다른 기쁨을 만끽할 수 있는 금전적 여유가 거의 없어진다.

우선, 보석과 같이 오래가는 물건을 사려면 많은 돈이 필요하다. 누군가 가 이런 품목에 투자하게 되면 다른 것을 살 수 있는 돈이 별로 없게 된 다. 더욱이, 오래 가는 물건은 대개 안전한 곳에 따로 보관하기 때문에 실제로 주인은 그것을 정말로 만끽하지 못한다. 예를 들어, 우리 아버지 의 친구분은 봉급으로 아내를 위해 고가의 목걸이와 귀걸이를 샀다. 물 론, 그녀는 행복했지만 잃어버릴 게 걱정이 되어 한 번도 착용한 적이 없다. 또한, 그들은 보석에 돈을 다 써버려서 자신을 위해 다른 좋은 것 들을 살 수도 없었다. 오래가는 물건에 돈을 써버리면 돈을 묶어버리는 셈이 되어 삶의 질이 떨어지게 된다.

또한, 오래가는 물건을 사는 사람들은 여행을 통해 삶을 만끽하는 즐거 움도 누릴 수 없다. 보석 같은 장신구에 돈을 다 써버리면 가령 세상 구 경을 한다든지 하는 것처럼 하고 싶은 일을 할 만한 돈이 남아 있지 않게 된다. 인생은 짧고 미래에는 어떤 일이 일어날지 아무도 모르기 때문에

이런 상황은 대단히 안타깝다. 사람들은 먼 미래의 즐거움이 아니라 현 재의 즐거움을 위해 돈을 써야 한다. 일례로, 우리 작은 할아버지는 가 족들과 휴가를 가서 시간을 보내는 대신 항상 돈을 고서에 투자하셨다. 이 때문에 작은 할아버지 가족은 한 번도 함께 여행을 가서 수년 동안 기 억될 만한 근사한 추억을 만들지 못했다. 오래가는 물건에 돈을 쓰는 대 신 사람들은 친구나 가족과 함께 재미있는 여행을 떠나는 데에 돈을 써 야 한다.

결론적으로, 보석처럼 오래가는 값비싼 물건에 돈을 쓰는 사람들은 자 신을 위해 다른 물건을 살 기회를 없애는 것이며 여행을 하고 삶을 진정 으로 만끽할 기회를 잃는 것이다. 미래에는 어떤 일이 일어날지 아무도 모르기 때문에 사람들은 재미있는 일에 돈을 써야 하며 그것이 단기간 의 즐거움이라는 사실에 염려하지 말아야 한다.

Unit 10 Culture & Leisure

Understanding the Topic
2   Cheaper & travel for a longer period /
    Not restricted by schedule → freedom to do whatever one wants
3   Older brother backpacked in Southeast Asia → more economical, could see more, & travel longer / Mom and Dad traveled to Europe on their own → more freedom & better overall experience

Brainstorming
1   cheaper
2   travel for a longer period
3   e.g. brother backpacked in Southeast Asia
4   no restrictions
5   free to do anything
6   e.g. Mom and Dad traveled independently in Europe

Outlining

B

1   Cheaper
    – travel for a longer time
    – e.g. older brother backpacked in Southeast Asia → traveled longer because saved money compared to group tour
2   No restrictions
    – freedom to do anything → eat and stay wherever you want
    – e.g. parents enjoyed independent travel over group tour in Europe.

Writing the Thesis Statement & Topic Sentences

B

Thesis statement I believe that it is much better for individuals to travel independently than to take a costly group tour.

Topic sentence 1 Traveling by oneself is much more economical than a group tour.

Topic sentence 2 Traveling by oneself is not as restrictive as going on a group tour.

Summary In conclusion, traveling by oneself is the best option because it is not as expensive or as restrictive as group tours. Traveling alone enables people to take longer trips and have more positive experiences than traveling in a large group.

Writing the Details

A

[도입문] 많은 사람들이 단체 여행이나 패키지 여행보다 혼자 여행하기를 좋아한다. 안타깝게도, 그런 사람들이 항상 최고의 휴가를 즐기는 것은 아니다. 대신에, 사람들은 단체 여행을 고려해 보아야 한다. [논제 진술] 단체 여행은 휴가를 생각하는 사람들에게 최고의 선택이다.

[주제문 1] 우선, 단체 여행에서는 여행의 전체 일정을 짠다. [일반 진술 1] 여행이 이미 계획이 짜여 있기 때문에 사람들은 목적지나 교통편에 대해서 걱정할 필요가 없다. 단지 편히 쉬면서 여행을 즐기기만 하면 될 뿐 어떤 것에 대해서도 스트레스를 받을 필요가 없다. [예 1] 예를 들어, 한번은 우리 가족이 중국으로 패키지 여행을 갔다. 여행사는 모든 것에 관한 계획을 짜 두었다. 호텔 예약, 교통편, 관광을 여행사가 다 처리했다. 우리 가족은 아무 것도 걱정할 필요가 없었다. 단지 여행사에서 준 일정표를 보고 따르기만 하면 되었다. 여행사 덕분에 우리는 편히 쉬면서 전체 여행을 즐길 수 있었다. 이로 인해 매 순간마다 다음은 어디로 갈지 걱정할 필요가 없었기 때문에 아버지가 한결 편해지셨다. 전체적으로, 우리는 즐거운 여행을 했다. [종결문 1] 단체 여행은 여행에서 매일 일정을 짜는 수고를 덜어주고 여행객들로 하여금 아무런 스트레스도 받지 않고 휴가를 즐기도록 해 준다.

[주제문 2] 단체 여행의 또 다른 이점은 여행을 하는 동안 다른 사람과 사귈 수 있다는 것이다. [일반 진술 2] 여행자들은 여러 날 동안 같이 여행을 하기 때문에 그렇지 않았더라면 만나지 못했을 사람들과 돈독한 우정을 쌓을 수 있다. [예 2] 예를 들어, 우리 부모님은 단체 여행으로 러시아로 신혼여행을 가셨다. 그들은 그 여행에서 다른 부부를 만났는데, 다 같이 즐거운 시간을 보냈다. 몇 년이 흐른 뒤에도 그들은 아주 친하게 지내며 가끔씩 여행도 같이 다니신다. 부모님이 두 분만 따로 여행을 하셨더라면 이 부부를 못 만났을 것이고 그런 끈끈한 우정도 쌓지 못했을 것이다. [종결문 2] 혼자서 하는 여행과는 달리 사람들은 단체 여행을 통해 다른 사람들을 만나고 돈독한 우정을 쌓기도 한다.

[요약] 결론적으로, 여행을 할 때는 단체 여행이 가장 좋다. 단체 여행은

모든 일정이 다 잡혀 있기 때문에 여행 동안 아무런 스트레스도 받지 않으며 개인들이 다른 사람을 만나 우정을 나누는 기회가 되기도 한다. [최종 논평] 단체 여행은 여행을 하는 가장 좋은 방법이다.

B

[Opening sentence] These days, more and more people are taking trips during their vacations. And group package tours are more popular than ever. [Thesis statement] However, I believe that it is much better for individuals to travel independently than to take a costly group tour.

[Topic sentence 1] First of all, traveling by oneself is much more economical than taking a group tour. [General statement 1] Since many people travel on budgets, it is often very important for them to save money. Additionally, with the money they save, people will be able to travel for longer periods of time if they choose. [Example 1] For example, my older brother once backpacked for a month in Southeast Asia. He said that if he had taken a group tour, he would only have been able to have traveled for less than a week. Because he went on the trip by himself, he was able to extend his stay for nearly a month and could therefore see more fascinating places. [Closing sentence 1] Because group tours are so expensive, people should travel independently and enjoy longer trips with the money they save from not taking a package tour.

[Topic sentence 2] Also, traveling by oneself is not as restrictive as going on a group tour. [General statement 2] When people travel by themselves, they are not restricted and have the freedom to choose where they will eat or stay, which can make for a more enjoyable experience. [Example 2] For instance, my parents have taken two trips to Europe: one on their own and the other with a group tour. On the group tour, they were forced to visit certain places that they were not interested in. When they got back home, they felt as if they had wasted much of their trip. However, they thoroughly enjoyed the trip that they took by themselves. The reason is that they felt free to change their schedule whenever they found something they wanted to see or do. They also found many interesting places on their own that a tour group would have never taken them to see. [Closing sentence 2] Clearly, traveling on one's own gives people more freedom, which is something people do not often have when they go on group tours.

[Summary] In conclusion, traveling by oneself is the best option because it is not as expensive or as restrictive as group tours. Traveling alone enables people to take longer trips and have more positive experiences than traveling in a large group. **[Final comment]** People who want to be free to determine their own trips should always avoid group tours and travel by themselves.

[도입문] 요즘에는, 점점 더 많은 사람들이 휴가 동안 여행을 떠난다. 그리고 단체 패키지 여행이 어느 때보다 인기를 얻고 있다. **[논제 진술]** 하지만, 나는 혼자 여행을 하는 것이 비싼 단체 여행을 하는 것보다 훨씬 낫다고 생각한다.

[주제문 1] 우선, 혼자 여행을 하면 단체 여행을 하는 것보다 훨씬 저렴하다. **[일반 진술 1]** 많은 사람들이 예산을 짜서 여행을 하기 때문에 흔히 경비를 절약하는 것이 대단히 중요하다. 게다가, 이렇게 절약한 돈으로 원하는 경우 더 오랜 기간 여행을 할 수도 있다. **[예 1]** 예를 들어, 한번은 우리 형이 한 달 동안 동남아시아로 배낭여행을 갔었다. 만약 단체 여행을 했더라면 1주일도 채 여행을 하지 못했을 거라고 그는 말했다. 형은 혼자 여행하는 쪽을 택했기 때문에 한 달 가까이 여행을 할 수 있었고, 그 덕분에 더 매력적인 장소들을 구경할 수 있었다. **[종결문 1]** 단체 여행은 너무 비싸기 때문에 사람들은 혼자 여행을 해야 하고 단체 여행을 하지 않아서 절약하게 된 돈으로 여행을 더 오래 즐길 수 있다.

[주제문 2] 또한, 혼자 여행을 하면 단체 여행을 하는 것에 비해 제약이 적다. **[일반 진술 2]** 혼자 여행을 하게 되면 제약이 없기 때문에 식당이나 숙소를 마음대로 선택할 수 있어서 더 즐거운 경험이 될 수 있다. **[예 2]** 예를 들어, 우리 부모님은 유럽으로 두 번 여행을 가셨는데, 한 번은 두 분만, 다른 한 번은 단체 여행을 가셨다. 단체 여행에서는 관심도 없는 특정 장소를 가야만 하셨다. 집으로 돌아오셨을 때 두 분은 마치 시간을 낭비한 듯한 느낌을 받으셨다. 하지만, 두 분만 떠났던 여행에서는 여행의 즐거움을 만끽하셨다. 그 이유는 보거나 하고 싶은 것을 발견하게 되면 일정을 마음대로 바꿀 수 있었기 때문이다. 두 분은 또한 단체 여행에서는 데려가지 않았던 많은 흥미로운 장소들을 스스로 발견하셨다. **[종결문 2]** 확실히, 혼자 여행을 하게 되면 사람들은 더 많은 자유를 누리게 되지만 단체 여행에서는 그렇지 못한 경우가 많다.

[요약] 결론적으로, 단체 여행만큼 비싸지도 않고 그만큼 제약도 심하지 않기 때문에 혼자 여행을 하는 것이 가장 낫다. 혼자 여행을 하게 되면 단체 여행을 할 때보다 더 오래 여행을 할 수 있고 더 긍정적인 경험을 할 수도 있다. **[최종 논평]** 자신만의 여행을 꿈꾸는 사람이라면 항상 단체 여행을 피하고 혼자서 여행하는 쪽을 택해야 한다.

Completing & Checking Your Essay

Agree

Movies and television play important roles in the lives of many people. However, when it comes to young people, the effects of movies and television are usually more negative than positive because they promote violence and laziness.

Visual media today is simply too violent for young people. Because of this violence, the young are taught that fighting and guns are solutions to their problems, and some of them may actually take similar violent actions themselves. They are too young to differentiate between the fiction of TV and movies and the reality of their lives. Furthermore, young people become desensitized to violence because it is all over television and movies. One example is the increase of violence at my school over the past few years. One of my teachers told us that when she started working at the school, there were hardly ever any fights. Yet today, there are more and more of them. She believes the reason for these fights is the excessive violence students see in movies and on television. It is obvious that they have negative effects on young people when it comes to violence.

Another negative effect movies, and especially television, have on young people is that they make children and teens lazy. Young people watch too much television instead of doing other activities like their homework or interacting with their families. In fact, these days, many articles on the Internet discuss how people watching too much television is one of the major causes of this situation. Students are spending more time in front of their TVs than they are reading books or doing their homework, and their grades are suffering from it. If they continue with this situation, they will not perform well in their jobs later in their lives, and they will lack the motivation to improve their lives. Clearly, TV and movies are making young people much less diligent.

In conclusion, movies and television have negative effects on young people today because children and teens often imitate the violence they view and they simply spend too much time watching television instead of focusing on their studies. Watching fewer movies and TV programs would probably have a more positive impact on young people in general these days.

영화와 TV는 많은 사람의 삶에 중요한 역할을 한다. 하지만 청소년의 경우에는 영화와 TV가 폭력과 나태를 조장하는 탓에 긍정적인 효과보다는 부정적인 효과가 더 크다.

오늘날 시각 매체는 청소년이 보기에 너무 폭력적이다. 이러한 폭력성 때문에 청소년은 싸움과 총이 문제를 해결하는 방법이라고 생각하고 일부는 실제로 비슷한 행동을 하기도 한다. 청소년은 나이가 너무 어린 탓에 TV와 영화에 나오는 가싱과 현실 사이를 잘 구별하지 못한다. 그뿐만 아니라, 영화와 TV에 끊임없이 폭력이 등장하기 때문에 청소년들은 폭력에 무디어진다. 한 가지 예가 지난 몇 년 동안의 교내 폭력의 증가이다. 우리 선생님 가운데 한 분은 갓 부임하셨을 때는 싸움을 거의 볼 수 없었다고 말씀하셨다. 하지만 요즘은 싸움이 점점 더 빈번해지는데, 이것이 영화와 TV에 나오는 지나친 폭력 때문이라고 선생님은 믿고 계신다. 폭력 면에서 영화와 TV는 청소년에게 확실히 부정적인 영향을 미친다.

영화 그리고 특히 TV가 청소년에게 미치는 또 다른 부정적인 영향은 어린 아이와 십대에게 나태를 조장한다는 것이다. 청소년들은 숙제를 하거나 가족들과 시간을 보내는 대신 TV를 너무 많이 시청한다. 사실, 오늘날 인터넷에 오르는 많은 기사들은 어떻게 해서 너무 긴 TV 시청 시간이 이런 상황의 주된 원인이 되는지를 다룬다. 학생들은 책이나 숙제보다는 TV 앞에서 너무 많은 시간을 보내는 탓에 성적이 점점 떨어진다. 이런 상황이 지속되면 학생들은 나중에 직장 생활에도 문제가 생기게 되고 더 나은 삶을 살고자 하는 동기부여도 받지 못하게 될 것이다. 확실히, TV와 영화는 청소년들을 훨씬 게으르게 만든다.

결론적으로, 영화와 TV는 어린 아이와 십대가 폭력을 모방하게 만들고 공부에 집중하는 대신 TV 시청에 너무 많은 시간을 보내게 한다는 점에서 그들에게 부정적인 영향을 미친다. 영화와 TV를 덜 보게 되면 요즘의 청소년 전반에게 더욱 긍정적인 영향이 미칠 것이다.

Disagree

Many people today blame movies and TV for having negative effects on young people. I completely disagree with this notion because the right kind of movie or television program can be highly educational as well as motivational.

Of course, there is a lot of trash on TV and the big screen these days. However, if parents guide their kids and have them watch worthwhile programs such as documentaries or even the news, their children can learn important information instead of just being entertained. For example, my father has always enjoyed watching the documentary *Animal Planet*, and he has gotten me into it as well. I never realized how much I was fascinated by animals and how complex their lives really are. Actually, I have even considered becoming a veterinarian mainly because of my exposure to *Animal Planet*. Without TV, I may never have found what I want to do as my career. Television and movies can definitely have positive effects on young people these days.

Also, movies and television can open up our eyes to the world. Without visual media, our world would be a much smaller place, and certain shows can motivate us to make the world we live in a better place. In this sense, they can have very positive effects on young people by encouraging them to change the world. For example, I often watch the Discovery Channel, which has programs on problems such as diseases and food shortages that people face in Africa. Eventually, with my parent's help, I began to donate some money each month to help people in Africa. Without television, I would not have known how serious the situation was there and would never have tried to help. In this way, because of TV, I

was motivated to help poor and desperate people in far-off lands whom I do not even know.

In summary, television and movies can have very positive effects on young people because they can educate them about the world and motivate them to do good deeds. Television opens up the world around us and can be a positive aspect in anyone's life so long as that person avoids all of the trivial programming.

오늘날 많은 사람이 영화나 TV가 청소년에게 부정적인 영향을 미친다고 말한다. 좋은 영화나 TV 프로그램은 동기 부여가 될 뿐만 아니라 대단히 교육적이기 때문에 나는 이 견해에 전적으로 반대한다.

물론, 요즘에 TV나 영화에 쓰레기 같은 장면이 많은 건 사실이다. 하지만, 부모가 자녀들로 하여금 다큐멘터리나 뉴스 같이 가치 있는 프로그램을 보도록 지도한다면 그들은 단지 오락만 즐기는 게 아니라 중요한 정보를 배울 수 있다. 예를 들어, 우리 아버지는 항상 "동물의 왕국"이라는 다큐멘터리를 즐겨 보셨는데, 나도 그 프로그램을 좋아하게 되었다. 나는 동물이 얼마나 매력적인지 그리고 실제로 동물의 삶이 얼마나 복잡한지 전혀 몰랐다. 사실, "동물의 왕국"을 본 덕분에 나는 수의사가 되는 것도 생각하고 있다. TV가 없었더라면 나는 어떤 직업을 선택할지 몰랐을지도 모른다. TV와 영화는 확실히 요즘 청소년들에게 긍정적 영향을 줄 수 있다.

또한, 영화와 TV는 세상에 눈을 뜨게 해 준다. 시각 매체가 없다면 우리의 세계는 훨씬 좁아졌을 테지만 어떤 프로그램은 우리가 사는 세상을 더 나은 곳으로 만들도록 동기를 부여해 주기도 한다. 이런 의미에서, 영화와 TV는 청소년들에게 세상을 변화시키도록 하는 아주 긍정적인 영향을 미친다. 예를 들어, 나는 디스커버리 채널을 즐겨 보는데, 이 채널에는 질병이나 기근과 같은 아프리카가 직면한 문제들에 대한 프로그램이 많다. 결국, 나는 부모님의 도움을 받아 매달 아프리카에 있는 사람들을 위해 약간의 돈을 기부하기 시작했다. TV가 없었다면 나는 그곳에 있는 사람들의 생활이 얼마나 심각한지 결코 알지 못했을 것이고 도우려는 시도도 하지 않았을 것이다. 이렇듯, TV가 있어 나만큼 행복한 삶을 누리고 있지 못한, 심지어 내가 알지도 못했던 사람들을 도울 수 있었다.

요약하자면, 영화와 TV는 청소년들에게 세상에 대해서 알 기회를 주고 선행을 할 수 있는 동기를 부여해 주기 때문에 매우 긍정적인 효과를 낼 수 있다. TV는 우리로 하여금 주변 세상에 눈을 뜰 수 있는 기회를 주고 모든 하찮은 프로그램들을 걸러내는 한 모든 이의 삶에 긍정적인 영향을 줄 수 있다.

Unit 11 School & Education I

Understanding the Topic

4   Have more free time → more study time for harder classes /
    Get a higher GPA → more scholarship money

5   Easy course load → do well in ethics class, my most difficult class /
    Older sister got high grade → got scholarship

Brainstorming

1 have more free time
2 more study time for harder classes
3 e.g. did well in difficult ethics class
4 get a higher GPA
5 more opportunity for scholarships
6 e.g. older sister boosted GPA & got a scholarship

Outlining

B

1 Have more free time
   – extra study time for harder classes
   – e.g. easier classes helped me do well in ethics class
2 Easier class boosts GPA
   – more opportunity for scholarships
   – e.g. older sister got high grade → money for graduate school

Writing the Thesis Statement & Topic Sentences

B

Thesis statement High grades are the most important objectives at college or university, and a good GPA can only be maintained by taking some easy courses.

Topic sentence 1 Taking easier classes will free up time for students.

Topic sentence 2 Taking easier classes will boost students' GPAs.

Summary It is clear that taking easier courses is beneficial for students because it will give them more time to study for their most difficult classes, thereby helping them get good GPAs.

Writing the Details

A

[도입문] 많은 학생이 일단 대학에 들어가면 학점이 잘 나올 수 있는 가장 쉬운 과목만을 선택한다. [논제 진술] 하지만, 성적이 잘 나오지 않는다고 해도 만만치 않은 어려운 과목을 택하는 것이 잠재력을 최대한 실현할 수 있는 최선의 방법이라는 게 내 생각이다.

[주제문 1] 우선, 만만치 않은 어려운 과목을 선택하면 더 많이 배우고 더 나은 학습 역량을 갖추게 된다. [일반 진술 1] 그런 수업에서는 교수님들이 훨씬 더 많은 것을 요구하고, 최고의 결과를 기대한다. [예 1] 예를 들어, 한번은 내가 수학 수업을 들었는데, 선생님이 까다롭기로 유명한 분이셨다. 선생님은 명성에 걸맞는 수업을 진행하셨다. 매일 밤 많은 과제

물을 해야 했고 때로는 힘든 순간도 있었다. 하지만, 나는 그런 빡빡한 일정에 익숙해졌고 까다롭긴 해도 선생님은 공정하게 대해 주셔서 나는 이전 수업에 비해 그 수학 수업에서 배운 것이 더 많았다. [종결문 1] 어려운 수업을 들으면 확실히 더 많은 것을 배울 수 있다.

[주제문 2] 더욱이, 스스로 목표를 더 높이 잡기 때문에 목표를 낮게 잡거나 아예 목표가 없는 경우보다 학생으로서 그리고 개인으로서 더 많은 것을 성취하게 된다. [일반 진술 2] 최종 성적과 무관하게 어려운 수업을 듣고 나면 자신감도 생기고 좋은 경험도 얻게 된다. [예 2] 작년에 나는 처음으로 프랑스어 수업을 들었다. 처음에 나는 초조했고 수업은 해야 할 게 많았다. 하지만 시간이 가면서 나는 이 수업을 통해 많은 자신감을 얻었다. 올해도 프랑스어 수업을 계속 듣고 있는데, 내 경험 덕분에 훨씬 쉬워졌다. 내게 있어 중요한 것은 완벽한 성적이 아니라 경험과 자신감이다. [종결문 2] 대학에서 더 어려운 수업을 듣게 되면 쉬운 수업을 듣는 것보다 확실히 도움이 된다.

[요약] 성적이 전부는 아니다. 학생으로서 더 많은 것을 배우고 자신감과 경험도 늘릴 수가 있기 때문에 어려운 수업을 듣는 것이 더 낫다. 이것은 쉬운 수업을 들어 좋은 성적을 얻는 것보다 미래에 더 큰 도움이 된다. [최종 논평] 쉬운 수업을 들으면 성적은 잘 나올지 모르지만 어려운 수업을 들으면 삶에 대한 준비가 된다.

B

[Opening sentence] Some university students take difficult courses, and their GPAs, as well as their lives, begin to suffer. [Thesis statement] High grades are the most important objectives at college or university, and a good GPA can only be maintained by taking some easy courses.

[Topic sentence 1] To begin with, taking easier courses will free up time for students. [General statement 1] Easier classes will give them more time to study for their tougher mandatory subjects and also let them get out and meet new people. [Example 1] For instance, my ethics class is the only hard class I currently have. Because I don't really have to study for my other classes too much, I can focus more attention on my ethics class and therefore do better in it. If all of my classes were hard, I would never have enough time to do well in every one of them. [Closing sentence 1] All in all, easy classes are the best bet because they will give students more time to focus on the classes they find difficult.

[Topic sentence 2] Also, taking easier classes will boost students' GPAs. [General statement 2] Having high grades will allow students to gain more scholarships and fund their educations. However, if students took only hard classes, their GPAs would decrease, and funding would not be available to them. [Example 2] For example, my older sister took a basic math class in college and got an A⁺ in it. This high grade made her GPA skyrocket and helped her get an academic scholarship the next semester. If she had taken an advanced math course, she probably would have gotten a lower grade and would not have received the scholarship. **[Closing sentence 2]** Taking easier classes is therefore necessary to get a high GPA.

[Summary] It is clear that taking easier courses is beneficial for students because it will give them more time to study for their most difficult classes, thereby helping them get good GPAs. **[Final comment]** Top-notch grades can only be secured by taking the easiest classes available and avoiding the difficult ones.

[도입문] 일부 대학생들은 어려운 수업을 들으면서 학점뿐만 아니라 인생도 기울기 시작한다. **[논제 진술]** 대학에서는 성적이 가장 중요한 목표이고 좋은 성적을 얻으려면 쉬운 과목 위주로 선택하는 수밖에 없다.

[주제문 1] 우선, 쉬운 과목을 선택하면 시간에 여유가 생긴다. **[일반 진술 1]** 쉬운 과목을 들으면 외출을 하고 친구를 사귈 수 있는 시간뿐만 아니라 다른 더 어려운 필수 과목을 공부할 수 있는 시간도 생긴다. **[예 1]** 예를 들어, 현재로는 내가 듣는 과목 가운데 윤리가 유일하게 어려운 과목이다. 다른 과목들은 사실상 공부를 많이 하지 않아도 되기 때문에 윤리 과목을 집중적으로 더 열심히 공부할 수 있다. 만약 수업 전부가 어려운 과목이라면 한 과목 한 과목 다 잘 할 수 있는 충분한 시간이 없었을 것이다. **[종결문 1]** 전반적으로, 쉬운 과목 위주로 수업을 들으면 어렵다고 생각되는 과목을 공부할 수 있는 시간이 더 많이 생긴다는 점에서 최선의 선택이다.

[주제문 2] 또한, 쉬운 과목을 들으면 학점도 올라간다. **[일반 진술 2]** 높은 학점을 받을 경우 장학금을 받아 학비에 보탤 수도 있다. 하지만, 어려운 수업을 듣는다면 성적은 내려가고 그런 장학금 혜택을 받지 못하게 될 것이다. **[예 2]** 예를 들어, 우리 누나는 대학에서 기초 수학 수업을 들었는데 A⁺를 받았다. 이 덕분에 학점이 쭉 올라갔고 그 다음 학기에 성적 장학생이 되었다. 고급 수학 수업을 들었더라면 아마도 성적은 더 낮았을 것이고 장학금도 받지 못했을 것이다. **[종결문 2]** 학점을 높게 관리하려면 쉬운 수업들을 들어야 한다.

[요약] 쉬운 수업을 들으면 가장 어려운 과목을 공부할 수 있는 시간적 여유가 더 생겨 높은 학점을 받을 수 있기 때문에 쉬운 수업 위주로 수업을 듣는 것이 확실히 유리하다. **[최종 논평]** 가능한 한 쉬운 과목 위주로 수업을 듣고 어려운 과목은 피해야만 최고의 성적을 받을 수 있다.

Completing & Checking Your Essay

A

Agree

Most students rush directly from high school to college without taking a break. However, I believe it is more beneficial to take a yearlong break before entering university because it will give me a chance to read many books and to earn extra money for college.

A yearlong break between high school and university would give me time to read various books before entering university. Before I enter university, I will have to spend most of my time preparing for the college entrance exam and will not have much time to read as I would like. A year's break will give me a chance to read as well as recharge my batteries to get ready for a demanding university schedule. I usually use my summer and winter vacation to catch up on my reading and keep my mind active. Still, there are many books that I have not read. A yearlong break would give me ample opportunity to catch up on my reading and prepare me for a college reading load.

Also, the yearlong break would give me a chance to do a part-time job to save money for college. I know my parents can pay for my tuition with little problem, but I would like to take some responsibility and save some money myself at least to help out. My sister is a good example of this. Before she entered college, she worked for a year to save money for college. She said the money came in very handy once she was in school. She also felt good about not having to ask our parents for spending money all the time. Therefore, in my opinion, a yearlong break is a good idea for students to work and save some money for college.

In summary, taking a year's break would definitely be beneficial to me because it would give me time to read extensively and earn supplemental money for college. Reading will prepare my mind for college, and working will allow me to save extra money without having to rely on my parents. Without a year's break, these two excellent opportunities would not be available to me.

대다수 학생들은 고등학교를 졸업하자마자 여유를 갖지 않고 대학에 진학한다. 하지만, 나는 대학 진학에 앞서 1년 간의 휴식을 갖는 것이 책도 많이 읽을 수 있고 학비를 위한 돈도 벌 수 있기 때문에 더 유익하다고 생각한다.

고등학교와 대학 사이에 1년 간의 휴식을 가지면 대학 진학에 앞서 다양한 책을 읽을 수 있다. 나는 대학에 들어가기 전에 대부분의 시간을 대학 입시 공부에 써야 하기 때문에, 읽고 싶은 만큼 많은 책을 읽을 시간이 없을 것이다. 1년 간의 휴식은 빡빡한 대학 일정을 위한 충전의 시간도 되고 독서를 할 수 있는 기회도 될 것이다. 나는 보통 여름 방학과 겨울 방학을 이용해 독서를 하고 머리를 충전한다. 하지만 아직도 읽지 못한 책이 너무 많다. 1년 간의 휴식은 그런 책을 읽고 대학에 필요한 독서량을 채우는 데 충분한 시간이 될 것이다.

또한, 1년 간의 방학을 이용해 학비에 도움이 되도록 아르바이트를 할 수도 있다. 물론 부모님이 등록금을 내주실 수도 있지만 나도 어느 정도의 책임을 지고 적어도 일부라도 도움이 되고 싶다. 우리 누나가 좋은 예이다. 그녀는 대학에 들어가기 전에 1년 정도 일을 하면서 학비를 모았다. 그녀는 대학에 진학해서 그 돈을 아주 요긴하게 썼다고 했다. 또한 그녀는 돈을 쓸 때마다 부모님께 부담을 안겨 드리지 않아도 되어서 좋았다. 1년 간의 휴식은 일을 하면서 학비를 모을 수 있기 때문에 좋은 생각이다.

요약하자면, 1년 간의 휴식을 가지면 광범위하게 책도 읽고 대학 학비도 벌 수 있는 시간이 주어지기 때문에 확실히 유익하다. 독서를 통해 대학 진학을 위한 수양을 쌓을 수도 있고 부모님께 의존하지 않도록 일을 통해 여윳돈을 모아둘 수도 있다. 1년 간의 방학이 없다면 이 두 가지 멋진 기회는 사라질 것이다.

Disagree

While some students might think it is good idea to take a yearlong break before entering university, I completely disagree for a number of reasons. First, if a student takes a yearlong break, he might forget much of what he learned at school. Second, a student who takes a break from school may never enroll in university at all.

To begin, a year is a long time for a young person, so it may cause the person to lose much of the knowledge he worked so hard to attain. Because of the large time gap between high school and college, once a student enters college, he will have a hard time readjusting to the classroom. He also runs a high risk of doing poorly in university or college and perhaps may even drop out permanently. For example, I read a magazine article about a student who took a yearlong break between high school and university. He regretted that he ever did such a thing. By the time he finally entered college, he could not readjust to the classroom atmosphere. He said he lacked the necessary discipline because he had taken such a long break. Unfortunately, he failed most of his classes and finally dropped out of school. Obviously, continuous schooling is the best strategy.

Furthermore, if a student takes a long break, he may lose interest in university altogether or simply never enroll. Some students who take time off and get jobs become obsessed with making money. Money, not education, rules their world, so they forget about college, which would give them a better quality of life in the long run. My neighbor always tells me to stay in school because, with the education I will receive there, I will have a more lucrative career in the future. My neighbor had the opportunity to go to college but did not go immediately, so he eventually gave up school for a full-time job. Though he likes his job, he has fewer opportunities for promotions because he never graduated from university. Staying in school removes the risk of becoming sidetracked and missing out on better, higher paying jobs.

In conclusion, students who take yearlong breaks between high school and university run the risks of being unable to adapt to the university climate and failing their classes. They may also have to settle for jobs that are not as profitable as those which college graduates can find. Such a decision will only work against them later in life.

일부 학생들은 대학에 진학하기 전에 1년 간의 긴 휴식 시간을 갖는 것이 좋다고 생각하지만 나는 여러 가지 이유에서 전적으로 반대한다. 우선, 1년 간 휴식 시간을 가지면 학교에서 배운 내용을 완전히 잊어버릴 수도 있다. 두 번째로, 휴학을 하는 학생은 아예 대학 등록을 하지 않을 수도 있다.

우선, 1년이라는 시간은 청소년에게 긴 시간이다. 따라서 열심히 얻은 지식의 상당 부분을 잊어버릴 수도 있다. 고등학교와 대학 사이의 공백이 커서 일단 대학에 들어가 강의에 다시 적응하는 데 어려움을 겪을 수도 있다. 또한 대학에서 성적이 잘 안 나올 가능성도 크고 어쩌면 영원히 학교를 그만둬야 할지도 모른다. 일례로, 나는 고등학교와 대학 사이에 1년 간의 휴식 시간을 가진 학생에 관한 기사를 잡지에서 읽은 적이 있다. 그는 자신이 한 일을 후회했다. 마침내 대학에 들어갔을 때 그는 강의실 분위기에 적응할 수 없었다. 그는 그렇게 긴 휴식 시간을 가진 탓에 학업에 필요한 준비가 부족했다고 말했다. 안타깝게도, 그는 대부분의 수업에서 낙제점을 받았고 결국 대학을 중퇴했다. 확실히, 학업을 중단 없이 진행하는 것이 최선의 전략이다.

더욱이, 학생이 긴 휴식 시간을 갖게 되면 아예 대학에 흥미를 잃게 되어 등록을 하지 않을 수도 있다. 휴학을 하고 직업을 갖는 학생들 가운데는 돈을 버는 데만 관심을 쏟는 학생들도 있다. 교육이 아닌 돈이 세상을 지배하다 보니 학생들은 결국에는 더 나은 삶의 질을 보장해 줄 대학에 대해서는 잊어버리게 된다. 우리 이웃에 사는 사람은 대학에서 받는 교육 덕분에 나중에는 훨씬 나은 직장을 구하게 될 테니 학업을 계속하라고 항상 말한다. 그는 대학에 갈 기회가 있었지만 곧바로 대학을 가지 않았다가 결국 전일제 직장을 위해 진학을 포기했다. 그는 자신의 일을 좋아했지만 대학을 다니지 않았기 때문에 승진의 기회가 적었다. 대학을 다니면 더 낫고 봉급이 많은 직장을 놓치는 위험 부담을 안지 않아도 된다.

결론적으로, 고등학교와 대학 사이에 1년 간의 긴 휴식을 갖는 학생은 대학 분위기에 적응을 못하고 수업에 낙제를 할 위험이 더 커진다. 또한 대학 졸업자가 구할 수 있는 것보다 못한 일자리에 만족해야 할지도 모른다. 그런 경솔한 판단은 미래의 삶에 도움이 되지 않는다.

Unit 12 School & Education II

Understanding the Topic

4   Can be faithful to their original duty → fill students with information /
Make their classes more valuable

5   Some teachers – not friendly but taught the best /
A young teacher in high school → friendly but had no authority

Brainstorming

1   not paid to be friendly with students
2   my only concern → what a teacher can teach me
3   e.g. some teachers – not friendly but the best teachers ever
4   some friendly teachers = the worst teachers
5   try to be cool but don't focus on teaching
6   e.g. a young teacher in high school – hung out with students → had no authority

Outlining

B

1   Teachers are not paid to be friendly with students.
    – my only concern → what a teacher can teach me
    – e.g. some teachers in my school days → were not friendly but taught the best
2   Some teachers who try to be friendly with the students = the worst teachers
    – do not focus on teaching → their classes = wastes of time
    – e.g. a young teacher in high school → friendly with the students but no discipline

Writing the Thesis Statement & Topic Sentences

B

Thesis statement My best teachers have been people who did not relate to the students but who instead managed to teach the class a lot.

Topic sentence 1 Teachers are not being paid to be friends with students but should instead be filling them with information.

Topic sentence 2 Teachers who try to be friendly with the students are often the worst ones I have ever had.

Summary It is better for a teacher to pass on knowledge to the students than to be able to relate well to them since it is what he/she is paid for and at least it will keep him/her from being a bad teacher.

Writing the Details

A

[도입문] 어떤 사람들은 학생에게 지식을 전달하는 교사의 능력이 교사의 가장 중요한 자질 가운데 하나라고 생각한다. [논제 진술] 하지만, 요즘 같은 시대에는 학생들과 어울리지 못하는 교사는 학생들의 관심을 끌 수도 없고 존경을 받지도 못하는데, 이 두 가지는 교사에게 대단히 중요한 자질이다.

[주제문 1] 요즘에는 교사들이 학생들을 가르치기 위해서는 학생들의 관심을 끄는 법뿐만 아니라 관심을 유지하는 법도 알아야 한다. [일반 진술 1] 지난 10년 동안 세상은 아주 많이 바뀌었고, 요즘 학생들은 10년이나 20년 전과 똑같은 것에 관심을 갖지 않는다. [예 1] 예를 들어, 우리는 전자제품, 특히 컴퓨터가 지배하는 시대에 살고 있다. 내 또래의 대다수 학생들은 최신 제품을 사용하는 법을 전부 알고 있다. 안타깝게도, 많은 교사들은 기계에 서투르기 때문에 그런 면에서 학생들과 어울리는 데 어려움이 있다. 대다수 교사들은 수업에 과학기술을 접목하지 않는다. 대신에, 그냥 강의만 하기 때문에 수업이 지겨워진다. 하지만 일부 교사들은 파워포인트 발표와 같이 컴퓨터를 사용하기도 하는데, 이는 대다수 학생들의 관심을 끄는 데 정말로 도움이 된다. [종결문 1] 과학기술과 같은 분야에서 학생들과 잘 어울리는 선생님은 확실히 학생들의 관심을 더 끌 수 있다.

[주제문 2] 교사는 또한 학생들과 잘 어울리기 위해서 학생들의 존경을 받을 수 있어야 한다. [일반 진술 2] 교사는 수업 시간에 엄격하게 해야 하지만 어떤 이유로든 언제 학생들이 최선으로 공부하지 못하는지도 알아야 한다. [예 2] 예를 들어, 나는 아주 엄하고 어렵게 수업을 했던 몇몇 선생님을 겪었다. 하지만, 항상 그런 선생님들을 존경했다. 그분들은 자신이 언제 학생을 너무 심하게 몰아붙이고 있는지 아셨기 때문이다. 시험이 너무 많아서 우리가 힘들어 할 때는 숙제를 내주지 않는다든지 우리를 위해 수업을 재미있게 해주곤 하셨다. 또한, 어떤 선생님들의 경우에는 개인적인 문제로 상담도 할 수 있었다. 나는 선생님들이 내 문제를 이해하고 충고도 해줄 수 있다고 느꼈다. [종결문 2] 이러한 교사들은 학생과 아주 잘 어울리기 때문에 학생들은 다른 교사들보다 그들을 더 존경한다.

[요약] 내가 겪어본 바로는, 최고의 교사는 학생들과 잘 어울리는 교사이다. 그렇게 함으로써 교사는 수업에서 학생들의 관심을 얻고 존경을 받을 수 있다. [최종 논평] 학생들과 잘 어울리지 못하는 교사는 수업 시간에 학생들 때문에 어려움을 더 많이 겪는 경향이 있다.

B

[Opening sentence] Is a teacher's ability to relate well with the students more important than the ability to teach them well? [Thesis statement] My answer to this question is definitely negative. In my experience, my best teachers have been people who did not relate to the students but who instead managed to teach the class a lot.

[Topic sentence 1] Teachers are not being paid to be friends with students but should instead be filling them with information. [General statement 1] I am not interested in hanging out with a teacher but am only concerned with what he can teach me. [Example 1] During my school years, I have had many teachers who were not friendly to the students. In fact, some students were quite intimidated by them. The students would never have dreamed of talking to these teachers about personal matters. However, these teachers were some of the best I ever had. The lessons they taught me have stayed with me for years, and I have never forgotten their classes. In fact, some of them even influenced me to study more on my own outside of class. **[Closing sentence 1]** With these teachers, the fact that they were unfriendly had nothing to do with how much I learned in their classes.

[Topic sentence 2] Additionally, teachers who try to be friendly with the students are often the worst ones I have ever had. **[General statement 2]** These teachers are typically more concerned with being cool and having students like them, so they do not focus on teaching, which makes their classes complete wastes of time. **[Example 2]** Here is one example. One of my teachers in high school had only graduated from college a few years earlier. So he was not much older than the students. He thought he could be friends with the students and hang out with them. Unfortunately, when he tried to enforce discipline in the classroom, everyone ignored him. Also, since he was more concerned with his image, he never taught very demanding lessons. He almost never gave homework, and his tests were easy. While getting a high grade was nice, I realized I had learned almost nothing in his class and that it had been a waste of time. **[Closing sentence 2]** Because of him, I realized that having a cool teacher is less important than having a teacher who takes his classes seriously.

[Summary] In conclusion, I strongly feel it is better for a teacher to pass on knowledge to the students than to be able to relate well to them since it is what he is paid for, and at least it will keep him from being a bad teacher. **[Final comments]** A teacher that relates well might be fun for a while, but I go to school to learn, not to hang out with a teacher and be friends with him

[도입문] 학생들과 잘 어울리는 교사의 능력이 학생들을 잘 가르치는 능력보다 중요할까? **[논제 진술]** 이 질문에 대한 나의 대답은 분명히 부정적이다. 내 경험상, 최고의 교사는 학생들과 잘 어울리는 사람이 아니라 어떻게든 학생들에게 많은 것을 가르치는 교사이다.

[주제문 1] 교사는 학생들과 친구가 되라고 월급을 받는 게 아니라 학생들에게 지식을 전달하라고 월급을 받는다. **[일반 진술 1]** 나는 교사와 어울려 시간을 보내는 데 관심이 있는 게 아니라 그가 내게 무엇을 가르칠 수 있는지에만 관심이 있다. **[예 1]** 학창 시절 동안 나는 학생들에게 다정하지 않은 많은 교사를 만났다. 사실, 어떤 학생들은 그분들을 무서워하기도 했다. 학생들은 이 선생님들께 개인적인 문제에 관해 말할 엄두도 못 냈을 것이다. 하지만, 이러한 교사들 중에 내가 만난 최고의 교사들도 있었다. 그분들이 가르쳐 주었던 내용은 수년 동안 기억에 남았고 그분들이 했던 수업은 잊혀지지 않았다. 사실, 일부 교사들은 내가 교실 밖에서 혼자 더 공부할 수 있도록 영향을 주기도 했다. **[종결문 1]** 이러한 교사들의 경우 다정하지 않은 것이 내가 수업 시간에 얼마나 많은 것을 배

우는지와 아무런 관련이 없었다.

[주제문 2] 게다가, 학생들과 친하게 지내려고 하는 교사들이 제일 형편없는 교사인 경우도 자주 보았다. **[일반 진술 2]** 이러한 교사들은 대개 멋있어 보이고 학생들의 환심을 사는 데에만 관심이 있어서 가르치는 데 집중하지 않기 때문에 수업 시간을 완전히 낭비한다. **[예 2]** 한 가지 예를 들겠다. 나의 고등학교 선생님들 가운데 한 분이 몇 년 전에 대학을 갓 졸업하신 분이었다. 그래서 학생들과 나이 차가 별로 없었다. 그 선생님은 학생들과 친구가 되어서 같이 어울릴 수 있다고 생각했다. 안타깝게도, 수업 시간에 엄하게 하려고 했을 때는 학생들이 하나같이 선생님을 무시했다. 게다가, 선생님의 이미지 관리에 더 신경을 썼기 때문에 한 번도 수업을 빡빡하게 진행하지 않았다. 숙제는 거의 내주지 않았고 시험도 쉬웠다. 점수가 잘 나와서 좋기는 했지만 수업에서 배운 게 거의 아무 것도 없었고 수업은 시간 낭비였다는 것을 깨달았다. **[종결문 2]** 그 선생님 때문에 나는 멋진 선생님보다는 수업을 진지하게 생각하는 선생님이 낫다는 것을 알게 되었다.

[요약] 결론적으로, 나는 교사가 학생들과 잘 어울리기보다는 학생들에게 지식을 전달하는 것이 더 낫다고 확신한다. 그것이 바로 교사가 월급을 받는 이유이고 적어도 형편없는 교사가 되지 않게 해주는 것이기 때문이다. **[최종 논평]** 학생들과 잘 어울리는 교사는 잠시 동안은 재미있을지 모르지만 나는 학교에 배우러 가는 것이지 교사와 어울리며 친구가 되기 위해 가지는 않는다.

Completing & Checking Your Essay

Agree

I entirely agree with the statement that parents make the best teachers. In the course of my life, I have learned a number of important lessons that were taught to me by my parents and that I could not have learned anywhere else.

To begin with, my parents have taught me about how to live with others and get along well with them. Thanks to my parents teaching me that social lesson, I have been able to get along well with everyone in my family. Not only do I have a mother and father, but I also have a brother and sister. My siblings and I usually get along well, but sometimes we argue and fight with each other. However, my parents taught us that we should learn to look at the other person's point of view, so, many, times instead of fighting with one of my siblings, we are able to sit down with each other and calmly talk about our problems. This enables us to solve all of our problems easily. Thanks to my parents, I have learned how to compromise and get along well with others.

Another thing that my parents have taught me is the value of hard work. Because of my parents, I know that I have to work hard if I want to be successful in life. For example, when I was younger, I never really enjoyed school, so I often did not do my homework. Naturally, my grades were very low. My parents told me that I needed to study hard if I wanted to be successful in life. They worked with me to improve my grades. I started working hard, and my grades improved considerably. Now, I get pretty good grades in school, and it is all thanks to my parents for teaching me to work hard.

I truly believe that parents are the best teachers. Of course, we all have many teachers throughout our lifetimes, but our parents can affect us in so many different ways that they are definitely our best teachers.

나는 부모가 최고의 교사라는 의견에 전적으로 동의한다. 나는 살면서 다른 어느 곳에서도 배우지 못했을 많은 중요한 교훈을 부모님께 배웠다.

우선, 우리 부모님은 내게 다른 사람과 어떻게 함께 살아가고 지내야 하는지를 알려 주었다. 그와 같은 부모님의 사회적 가르침 덕분에 나는 가족들과 잘 지낼 수 있었다. 내게는 부모님뿐만 아니라 형과 누나도 있다. 형제들과 나는 대체로 잘 지내지만 때로는 말다툼도 하고 싸우기도 한다. 하지만, 부모님이 우리에게 상대방의 입장을 생각해 보라고 가르치셨기에 우리는 많은 경우 서로 싸우기보다는 함께 앉아 우리 문제에 대해서 차분히 대화를 나눌 수 있다. 이렇게 해서 우리는 언제나 문제들을 쉽게 해결할 수 있다. 부모님 덕분에 나는 다른 사람들과 타협하고 잘 지내는 법을 알게 되었다.

부모님이 내게 가르쳐 주신 또 다른 교훈은 열심히 일하는 것의 가치이다. 부모님 덕분에 나는 삶에서 성공하기 위해서는 열심히 일해야 한다는 것을 알게 되었다. 예를 들어, 내가 지금보다 어렸을 때 나는 정말로 학교 생활이 전혀 재미없어서 숙제를 안 한 적이 많았다. 당연히 성적도 형편없었다. 부모님은 인생에서 성공하고 싶다면 열심히 공부해야 한다고 말씀해 주셨다. 부모님은 내 성적을 끌어올리기 위해 나와 함께 공부해 주셨다. 나는 열심히 공부하기 시작했고 성적은 많이 향상되었다. 이제는 성적이 꽤 잘 나오는 편인데, 이 모든 것이 열심히 공부하도록 가르쳐 주신 부모님 덕분이다.

나는 진심으로 부모가 최고의 교사라고 생각한다. 물론, 우리 모두는 인생을 통틀어 많은 교사를 만난다. 하지만 부모는 아주 여러 가지 방식으로 우리에게 영향을 미치기 때문에 확실히 최고의 교사이다.

Disagree

While I understand the logic behind the statement, I must actually disagree with the statement that parents make the best teachers. In my case, I would have to say that my teachers at school have been much better teachers for me than my parents. Allow me to explain my feelings in more detail.

For one, I spend a lot of time with my teachers, and they often teach me lessons that are not so much about book learning but are about life learning. Several of my teachers make classes that are usually boring into fascinating classes that have shown me how the material they are teaching is relevant to life. One example is my history teacher, Mr. Patterson. Before I took Mr. Patterson's class, I never really enjoyed history that much. To me, it was just a lot of old names, dates, and places. However, Mr. Patterson made his classes seem to come alive by the way that he taught history. He also showed us how it is important to learn about the past because we can compare past events to present and even future ones. He has definitely been a great teacher for me.

Also, many of my teachers have encouraged me to be both a good student and an even better person. Through watching many of my teachers, I have learned how to conduct myself in a professional manner. For example, my English teacher, Mr. Thagard, is not only a great teacher but also an excellent person. He is also polite to everyone, even the students. He calls all of the students "Mr." or "Miss" even though we are much younger than he is. He never gets angry or yells at students even when they are impolite to him or forget to turn in their homework. He also always tries to help out students who are not doing well in the class. I have tried to model my behavior on his in an effort to become a real gentleman. He has truly been an excellent teacher in my life.

Throughout our lives many people, including our parents and friends, act as our teachers. However, I believe that the best teachers are those we have at school. They have taught me many lessons that I will never forget.

나는 그 진술 뒤에 깔린 논리는 이해하지만 부모가 최고의 교사라는 진술에는 사실상 반대한다. 내 경우에는, 학교 선생님들이 부모님보다 훨씬 나은 교사였다. 내가 느낀 바를 좀 더 자세하게 설명하겠다.

우선, 나는 많은 시간을 선생님들과 보내며 그분들은 종종 교재 학습보다는 인생에 관한 가르침을 주신다. 몇몇 선생님들은 일반적으로는 지겨울 수 있는 수업을 훌륭한 수업으로 만들어서, 내가 배우는 내용이 삶과 어떻게 관련되어 있는지 보여주셨다. 한 가지 예가 역사 선생님이셨던 패터슨 선생님이다. 나는 패터슨 선생님의 수업을 받기 전에는 역사를 그다지 좋아하지 않았다. 내게 역사 과목은 옛 사람들의 이름, 날짜, 장소의 나열에 지나지 않았다. 하지만, 패터슨 선생님은 자신만의 역사 교수법으로 수업이 살아있는 듯 느껴지게 하셨다. 또한 과거의 사건과 현재 그리고 심지어 미래의 사건을 비교해볼 수 있기 때문에 과거에 대해 배우는 것이 얼마나 중요한지 가르쳐 주셨다. 패터슨 선생님은 내게 확실히 훌륭한 선생님이셨다.

또한, 많은 선생님들이 더 나은 학생, 나아가 더 나은 인간이 되도록 나를 격려해 주셨다. 많은 선생님들을 지켜보면서 내가 어떤 길을 갈지에 대해서도 알게 되었다. 예를 들어, 영어 선생님이셨던 타가드 선생님은 훌륭한 선생님이기도 하셨지만 뛰어난 분이셨다. 그는 누구에게나, 심지어 학생에게도 예의를 갖추셨다. 학생들이 선생님보다 나이가 훨씬 어린데도 모든 학생들을 부를 때 "씨"라고 호칭을 붙이셨다. 학생들이 선생님께 버릇없이 굴거나 과제를 제출하지 않는 경우에도 학생들에게 화를 내거나 소리지르는 법이 없었다. 또한 수업을 제대로 따라가지 못하는 학생들에게는 항상 도움을 주셨다. 진정한 신사가 되기 위해서 나는 그의 행동을 본보기로 삼았다. 그는 진정 내 삶의 훌륭한 교사였다.

우리가 삶을 사는 동안 부모님과 친구들을 포함해 많은 사람들이 교사의 역할을 한다. 하지만, 나는 최고의 교사는 학교 선생님들이라고 생각한다. 그분들은 내가 결코 잊지 못할 많은 가르침들을 주셨다.

Unit 13 Environment & Science

Understanding the Topic

4   Maintain the biodiversity on Earth /
Commercial & medicinal benefits of some animals

5   Lack of wild animals in Africa → land is changing /
Some spider webs → strong fibers

Brainstorming

1   some animals – useful to people
2   commercial & medical benefits
3   e.g. some spider webs → strong fibers
4   need of biodiversity on Earth
5   too many or too few animals → imbalance of nature
6   e.g. lack of wild animals in Africa → land is changing

Outlining

1   Need a large biodiversity of animals
    – animals going extinct → imbalance of ecosystem
    – e.g. lack of animals in Africa → the land is changing
2   Some animals → valuable to people
    – provide both commercial and medical benefits
    – e.g. some spider webs → used to make strong fibers

Writing the Thesis Statement & Topic Sentences

Thesis statement It is imperative that humans set aside land for endangered animals to live on even if it means that human needs like farming, housing, and industry are ignored.

Topic sentence 1 As more and more animals become extinct, the biodiversity of the planet is getting smaller and smaller.

Topic sentence 2 Animals are important to humans and should not be allowed to go extinct.

Summary While the needs of humans are important, it is also crucial to set aside land upon which endangered animals may live without the threat of becoming extinct in order to maintain the biodiversity of the planet and human benefits.

Writing the Details

[도입문] 지구의 인구가 해마다 계속 늘고 있기 때문에 사람들은 농사를 짓고 주택을 건설하고 공장을 세울 땅이 점점 더 많이 필요하다. [논제 진술] 멸종 위기에 처한 동물들을 위한 땅을 따로 마련하는 것도 좋지만 이용 가능한 모든 땅을 인간을 위해 이용하는 것이 훨씬 더 중요하다.

[주제문 1] 우선, 인간은 접근 가능한 땅을 모두 이용할 필요가 있다. [일반 진술 1] 지구의 인구가 계속 늘어나면서 사람들은 이전에는 동물들만 살던 땅으로 옮겨가야 할 필요가 생겼다. [예 1] 많은 국가에는 인구가 백만 명이 넘는 도시가 많다. 사실 도쿄, 서울, 뉴욕과 같은 일부 도시들은 인구가 천만 명이 넘는다. 이러한 도시들은 인구 과잉으로 많은 사람들이 도시 외곽으로 새로운 곳을 찾아 나가야 한다. 멸종 위기에 처한 동물들이 서식하는 땅으로 이주하게 되는 경우도 있겠지만, 인간의 복지가 몇몇 멸종 위기종의 행복보다 훨씬 중요하다. [종결문 1] 점점 늘어나는 인구를 수용하고 편안하게 살도록 하는 최선의 방법은 동물이 서식하는 땅으로 이동하는 것이다.

[주제문 2] 또한, 동물은 지구상에 생명체가 존재했던 모든 시기 동안 지구 상에서 멸종되어왔다. [일반 진술 2] 번성하는 종이 있는 반면 멸망하는 종도 있다는 것은 삶의 진리이다. 동물의 멸종에 인간이 간섭해서는 안 되며 자연의 추세를 따라야 한다. [예 2] 사실, 일부 국가에서는 멸종 위기종이 살 수 있는 생물 보호구역을 정하는데, 이는 자연에 간섭하는 짓이다. 인간은 지구상의 우점종인 까닭에 인간 때문에 일부 종이 멸종되는 것은 불가피하다. [종결문 2] 이들 보호구역에 멸종 위기종을 살게 하는 것은 자연이 스스로 일부 종을 도태시키고 일부 종을 살리는 것을 거부하는 짓일 뿐이다.

[요약] 일부 멸종 위기종이 멸종되는 것은 안타깝지만 우리는 인간에 대해 더 신경을 써야 하고 인간이 살아남을 수 있도록 해야 한다. [최종 논평] 멸종 위기종을 걱정하기보다는 인류 문명을 걱정하는 일이 훨씬 더 중요하다.

[Opening sentence] An enormous number of endangered species of animals live on the planet. [Thesis statement] It is imperative that humans set aside land for these endangered animals to live on even if it means that human needs like farming, housing, and industry are ignored.

[Topic sentence 1] As more and more animals become extinct, the biodiversity of the planet is getting smaller and smaller. **[General statement 1]** It is important that Earth have large numbers of different species so as to maintain a diverse population of animals. **[Example 1]** Nature is very delicate. In every ecosystem, all of the animals are important. If there are too many or too few of one species, it could upset the entire balance of the ecosystem. This is already happening in places like Africa, where wild animals like lions, tigers, and elephants are endangered. Because there are fewer of these animals, the land itself is changing, and this is upsetting the balance of nature. **[Closing sentence 1]** By setting aside land for endangered animals to live on, people can help to maintain the diversity of nature while not upsetting local ecosystems.

[Topic sentence 2] Second of all, animals are important to humans and should not be allowed to go extinct. **[General statement 2]** Scientists often learn very much by studying animals in their natural habitats, and many animals can actually benefit humans. **[Example 2]** For example, some spiders spin webs that humans can use to make very strong fibers with. If these spiders were to become extinct, humans would not be able to make use of them at all. There are countless other animals that benefit humans both commercially and medicinally. Besides, many scientists do not yet know how some endangered animals could help people. **[Closing sentence 2]** By setting aside land for endangered animals, scientists could keep these animals alive and then be able to learn how they could be used to benefit humans.

[Summary] While the needs of humans are important, it is also crucial to set aside land upon which endangered animals may live without the threat of becoming extinct in order to maintain the biodiversity of the planet and human benefits. **[Final comment]** Having a diverse amount of animal species benefits both the planet and people in the long run, making it important to keep every species from becoming extinct.

[도입문] 지구상에는 엄청난 수의 멸종 위기종 동물들이 산다. **[논제 진술]** 농업, 주택, 산업 등에 대한 인류의 욕구를 저버리는 한이 있더라도 이러한 멸종 위기종이 서식할 수 있는 땅을 따로 마련해야 하는 것은 인간의 의무이다.

[주제문 1] 점점 더 많은 동물들이 멸종되면서 지구 생태계의 다양성이 점점 줄어들고 있다. **[일반 진술 1]** 지구가 다양한 생물 개체군을 유지하기 위해서는 다양한 종이 필요하다. **[예 1]** 자연은 대단히 민감하다. 모든 생태계에서 모든 동물들이 중요하다. 만약 어떤 한 종의 수가 너무 많거나 적을 경우 생태계의 전체적 균형을 깨뜨리게 된다. 사자나 호랑이, 코끼리 같은 야생동물들이 멸종할 위기에 처한 아프리카에서는 이미 이런 일이 일어나고 있다. 이러한 동물들의 수가 예전보다 적어져 토지가 바뀌고 있으며, 이로 인해 자연의 균형이 깨지고 있다. **[종결문 1]** 멸종 위기종의 서식지를 따로 정함으로써 사람들은 지역 생태계를 파괴하지 않고 자연의 다양성을 유지할 수 있다.

[주제문 2] 두 번째로, 동물은 인간에게 중요한 역할을 하기 때문에 멸종되도록 해서는 안 된다. **[일반 진술 2]** 과학자들은 흔히 서식지에서 생활하는 동물을 연구함으로써 아주 많은 것을 배울 수 있고 많은 동물들이 실제로 인간에게 이롭다. **[예 2]** 예를 들어, 어떤 거미들이 잣는 거미줄로 인간은 아주 튼튼한 섬유를 만들 수 있다. 만약 이 거미가 멸종된다면 인간은 거미줄을 전혀 이용할 수 없을 것이다. 상업이나 의료 면에서 인간에게 이익을 주는 수많은 다른 동물들이 있다. 게다가, 많은 과학자들은 일부 멸종 위기 종이 어떻게 인간에게 도움을 줄 수 있는지 아직까지 알지 못하고 있다. **[종결문 2]** 멸종 위기종을 위한 지역을 정함으로써 과학자들은 이런 위기종을 구할 수 있고 인간에게 도움을 주기 위해 어떻게 이 동물들을 활용할 수 있는지 알아낼 수 있다.

[요약] 인간의 욕구도 중요하지만 지구의 생물다양성과 인간의 이익을 유지하기 위해 멸종 위기종이 멸종될 위험 없이 살 수 있는 땅을 마련하는 일 역시 매우 중요하다. **[최종 논평]** 다양한 수의 동물 종이 존재할 경우 결국 지구와 인간에게 도움이 되기 때문에 모든 종이 멸종되지 않도록 하는 것이 중요하다.

Completing & Checking Your Essay

Agree

I fully agree with the statement that renewable sources of energy like solar and wind power will soon replace fossil fuels like coal, oil, and gas. There are several reasons why I feel this way.

First of all, many people now realize that Earth's supply of fossil fuels is going to run out within a few decades. Because people are going to exhaust these fossil fuels soon, we will have no choice but to make the transition to renewable sources of energy. During the twentieth century, people all over the world began using fossil fuels more than ever before. Mostly, they were used for running cars and other forms of transportation and for heating homes and buildings. Fossil fuels were very important during the twentieth century, yet people used them too much. Now geologists are telling people that Earth's supply is running out. Since we need energy to keep our economies running, we will have to work to develop renewable sources of energy.

Second of all, people are more concerned about the environment these days. Fossil fuels often pollute the environment, but renewable sources of energy cause virtually no pollution. In the twenty-first century, many people are focusing on cleaning up the Earth. Also, people are worried about the greenhouse effect, which some scientists believe is caused by the release of carbon dioxide—created by burning fossil fuels—into the atmosphere. The greenhouse effect is believed to be causing global warming, so something needs to be done about this. If people use solar, water, or wind power, they will not be adding any greenhouse gases to the atmosphere. This should help to prevent global warming, and it will also make Earth a much cleaner place.

In the near future, it is highly likely that renewable sources of energy will replace fossil fuels. Considering that the supply of fossil fuels is running out and that they pollute the environment, unlike renewable sources of energy, it is inevitable that people will start relying upon renewable sources of energy soon.

나는 태양력, 풍력과 같은 재생 에너지가 석탄, 석유, 천연가스와 같은 화석연료를 곧 대체하게 되리라는 의견에 전적으로 찬성한다. 이렇게 느끼는 이유는 여러 가지가 있다.

첫 번째로, 많은 사람들이 이제 지구의 화석연료 공급량이 수십 년 내에 바닥을 드러낼 것이라는 사실을 깨닫고 있다. 빠른 시간 내에 화석연료가 고갈될 것이기 때문에 재생 에너지로 방향을 전환하는 수밖에 없다. 20세기 동안 전 세계 사람들은 과거 어느 때보다 많은 화석연료를 사용하기 시작했다. 화석연료는 주로 자동차나 다른 형태의 교통 수단 그리고 주택과 건물의 난방에 사용되었다. 화석연료가 20세기 동안 매우 중요하긴 했지만 사람들은 너무 많은 양의 화석연료를 사용했다. 이제 지질학자들은 지구의 공급량이 바닥나고 있다고 말한다. 지구 경제가 돌아가기 위해서는 에너지가 필요하기 때문에 재생 에너지를 개발해야만 한다.

두 번째로, 사람들은 요즘 들어 환경에 더 많은 관심을 기울인다. 화석연료는 종종 환경을 오염시키지만 재생 에너지는 사실상 오염을 전혀 유발하지 않는다. 21세기에는 많은 사람들이 지구를 깨끗하게 만드는 데 관심을 쏟고 있다. 또한, 사람들은 온실효과에 대해서도 걱정한다. 일부 과학자들은 화석연료를 태울 때 나오는 이산화탄소가 대기 중에 배출되어서 온실효과가 일어난다고 믿는다. 온실효과는 지구 온난화를 야기한다고 알려져 있기 때문에 어떤 조치를 취해야 한다. 사람들이 태양 에너지, 수력, 풍력을 사용한다면 대기 중에 온실가스가 배출되는 것을 막을 수 있다. 이것은 지구 온난화 방지에도 도움이 되며 훨씬 깨끗한 지구를 만들 수 있게 된다.

가까운 미래에 재생 에너지가 화석연료를 대체할 가능성이 대단히 높다. 화석연료 공급량이 바닥나고 있고 화석연료는 재생 에너지와는 달리 환경을 오염시킨다는 사실을 고려할 때 사람들이 곧 재생 에너지에 의존하기 시작해야 하는 것은 불가피하다.

Disagree

Nowadays, many people are talking about renewable sources of energy like solar, wind, and water power. They insist that renewable energy sources will replace fossil fuels in the near future. However, I disagree with these people. In my opinion, humans are going to be using fossil fuels to create energy for many years to come.

First of all, according to many scientists, there is still an enormous supply of fossil fuels on Earth. Many geologists estimate that Earth has gas and oil supplies of over 100 years. The coal supply is even higher. Also, teams of geologists are often announcing they have found new oil and gas fields all over Earth, especially because they can now dig deeper into the ground to extract these fossil fuels. Since there are still so many fossil fuels left on Earth, it is highly unlikely that people are suddenly going to change to renewable sources of energy. For one, people do not often change until they are forced to do so. In addition, machines like cars are becoming more fuel-efficient, and this development will actually help make the supply of fossil fuels last longer because machines are using less energy to operate. Simply put, until people are forced to change energy supplies, they are not going to.

Next, renewable sources of energy are still in their developmental stage. Some people use solar, wind, and water power, yet the number doing so is very small. Also, these renewable sources of energy are not yet very efficient. This means that they actually cost more than fossil fuels while providing less energy. Not only that, but their uses are also often limited. For example, people cannot use solar power if the weather is bad; people who do not live near a body of water cannot use water power; and people who live in areas with little wind cannot make use of wind power. Until researchers discover ways to make renewable energy more efficient and more ubiquitous, people are not going to start using it in place of fossil fuels.

Although many people are attracted to renewable sources of energy, I do not believe they are going to become the dominant form of energy and replace fossil fuels. People see no reason to replace fossil fuels, and the technology to create energy from renewable sources is currently not efficient enough.

요즘에는 많은 사람들이 태양력, 풍력, 수력과 같은 재생 에너지에 관해 이야기한다. 그들은 재생에너지가 화석연료를 대체할 것이라고 주장한다. 하지만 나는 이들과는 생각이 다르다. 나는 앞으로 오랫동안 사람들이 화석연료를 사용해 에너지를 얻을 것이라고 생각한다.

무엇보다도, 많은 과학자들에 따르면 지구에는 엄청난 양의 화석연료가 아직도 존재한다. 많은 지질학자들은 지구에 100년 이상 사용할 수 있는 천연가스와 석유가 있다고 추정한다. 석탄 공급량은 훨씬 많다. 또한, 지질학 연구팀들은 화석연료를 뽑아내기 위해 점점 더 깊이 땅을 팔 수 있게 되면서 지구 전역에서 새로운 유전과 가스전을 발견했다고 발표하고 있다. 지구상에는 아직도 많은 화석연료가 남아 있기 때문에 사람들이 갑자기 재생에너지로 눈길을 돌릴 것 같지는 않다. 우선, 사람들은 꼭 해야 하는 경우가 아니면 변화를 좋아하지 않는다. 그뿐만 아니라, 자동차와 같은 기계들이 점점 더 에너지 효율이 좋아지면서 기계 작동에 에너지를 덜 사용하기 때문에 화석연료의 공급량이 더 오래 갈 수 있다. 간단히 말해서, 사람들이 에너지 공급원을 마지못해 바꿔야만 하는 순간이 오기 전에는 에너지 공급원을 바꾸는 일은 일어나지 않을 것이다.

다음으로, 재생 에너지는 아직도 개발 단계에 있다. 몇몇 사람들은 태양력, 풍력, 수력을 사용하고 있지만 그것은 소수에 불과하다. 또한, 이러한 재생 에너지는 효율이 별로 높지 않다. 화석연료에 비해 실제로 비용은 많이 들지만 에너지는 덜 나온다는 얘기다. 그뿐만 아니라, 사용이 제한되는 경우도 많다. 예를 들어, 날씨가 궂은 날에는 태양에너지를 사용할 수 없다. 물이 있는 곳 근처에 살지 않으면 수력을 이용할 수도 없다. 바람이 거의 불지 않는 곳에 산다면 풍력을 이용할 수도 없다. 연구자들이 재생에너지를 더 효과적이고 장소에 덜 구애 받고 이용할 수 있는 방법을 찾아내기 전까지는 사람들이 화석연료 대신 재생 에너지를 사용하는 일은 없을 것이다.

많은 사람들이 재생 에너지에 매력을 느끼기는 하지만 나는 재생에너지가 주요 에너지원이 되어 화석연료를 대체하게 되리라고는 생각하지 않는다. 사람들이 화석연료를 대체해야 할 이유가 없고 재생 에너지를 생산하는 기술도 현재로서는 충분히 효율적이지 못하다.

Chapter 4 Preference

Unit 14 Family & Society

Understanding the Topic

4   Majority of time spent with friends → become like them in personality and actions /
Similar age & perspective → can relate well to one another & show more empathy

5   Father's experience → hung out with the wrong crowd in high school but made friends with smart, good students later in college /
Best friend broke up with her boyfriend → I supported her.

Brainstorming

1   majority of time spent with friends
2   become like them in personality & actions
3   e.g. father's high school vs. college experience
4   similar age & perspective
5   relate to one another better → more empathy & understanding
6   e.g. best friend - romantic relationship support

Outlining

1   Majority of time spent with friends
    – an important factor in shaping personality and actions
    – e.g. father with the wrong crowd in high school → a poor student vs. with the right crowd in university → graduated with top marks
2   Similar age and perspectives
    – relate to one another better → more empathy and understanding
    – e.g. best friend broke up with her boyfriend → I gave her support as a friend

Writing the Thesis Statement & Topic Sentences

Thesis statement Friends are by far the most important influence on young adults.

Topic sentence 1 Most young adults spend more time with their friends than anyone else, including their families.

Topic sentence 2 Young adults and their friends are of similar ages and perspectives.

Summary All in all, friends influence young adults more than anything else because they are around each other all the time and they share common viewpoints.

Writing the Details

A

[도입문] 청소년들은 감수성이 대단히 예민해서 친구 같은 다양한 방법에 의해 쉽게 영향을 받는다. [논제 진술] 그럼에도 불구하고, 나는 가족이야말로 청소년들에게 가장 큰 영향을 준다고 생각하는데, 그 이유는 교육 목표를 성취하도록 해주고 좋을 때나 나쁠 때나 진심 어린 충고를 해주기 때문이다.

[주제문 1] 무엇보다도, 부모는 젊은이의 교육 목표 달성에 도움을 줄 수 있는 유일한 존재이다. [일반 진술 1] 대다수의 청소년들은 부모의 경제적 도움이 없다면 대학에 다닐 수 없을 것이다. [예 1] 예를 들어, 내 사촌은 좋은 대학에 합격했는데, 그의 부모님이 융자를 받아 대학에 다닐 수 있게 해주었다. 또한, 부모님의 도움 덕분에 일을 하지 않고 공부에만 전념할 수 있었다. 마침내, 그는 가족 가운데 대학을 졸업한 최초의 인물이 되었다. [종결문 1] 부모들은 청소년인 자녀들이 대학에 다닐 수 있게 해준다.

[주제문 2] 그뿐만 아니라, 가족은 청소년들에게 좋을 때나 나쁠 때나 진심 어린 충고를 해준다. [일반 진술 2] 이것이 가능한 이유는 또래 친구들

과 달리 부모나 연장자인 가족 구성원은 이미 특정한 상황을 겪어보았기 때문에 자연스럽게 상담을 해줄 수 있기 때문이다. **[예 2]** 예를 들어, 내 형은 고등학교 때 참가했던 과학 경시대회에서 입상해 상당한 액수의 상금을 받았다. 친구들은 대부분 나가서 새 핸드폰이나 옷을 사라고 했다. 하지만, 부모님은 대학을 위해 은행에 저금해 놓는 것이 더 좋을 거라고 충고해 주셨다. 아버지는 언젠가는 그 돈이 유용하게 쓰일 거라고 말씀하셨다. 형은 부모님 판단이 옳았다는 것을 깨달았다. **[종결문 2]** 가족이 청소년에게 미치는 긍정적 영향을 대신할 수 있는 것은 없다.

[요약] 결론적으로, 가족은 청소년들이 고등학교를 졸업한 후에도 교육을 지원해 주고 나이가 더 어린 친구들은 해줄 수 없는 바람직한 충고를 해주기 때문에 청소년들이 가족에게서 가장 긍정적인 영향을 받는다는 것은 확실하다. **[최종 논평]** 가족이 없다면 청소년들은 삶을 살아나가는 데 훨씬 큰 어려움을 겪을 것이다.

B

[Opening sentence] There is no question that young adults are under a lot of stress and are influenced in many ways. **[Thesis statement]** Among other influences, friends are by far the most important influence on young adults because the majority of their time is spent with their friends, with whom they share similar ages and perspectives.

[Topic sentence 1] For one thing, most young adults spend more time with their friends than anyone else, including their families. **[General statement 1]** Therefore, a young person's friends can have profound effects on his personality and actions. **[Example 1]** A good example of this type of influence occurred with my father. As a high school senior, he tended to hang out with the wrong crowd, so his grades suffered to the point where he almost did not graduate. However, he managed to graduate from high school and eventually made it to college, where he chose his friends more carefully and spent time with serious, goal-oriented students. He ultimately graduated with top grades and still exhibits the positive personality traits he learned from his classmates. **[Closing sentence 1]** Being around friends can influence young adults constantly in both positive and negative ways.

[Topic sentence 2] Moreover, young adults and their friends are of similar ages and perspectives. **[General statement 2]** Therefore, they are able to relate to one another better and be more empathetic and understanding because they know what the others are going through. Sometimes even family members cannot relate to a person like his friends can. **[Example 2]** For instance, my best friend recently broke up with her boyfriend. Of course, she turned to me for support and comfort because she trusts me and knows I understand how she feels. I doubt she could have discussed her intimate feelings about him with her parents or little sister. **[Closing sentence 2]** In this way, friends are the biggest influence on young adults.

[Summary] All in all, friends influence young adults more than anything else because they are around each other all the time and they share common viewpoints. **[Final comment]** Friends have the most in common, and they make us who we are.

[도입문] 청소년들이 스트레스도 많이 받고 여러 가지 방식으로 영향을 받는다는 것은 의심의 여지가 없다. **[논제 진술]** 청소년들은 대부분의 시간을 친구와 함께 보내고 나이와 생각도 비슷하기 때문에 청소년기에는 다른 무엇보다도 친구에게서 가장 큰 영향을 받는다.

[주제문 1] 우선, 대다수 청소년들은 가족을 포함한 어느 누구보다도 친구와 많은 시간을 보낸다. **[일반 진술 1]** 그래서 친구들은 성격과 행동에 지대한 영향을 미친다. **[예 1]** 이러한 영향의 좋은 예를 우리 아버지에게서 볼 수 있다. 고등학교 3학년 때 아버지는 나쁜 친구들과 어울리면서 성적이 떨어져 졸업을 하기도 힘든 지경에 이르렀다. 하지만, 가까스로 고등학교를 졸업해 대학에 들어갔는데, 대학에서는 좀 더 신중하게 친구를 선택해 진지하고 목표 지향적인 학생들과 어울렸다. 아버지는 결국 우등생으로 대학을 졸업했고 지금도 친구들에게서 배운 긍정적인 성격을 지니고 계신다. **[종결문 1]** 친구들과 함께 어울리는 것은 청소년에게 긍정적 또는 부정적 방법으로 끊임없이 영향을 미친다.

[주제문 2] 더욱이, 청소년들은 친구들과 나이와 생각이 비슷하다. **[일반 진술 2]** 따라서, 그들은 상대방이 겪고 있는 상황을 이해하기 때문에 관계가 더 긴밀하고 공감대도 잘 형성되며 더 잘 이해한다. 때로는 가족들도 친구들만큼 긴밀한 관계를 형성하지 못 한다. **[예 2]** 예를 들어, 나와 가장 친한 친구는 최근에 남자친구와 헤어졌다. 물론, 그녀는 나를 믿고 내가 그녀의 기분을 이해하리라는 걸 알기 때문에 나에게 도움과 위안을 구했다. 남자친구에 대한 마음을 부모님이나 여동생과 이야기하기는 힘들 것이다. **[종결문 2]** 이렇듯이, 친구는 청소년들에게 가장 큰 영향을 미친다.

[요약] 전반적으로, 친구는 항상 어울려 다니고 공통된 관점을 갖고 있기 때문에 다른 무엇보다도 청소년에게 큰 영향을 미친다. **[최종 논평]** 친구는 우리와 가장 공통점이 많고 현재의 우리가 있게 해준다.

Completing & Checking Your Essay

A

Spending Time with One or Two Close Friends

People have many different preferences when it comes to their friends. Some like to have one or two close friends while others enjoy spending time with many people. Personally, I believe it is better to spend most of my time with one or two close friends because the bond between us is tighter, so we are like a family.

Spending time with one or two very close friends builds a tighter bond between people than it would by spending time with a large group. They have more in common and are more apt to understand each other completely. I spend almost all of my time with my best friend, and we have a very close relationship. We never argue and can rely on each other for anything because we are so tight. On the other hand, there are often more misunderstandings and conflicts within a large group of friends. However, I know my best friend will be with me for life. This type of longevity is not possible with a large group of friends.

In addition, having one or two close friends is like having an extended family. The reasons are that the relationship is more intimate and built on trust. I know my best friend will keep my most private secrets. For example, I did really poorly on my English exam, and I got really depressed about it. I would not have dared to have told a large group of friends about it because it was embarrassing, and I knew they would have told everyone in the whole school. However, I needed to talk about it with someone whom I could trust. That person was my best friend. She comforted me and helped me think positively. Plus, she never told anyone else about it. In this respect, spending time with one or two close friends is best.

In conclusion, spending time with one or two close friends is more desirable because the connection is closer than it would be with a group of friends and there is greater trust between these friends. I know I can absolutely count on them for anything.

사람들은 친구와 관련해 여러 가지 기호가 있다. 어떤 사람들은 여러 사람과 시간을 보내기를 좋아하는 반면 어떤 사람들은 절친한 친구 한두 명과 시간을 보내는 것을 좋아한다. 개인적으로, 나는 절친한 친구 한두 명과 대부분의 시간을 보내는 쪽을 좋아하는데, 친한 친구 사이의 유대감이 더 강하고 마치 가족 같은 느낌이 들기 때문이다.

한두 명의 절친한 친구와 시간을 보내면 큰 무리집단에 비해 더 끈끈한 정이 쌓인다. 공통점도 많고 서로 완전히 이해하기도 더 쉽다. 나는 거의 대부분의 시간을 절친한 친구와 보내는데, 우리는 아주 깊은 우정을 간직하고 있다. 말다툼을 하는 경우도 거의 없고 우정이 깊어 무엇을 할 때나 서로에게 의지한다. 반면에, 큰 집단에서는 흔히 더 많은 오해와 갈등이 있다. 하지만, 나는 내 친구가 평생 내 옆에 있어줄 것이라는 것을 안다. 이런 깊이 있는 우정은 큰 집단의 친구 사이에서는 불가능하다.

그뿐만 아니라, 한두 명의 절친한 친구가 생기는 것은 가족이 생기는 것과도 같다. 이것은 관계가 아주 긴밀해서 신뢰가 쌓이기 때문이다. 나는 내 절친한 친구가 나의 가장 개인적인 비밀을 지켜줄 것임을 안다. 한 가지 예로, 나는 영어 시험을 완전히 망쳐 정말 낙담해 있었다. 당황스러운 일이었기 때문에 큰 집단이었다면 말을 하지도 못했을 것이고, 말했다가는 그 애들이 우리 학교 학생 전부에게 떠벌렸을 것이라는 것을 안다. 하지만, 나는 누군가 믿을만한 사람에게 말을 해야 했는데, 그게 바로 내 절친한 친구였다. 그녀는 나를 위로해 주었고 긍정적인 생각을

갖도록 도와 주었다. 그뿐만 아니라, 누구에게도 발설하지 않았다. 이런 점에서, 절친한 친구 한두 명과 시간을 보내는 것이 가장 바람직하다.

결론적으로, 큰 집단의 친구들과 있을 때보다 유대감도 긴밀하고 신뢰감이 더 들기 때문에 한두 명의 절친한 친구와 시간을 보내는 게 더 낫다. 나는 거의 무슨 일에서든지 그 친구들을 믿을 수 있다는 것을 안다.

Spending Time with a Large Number of Friends

Some people really limit themselves by spending all of their time with just one or two close friends. I believe it is best to spend my time with a large number of friends. This will let me to get the most out of life because it will allow me to have an open mind and make me a more outgoing person.

When I spend a lot of time with a large group of friends, my mind becomes open to new worlds. The reason is that a large group offers me many different opinions about life that I have never even thought of. For example, I was always nervous about traveling to a foreign country. But, after listening to the travel experiences and opinions of numerous friends, I decided to give it a shot. What an amazing experience I had in Norway! Without my friends' influence, I would never have made such a bold move. Because of them, I was able to find the courage to go on my trip and also grew as a person.

Moreover, spending time with a large number of friends makes me a more personable and outgoing person. Because I have a large, diverse group of friends, I am continuously exposed to different personalities, and I have learned how to interact with people better. A good example of this is when my family moved to a new city because of my father's job. Of course, I had to start a new school. I was alone and did not know anyone. Yet, because I was used to meeting and talking to lots of people, it was easy for me to form new friendships. If I had only spent time with one or two good friends, I would have been shy and less assertive when it came to making new friends. However, since I was used to dealing with lots of different types of people, I was able to make new friends rather easily.

Ultimately, it is better to spend the most time with a large group of friends because they can help open our minds and help us to be more outgoing and sociable. Without them, my life would probably be pretty boring.

어떤 사람들은 자신이 가진 시간을 한두 명의 친한 친구와만 보냄으로써 자신의 세계를 제한한다. 나는 여러 친구들과 시간을 보내는 것이 가장 바람직하다고 생각한다. 이렇게 되면 열린 마음을 가지고 더 외향적인 사람이 될 수 있기 때문에 삶을 최대한 활용할 수 있다.

여러 친구와 함께 많은 시간을 보내다 보면 내 마음이 새로운 세계로 열리게 된다. 왜냐하면 여러 친구들은 내가 생각지도 못했을 삶에 대한 다양한 의견을 제공해 주기 때문이다. 한 가지 예로, 나는 항상 외국 여행을 하는 것을 두려워했다. 하지만, 많은 친구들의 여행 경험과 의견을 들은 뒤 나는 한번 시도해 보기로 했다. 노르웨이에서의 여행은 정말 멋진 경험이었다! 친구들의 영향이 없었다면 그런 대담한 시도는 엄두도 못냈을 것이다. 그들 때문에 나는 여행을 떠나고 한 인간으로 성장할 수 있었다.

그뿐만 아니라, 여러 친구들과 시간을 보내다 보면 더 매력적이고 외향적인 사람이 된다. 여러 명의 다양한 친구들이 있기 때문에 계속해서 다른 성격의 소유자들과 만나게 되고 다른 사람과 더 잘 지내는 법도 알게 된다. 이것을 보여주는 좋은 예가 우리 가족이 아버지의 일 때문에 새 도시로 이사를 가야 했을 때이다. 물론, 나는 전학을 해야 했다. 나는 혼자였고 친구가 없었다. 하지만, 많은 사람들을 만나고 이야기하는 것에 익숙해 있었기 때문에 새 친구를 찾는다는 것이 어려운 일이 아니었다. 만약 내가 항상 한두 명의 친한 친구와만 지냈다면 새 친구를 사귀는 것에 대해 소심했을 것이고 확신도 없었을 것이다. 하지만, 다양한 사람들을 만나는 것에 익숙해 있었기 때문에 비교적 쉽게 친구를 사귈 수 있었다.

결국, 여러 명의 친구를 사귀면 마음이 열리고 더 외향적이고 사교적인 성격이 되기 때문에 여러 친구를 사귀는 것이 더 낫다. 그들이 없다면 내 인생은 아마도 꽤나 따분할 것이다.

Unit 15 Environment & Technology

Understanding the Topic

2   Coal plants increase output for power → acid rain harms water supplies & ecosystems /
More housing developments → destroy habitat of animals & make them extinct

3   Lakes near coal plants affected by acid rain → now off-limits for recreation due to pollution /
Increased populations in areas near rainforests → many species of animals become extinct

Brainstorming

1   continued use of coal plants
2   acid rain harms water supplies & ecosystems
3   e.g. local lakes once popular for swimming & fishing → now off-limits
4   more housing developments
5   destroys ecosystems
6   e.g. rainforests cleared for new houses → extinct animals

Outlining

1   Continued use of coal plants
    – acid rain from coal plant toxin harms lakes and rivers
    – e.g. local lakes, once popular recreation spots → now off-limits to people
2   More housing developments
    – destroy habitats for animals, so they become extinct
    – e.g. rainforests cleared for houses → animals have no homes are & are lost forever

Writing the Thesis Statement & Topic Sentences

Thesis statement Human activity continues to harm the Earth in a number of ways.

Topic sentence 1 Coal power plants, which hurt the environment, continue to be used to produce eletricity for people.

Topic sentence 2 More and more homes are being constructed to house increasing populations, which destroys ecosystems.

Summary In conclusion, human activity continues to damage the Earth through the use of coal power plants and the construction of homes. Coal plants create toxins that cause acid rain, which harms bodies of water, and jungles and forests are being cleared to build houses, which reduces animal habitat.

Writing the Details

[도입문] 내가 뉴스에서 자주 보는 것은 사람들이 지구를 얼마나 파괴하고 있는지에 대한 얘기이다. [논제 진술] 하지만, 인간은 지구에 도움이 되는 유익한 일들을 계속하여 지구를 더 살기 좋은 곳으로 만든다.

[주제문 1] 우선, 의사들은 시간을 투자해 제3세계 국가들에 자선 활동을 한다. [일반 진술] 아프리카 국가들은 그들의 도움을 받아 이전보다 건강한 지역이 되었다. [예 1] 예를 들어, "국경 없는 의사회"라는 단체가 있다. 이 단체에서는 휴가를 내어 세계에서 도움을 필요로 하는 곳을 찾아 무상 의료를 제공한다. 그러한 지역들은 단지 의료 면에서만이 아니라 여러 가지로 그들의 도움을 받고 있다. 그들의 도움으로 사람들의 삶의 질이 대단히 향상되었다. [종결문 1] "국경 없는 의사회" 같은 단체의 사람들 덕에 지구는 더 살기 좋은 곳이 되었다.

[주제문 2] 더욱이, 세계의 많은 도시에 사는 사람들은 요즘에 와서 점점

더 자동차 사용을 자제한다. **[일반 진술 2]** 이로 인해 대기 중에 배출되는 유해 오염물질도 줄고 환경의 질도 향상된다. **[예 2]** 한 가지 예로, 어떤 도시의 사람들은 자동차 사용을 자제하고 대중교통을 더 이용하려고 한다. 그렇게 하는 과정에서 도시 대기의 질이 대단히 향상되었다는 결과가 나왔다. 이런 것들을 볼 때 인간 활동은 지구에 유익한 결과를 가져올 수 있다. **[종결문 2]** 만약 더 많은 사람들이 일상 생활에서 이와 비슷한 변화를 계속 시도한다면 지구는 더 살기 좋은 곳이 될 것이다.

[요약] 결국, 인간은 지구를 더 나은 곳으로 만들기 위해 여러 가지 좋은 일을 하고 있다. 이러한 행동 가운데 두 가지가 의료 기술을 나누는 의사들과 자동차를 적게 쓰는 사람들이다. 의사들은 가난한 사회에 사는 사람들의 건강을 개선하고 사람들이 자동차에 덜 의존하는 지역에서는 대기의 질이 향상되었다. **[최종 논평]** 인간의 활동은 지구와 거기에 사는 삶의 질을 향상시킬 수 있다.

B

[Opening sentence] Since the start of the Industrial Revolution, the polluting of the Earth has increased greatly. Lately, however, many people have been trying to clean up the environment. In fact, some believe that the Earth is being mended from the damage done by humans. But this is actually not true. **[Thesis statement]** In fact, human activity is continuing to harm the Earth in a number of ways.

[Topic sentence 1] One example of this is that coal power plants, which hurt the environment, continue to be used to produce electricity for people. **[General statement 1]** The toxins these power plants release into the atmosphere cause acid rain, which harms lakes and rivers. **[Example 1]** In many industrialized countries, lakes that used to be popular for swimming or fishing are now closed because they have been polluted by acid rain. Coal power plants should take much of the blame for this. Many experts say that lakes and rivers, as well as water supplies that people depend on, have been polluted by acid rain caused by greenhouse gases like those emitted from coal power plants. **[Closing sentence 1]** The continued reliance of people on fossil-fuel-burning coal power plants is causing the destruction of the environment.

[Topic sentence 2] Also, more and more homes are being constructed to house increasing populations of people. The building of these homes requires the destruction of various ecosystems. **[General statement 2]** Builders often destroy the habitats of many animals and therefore cause them to become extinct. **[Example 2]** For example, in areas near the rainforests of South America and Africa, populations are increasing, so construction companies must clear away the jungle to build more and more homes. When they do this, they

are destroying the habitats of many species of animals. Without a place to live, many species on Earth have become extinct. And many more will become extinct in the future. Once this happens, certain types of animals are lost forever. The reason for this is human negligence. **[Closing sentence 2]** Human homes are replacing animal ones, which is harming the Earth in general.

[Summary] In conclusion, human activity continues to damage the Earth through the use of coal power plants and the construction of homes. Coal plants create toxins that cause acid rain, which harms bodies of water, and jungles and forests are being cleared to build houses, which reduces animal habitats. **[Final comment]** Humans should be more careful of how their actions affect the Earth than they are now.

[도입문] 산업혁명이 시작된 이래로 지구의 오염은 대단히 심각해졌다. 하지만, 최근에 와서는 많은 사람들이 환경을 깨끗하게 하기 위해 노력하고 있다. 사실, 어떤 사람들은 지구가 인간이 끼친 피해로부터 회복되고 있다고 믿는다. 그러나 이는 사실과 거리가 멀다. **[논제 진술]** 사실상, 인간 활동은 계속해서 여러 가지로 지구에 피해를 미치고 있다.

[주제문 1] 이것의 한 예가 화력 발전소로, 이는 환경에 피해를 끼치며 계속해서 전기를 생산해내고 있다. **[일반 진술 1]** 이 발전소에서 대기 중으로 내 뿜는 독소는 산성비를 내리게 하며 산성비는 강과 호수에 해를 끼친다. **[예 1]** 많은 산업 국가에서는 수영이나 낚시 때문에 사람들이 즐겨 찾곤 했던 호수가 산성비에 오염이 되어 지금은 폐쇄가 된 상태다. 화력 발전소는 많은 부분 그 책임이 있다. 많은 전문가들은 화력 발전소에서 내보낸 배기 가스와 같은 온실 가스 때문에 생긴 산성비에 의해 사람들이 먹는 식수원뿐만 아니라 강이나 호수가 오염되었다고 입을 모은다. **[종결문 1]** 사람들이 화석연료를 태우는 화력 발전소에 계속 의존함으로써 환경 파괴가 야기된다.

[주제문 2] 또한, 점점 불어나는 인구를 수용하기 위해 점점 더 많은 주택이 건설되고 있다. 이러한 주택의 건설에는 다양한 생태계의 파괴가 수반된다. **[일반 진술 2]** 건축업자들은 종종 많은 동물의 서식지를 파괴해 동물이 멸종되게 만들기도 한다. **[예 2]** 예를 들어, 남아메리카와 아프리카의 열대우림 인근 지역에는 점점 인구가 늘어나고 있어 건설 회사들은 더 많은 주택을 건설하기 위해 정글을 밀어야 한다. 이렇게 하면 많은 종의 동물이 서식지를 잃게 된다. 지구상의 많은 종들이 서식지가 없어 멸종되었다. 그리고 미래에는 더 많은 종이 멸종될 것이다. 이렇게 되면 어떤 종은 완전히 자취를 감추게 될 것이다. 이런 일이 일어나는 이유는 인간의 무관심 때문이다. **[종결문 2]** 인간의 거주지가 동물의 서식지를 빼앗아 지구 전체에 피해를 주고 있다.

[요약] 결론적으로, 인간 활동은 화력 발전소나 주택 건설로 지구에 피해를 미치고 있다. 화력 발전소는 산성비를 유발하는 독소를 배출하고 산성비는 수원에 피해를 주며, 주택 건설을 위해 정글과 숲이 파괴되어 동물의 서식지가 감소되고 있다. **[최종 논평]** 인간은 인간 활동이 어떻게 지구에 영향을 미치는가에 대해 현재보다 더 많은 신경을 써야 한다.

Completing & Checking Your Essay

The Internet Provides Valuable Information

There is no question that the Internet has changed modern life forever. It provides us with a lot of valuable information, such as instant price comparison shopping and facts for students doing research papers.

Before the creation of the Net, people would go to one or two stores before buying an item. But now, they can price comparison shop online in order to get the best prices on goods. This way of shopping can save them a lot of money. For example, last month, I was in the market for a computer. I went to a couple of stores and thought the prices were a bit high. Later, after checking some websites, I found that I was right. I actually ended up purchasing the exact computer that I saw in the store; however, I got it online for three hundred dollars cheaper than the store was selling it for. Because of my ability to compare prices online, I saved a large amount of money. This would not have been possible before the Internet became widespread. The Internet clearly saves people a lot of money in the long run.

Also, the Internet has a wealth of quick facts and information for students doing research or writing papers. Previously, students would have to be satisfied with the limited number of books on various topics at their local or school library. But, thanks to the Internet, they have access to a virtually unlimited amount of information on anything they could ever think of. Plus, the Internet saves them time while researching their papers as well as when they are actually writing them. Today, the Internet increases the amount of information available to students and cuts down on both their research and writing time.

Overall, the Internet is a valuable tool for gathering information for anyone, no matter if that person is a shopper or a student. It saves people money by price comparison shopping and is an excellent, swift research tool. It is amazing that anyone was ever able to do anything before the Internet.

인터넷으로 인해 현대의 삶이 완전히 바뀌었다는 데는 의문의 여지가 없다. 인터넷은 즉각적인 가격 비교가 가능한 쇼핑이나 학생들이 조사 과제물을 하는 데 필요한 사실과 같은 많은 소중한 정보를 제공해 준다.

인터넷이 나오기 전에는 사람들은 한 가지 물건을 사기 위해서도 한두 곳의 가게를 가야 했다. 하지만 이제는, 온라인 상에서 가격 비교 쇼핑을 통해 제일 싼 가격에 물건을 살 수 있다. 이런 식으로 쇼핑을 하면 많은 돈을 절약할 수 있다. 예를 들어, 지난달에 나는 컴퓨터를 사야 했다.

가게 몇 곳을 둘러 보았는데, 가격이 약간 높아 보였다. 나중에 인터넷을 검색해 보고서 나는 내 생각이 옳았음을 알게 되었다. 결국 나는 가게에서 봤던 것과 정확하게 똑같은 컴퓨터를 300달러나 싸게 온라인으로 구입했다. 온라인으로 가격 비교를 한 덕분에 많은 돈을 아낄 수 있었던 것이다. 인터넷이 보급되지 않았다면 불가능했을 일이다. 확실히 인터넷은 궁극적으로 많은 돈을 절약하게 해준다.

또한, 인터넷은 학생들이 조사를 하거나 논문을 쓰는 데 필요한 빠른 사실과 정보를 제공해준다. 이전에는 학생들이 동네 도서관이나 학교 도서관에 있는 여러 가지 주제에 관한 한정된 분량의 책에 만족해야 했다. 하지만, 인터넷이 생기면서 생각할 수 있는 거의 모든 주제에 대해 사실상 무한한 정보를 가질 수 있게 되었다. 게다가, 인터넷은 실제로 논문을 쓸 때뿐만 아니라 조사 시간도 줄여 주었다. 오늘날에는 인터넷에 나와 있는 정보의 양이 많아져 조사와 보고서 작성 시간을 줄일 수 있다.

전체적으로, 인터넷은 쇼핑을 하는 사람이건 학생이건 누구에게나 정보를 수집하는 중요한 도구이다. 가격 비교 쇼핑으로 많은 돈을 절약할 수도 있고 훌륭하고 신속한 조사 도구가 되기도 한다. 인터넷이 나오기 전에 사람들이 뭔가를 할 수 있었다는 게 놀라울 뿐이다.

Information on the Net Causes Many Problems

Many people believe the Internet is the answer to everything. In reality, the abundance of information on the Internet causes many problems because it takes a long time for someone to sift through all of it to find exactly what the person is looking for and also because there are many fictitious and deceitful websites that attempt to trick people and take advantage of them.

Whenever I surf the Internet for specific information, I sometimes spend hours clicking on links that lead to dead ends. This is really frustrating because it wastes my time if I am in a hurry. For example, one day I wanted to find a simple map of Switzerland. After a quick search, I had over 1,000 webpage hits for my search. Most of the maps were not of Switzerland itself but were of specific regions of the country or city maps. An hour later, I finally randomly hit a link which led me to a general map of Switzerland. If I had known it was going to have taken that long, I would have just gone down to my local library, which would have been much faster. Sometimes the abundance of information on the Internet can be too much.

Furthermore, the Internet is full of information which is designed to take advantage of people and get their money. Advertising for winning lottery numbers and spam mail are a couple of the most common examples of this type of misleading information on the Internet. For example, my mother was surfing the Internet and came across a webpage that said she had won a flat screen TV. She immediately called the number, and the person said that she had to buy something from them in order to have her name placed in a contest for the new television. Of course, she was quite upset and immediately hung up. Still, the abundance of information on the Internet can be very misleading to some people and can cause lots of problems, like the one that happened to my mother.

In conclusion, the Internet might seem to be a wonderful world of information, yet when it comes down to it, it is also a sea of misinformation and deceptive links which can lead to frustration and many problems. The Internet could be much more efficient if there were a way to limit the amount of false information on it.

많은 사람들은 인터넷이 모든 것에 대한 해답이라고 생각한다. 사실, 인터넷의 정보가 많아지면서 많은 문제가 발생한다. 사람들이 자신들이 원하는 정확한 정보를 찾는 데도 시간이 많이 걸리고 사람들을 현혹시키거나 이용하는 거짓 내용도 많기 때문이다.

나는 특정 정보를 얻기 위해 인터넷을 검색할 때마다 여러 시간을 클릭했는데, 결국 막다른 골목에 이른 경우가 가끔 있다. 여유가 없는 상태에서 이런 경험은 시간 낭비이기 때문에 정말 짜증이 난다. 일례로, 하루는 스위스의 전국 지도를 찾아야 했다. 잠시 검색을 하는 동안 나는 천 개 이상의 웹페이지를 뒤져야 했다. 대부분의 지도는 스위스 지도가 아니라 그 나라의 특정 지역 또는 도시 지도였다. 한 시간이 지나서야 나는 우연히 스위스의 전국 지도가 있는 링크를 찾았다. 만약 그렇게 오래 걸릴 줄 알았다면 우리 동네 도서관을 찾았을 것이다. 그러는 편이 적어도 시간상으로 훨씬 절약이 되었을 테니까 말이다. 때로는 인터넷의 풍부한 정보가 필요 이상일 경우도 있다.

더욱이, 인터넷은 사람들을 이용해 돈을 갈취하고자 하는 정보들로 넘쳐난다. 인터넷에서 볼 수 있는 이러한 종류의 그릇된 정보 가운데 가장 흔한 두 가지 예가 복권 당첨 광고나 스팸 메일이다. 한 가지 예로, 우리 어머니께서 인터넷 검색을 하다가 한 웹사이트에서 무료 평면 TV에 당첨되었다는 얘기를 들으셨다. 어머니는 즉시 그 번호로 전화를 걸었는데, 담당자가 새 TV 당첨자 명단에 이름이 오르려면 물건을 사야 한다고 말했다. 물론, 어머니는 꽤 화가 나셔서 곧바로 전화를 끊어 버리셨다. 여전히, 인터넷의 많은 정보는 여러 사람을 현혹시킬 수 있고 우리 어머니의 경우와 같이 많은 문제를 야기할 수 있다.

결론적으로, 인터넷은 정보로 가득한 멋진 세상처럼 보일지 모르지만 깊이 들어가 보면 잘못된 정보의 바다이며 실망과 많은 문제를 야기하는 기만적인 링크의 바다이다. 인터넷에 오르는 그릇된 정보를 제한할 방법이 있다면 인터넷은 훨씬 더 효과적일 것이다.

Unit 16 Business & Economy

Understanding the Topic

4 Full benefits → complete health insurance & retirement benefits /
More opportunities for advancement → higher salaries & more benefits

5 Recent Internet survey → a majority of large companies provide retirement & comprehensive health care plans /
Three or four promotions at large companies vs. just one promotion at small companies over the same period of time

Brainstorming

1 full benefits
2 complete health insurance & retirement plans
3 e.g. Internet survey - most large companies provide full benefits
4 more opportunities for advancement
5 higher salaries & more benefits
6 e.g. 3 or 4 promotions at large companies vs. 1 promotion at small companies

Outlining

1 Full benefits packages
- workers have complete health insurance & retirement plans
- e.g. Internet survey → a majority of large companies provide retirement & health care plans
2 More opportunities for advancement
- employees receive higher salaries & more benefits
- e.g. 3 or 4 promotions at large companies vs. 1 promotion at small companies over the same period of time

Writing the Thesis Statement & Topic Sentences

Thesis statement While small companies might initially seem enticing because of their more relaxed environments, large companies are actually better places to work at due to the greater financial benefits and opportunities for advancement that they offer.

Topic sentence 1 Unlike many small companies, nearly all large companies provide generous benefits packages to their employees.

Topic sentence 2 Another way in which large companies are better than small ones is that large companies provide their workers with more opportunities for advancement.

Summary In conclusion, large companies are definitely better places to work at than small companies. First, they provide better financial packages, and second, they give their employees more chances to get promotions and higher status.

Writing the Details

A

[도입문] 요즘에는 많은 사람들이 대기업에서 일하고 싶어하는 것 같다. 그들 생각에는 큰 것이 좋은 것이다. [논제 진술] 하지만 대기업이 월급이 많을지는 몰라도 작은 회사가 직원들에게 더 나은 근로 환경을 제공한다.

[주제문 1] 한 가지 큰 장점은 직무 만족도이다. 직무 만족도와 관련해서는 대기업이 작은 회사에 비교가 되지 않는다. [일반 진술 1] 회사의 규모 때문에 직원들은 작은 회사에서 일할 때는 대기업에서 일할 때에 비해 더 큰 기여를 하고 있다고 느끼게 된다. 대기업에서 직원들은 종종 자신들을 익명의 존재로 느낀다. [예 1] 최근에 있었던 전국 규모의 조사에서 대기업과 소규모 회사 직원들을 대상으로 전반적인 직무 만족도에 관한 질문을 했다. 소규모 회사의 경우 직원의 반 이상이 긍정적인 답을 했는데, 자신들이 회사에서 핵심적 역할을 하고 있다고 말했다. 이와는 대조적으로, 대기업 직원 가운데 자신들이 중요한 기여를 하고 있다고 대답한 사람은 3분의 1 이하였다. [종결문 1] 이 조사 결과를 볼 때 작은 회사의 직원들이 대기업 직원들에 비해 훨씬 더 만족도가 큰 것을 알 수 있다.

[주제문 2] 또 다른 중요한 요소는 작은 회사에서는 대기업과는 달리 직원들의 유연성을 인정한다는 것이다. [일반 진술 2] 작은 회사의 직원들은 대단히 다양한 업무를 하기 때문에 관심과 활력을 항상 높게 유지할 수 있다. [예 2] 지난해에 한 TV 다큐멘터리에서는 작은 기업의 많은 직원들이 대기업에 비해 다양한 업무를 소화해내고 이로 인해 더 활기에 넘친다는 것을 보여주었다. 간단히 말해, 다양한 업무로 인해 작은 회사의 사원들은 직무에 대한 관심을 유지할 수 있다. 그 프로그램에 따르면, 다양한 업무를 함으로써 기력이 소진되거나 권태를 느끼는 일이 적다고 한다. 안타깝게도, 대기업의 직원들은 다양한 업무를 할 수 있는 기회가 없는 경우가 많다. [종결문 2] 업무의 유연성으로 인해 작은 회사의 직원들은 훌륭한 근로 환경을 누릴 수 있다.

[요약] 요약하자면, 작은 회사는 대기업에 비해 만족도가 더 높고 유연하기 때문에 사람들에게 더 나은 근로 조건을 제공한다. [최종 논평] 사람들은 성인기의 상당 부분을 직장에서 보내는데, 작은 회사에서 근무함으로써 직무 만족도를 높일 수 있다.

B

[Opening sentence] Many people opt to work at small companies, where the atmospheres are not as fast paced as they are at large companies. [Thesis statement] While small companies might initially seem enticing because of their more relaxed environments, large companies are actually better places to work at due to the greater financial benefits and opportunities for advancement that they offer.

[Topic sentence 1] Unlike many small companies, nearly all large companies provide generous benefits packages to their employees. [General statement 1] This saves money for employees and also provides them with health insurance and retirement benefits. On the other hand, many employees at small companies receive fewer benefits. Those employees may have to pay for their own health insurance, which can cost them thousands of dollars a year. [Example 1] A recent Internet survey conducted by a leading financial magazine showed that a significant majority of the large companies that responded provide retirement and comprehensive health care plans for their employees. In comparison, a very small number of small companies offered the same benefits to their workers. [Closing sentence 1] When it comes to offering more than just basic compensation, large companies provide much more than small ones.

[Topic sentence 2] Another way in which large companies are better than small ones is that large companies provide their workers with more opportunities for advancement. [General statement 2] Since there are more positions available at large companies, the workers can get promotions much faster than their counterparts at small companies can. [Example 2] For example, workers at large companies might get three or four promotions during a several-year period while a worker doing the same job at a small company may get just one promotion. Naturally, these promotions come with higher salaries and more benefits, so they can help to advance workers' careers. [Closing sentence 2] For ambitious employees who are eager to improve their status at their workplaces, large companies simply offer many more chances than small ones do.

[Summary] In conclusion, large companies are definitely better places to work at than small companies. First, they provide better financial packages, and second, they give their employees more chances to get promotions and higher status. [Final comment] Money and advancement are two of the main reasons that people work, so it seems natural that more people would want to be employed at large companies.

[도입문] 많은 사람들이 대기업만큼 업무 진행 속도가 빠르지 않은 소규모 회사에서 일하는 쪽을 택한다. [논제 진술] 작은 회사는 근로 환경이 더 여유로워 보이기 때문에 처음에는 더 매력적으로 보일지 모르지만 실제로는 경제적 혜택이 더 많고 발전의 기회가 많은 대기업이 일하기에는 더 낫다.

[주제문 1] 많은 작은 회사들과는 달리 거의 모든 대기업들은 직원들에게 많은 혜택을 제공한다. [일반 진술 1] 이는 직원 입장에서 볼 때 많은 돈을 절약하게 해주며 의료보험과 퇴직연금도 제공한다. 반면에 작은 회사에서 일하는 사람들은 대부분 더 적은 혜택을 받는다. 그러한 사람들은 자

신의 의료보험을 직접 들어야 하고 때로는 일 년에 수천 달러씩 비용이 들기도 한다. [예 1] 유명 경제 잡지에서 최근에 실시한 인터넷 조사에서 대답에 응한 대기업 대부분이 직원들에게 퇴직 연금 제도와 포괄적인 건강 의료 계획을 제공하는 것으로 나타났다. 그에 비해 작은 회사들 가운데는 아주 소수만이 직원들에게 동일한 혜택을 제공하고 있다고 답했다. [종결문 1] 기본 연봉 이상을 제공하는 데 있어서는 대기업이 작은 회사보다 훨씬 더 많은 혜택을 준다.

[주제문 2] 대기업이 작은 회사들보다 나은 또 하나의 이유는 직원들에게 더 많은 발전 기회를 제공한다는 것이다. [일반 진술 2] 대기업에는 더 많은 자리가 있기 때문에 직원들은 작은 회사에 비해 훨씬 더 고속으로 승진을 할 수 있다. [예 2] 예를 들어, 대기업의 직원은 작은 회사의 직원이 몇 년에 걸쳐 딱 한 번 승진을 하는 동안 서너 번의 승진이 가능하다. 당연히, 승진이 되면 월급이 오르고 혜택도 많아져서 경력에도 도움이 된다. [종결문 2] 직장에서 자신의 입지를 더 높이고자 하는 야심 있는 직원의 경우 대기업은 작은 회사에 비해 더 많은 기회를 제공한다.

[요약] 결론적으로, 대기업은 작은 회사에 비해 확실히 근무하기에 더 낫다. 첫 번째로 임금 수준이 더 높으며, 두 번째로는 승진을 해서 지위가 더 높아질 기회가 더 많다. [최종 논평] 보수와 승진은 사람들이 일을 하는 두 가지 중요한 이유이기 때문에 더 많은 사람들이 대기업에서 일하고 싶어하는 것은 당연해 보인다.

Completing & Checking Your Essay

Spending Money on Space Exploration

Many people are in favor of spending large amounts of money on exploring space, particularly the moon and other planets. I fully agree with these people for several different reasons. For one, we are running out of space on Earth and need to colonize other planets. And, second of all, exploring space will help people learn much more and increase their knowledge in many different fields.

The population of Earth continues to increase every year while Earth's natural resources are becoming depleted. For these reasons, we should consider moving off the planet and colonizing either the moon or some other planets. This will accomplish two things. It will allow large numbers of people to migrate to other planets, thereby easing the population crisis on Earth. And it will enable us to utilize the natural resources of other planets, thereby helping to preserve Earth's. By exploring space now, governments can obtain the knowledge they need to be able first to travel to other planets and then to colonize them. For example, recent unmanned visits to Mars have shown that, with the proper technology, Mars could be made inhabitable for humans. However, governments need to spend more money on the space program to be able to invent the necessary technology. By spending money now, the payoff in the future can be tremendous.

Second, governments should spend more money on exploring outer space simply because it will help increase human knowledge. The space program has already helped astronomers learn much about the universe and everything in it. Also, the space program has helped people learn more about Earth. By providing more funding for space programs, we can increase this body of knowledge. Indeed, many discoveries and inventions by the space program have helped to improve life on Earth in many different fields, including technology and medicine. By continuing to fund space programs, surely there will be even more advances made in these fields.

I strongly believe that governments should continue to fund their countries' space programs. These programs will not only help humans eventually leave Earth and colonize other planets but will also contribute to the knowledge that we on Earth possess. Countries should be encouraged to support their space programs. Doing so will improve the lives of people both on Earth and off of it.

많은 사람들이 우주 탐사, 특히 달과 기타 행성 탐사에 많은 돈을 쓰는 것을 찬성한다. 나 역시 여러 가지 이유로 이들의 의견에 전적으로 동의한다. 우선, 우리는 지구상에서 공간이 부족하며 다른 행성을 개척해야 한다. 그리고 두 번째로, 우주 탐사를 통해 사람들은 훨씬 더 많은 것을 배우고 여러 분야에서 지식을 늘릴 수 있다.

지구의 자원은 고갈되는 반면 인구는 해마다 계속해서 증가하고 있다. 이러한 이유로 우리는 지구 밖으로 나가 달이나 다른 행성을 개척하는 것을 고려해 보아야 한다. 이렇게 되면 두 가지를 이룰 수 있다. 많은 사람들이 다른 행성으로 이주해 지구 상의 인구 폭발 문제를 완화할 수 있다. 그리고 다른 행성의 천연자원을 활용해 지구의 자원을 보존할 수 있다. 현재 우주 탐사를 함으로써 정부는 먼저 다른 행성으로 갈 수 있고, 다음으로 그 행성을 개척하는 데 필요한 지식을 얻을 수 있다. 예를 들어, 최근에 화성에 보낸 무인우주선을 통해 적절한 기술이 있으면 화성도 인간이 거주할 수 있는 지역으로 만들 수 있다는 것을 알게 되었다. 하지만, 정부는 필요한 기술을 개발할 수 있도록 우주 계획에 더 많은 돈을 써야 한다. 지금 돈을 쓰면 미래의 언젠가는 엄청난 수익을 거둘 수 있을 것이다.

두 번째로, 우주 탐사가 인간의 지식을 증가시킨다는 이유만으로도 정부는 우주 탐사에 더 많은 돈을 써야 한다. 이미 우주 계획으로 인해 천문학자들은 우주와 우주 안의 모든 것에 관해 더 많은 정보를 알 수 있었다. 또한, 우주 계획은 지구에 관해서도 더 많은 것을 알게 해주었다. 사실, 우주 탐사 계획 덕분에 가능했던 많은 발견과 발명은 기술과 의학을 비롯한 여러 분야에서 지구에서의 삶을 향상시켰다. 우주 탐사 계획을 계속적으로 지원할 경우 이러한 분야들에 훨씬 많은 진전이 이루어질 것은 확실하다.

나는 정부가 자국의 우주 계획을 계속해서 지원해야 한다고 확신한다. 이러한 계획은 인간이 결국 지구를 떠나 다른 행성을 개척하도록 도울 뿐만 아니라 지구에 살고 있는 인간이 소유한 지식의 양을 늘리는 데도 기여할 것이다. 각국은 자국의 우주 계획을 지원해야 한다. 그렇게 함으로써 지구 안팎에 사는 사람들의 삶을 향상시킬 수 있다.

Spending Money on Basic Needs on Earth

While many governments like to spend large sums of money on space exploration, this actually does little to benefit the citizens of those countries. Governments instead should focus on spending the majority of their funds on the basic needs of the citizens of their countries.

One of the most basic needs for people is health care. Unfortunately, most governments have not ensured that their citizens have access to quality health care. If governments were to spend more money on even the most basic health care, the quality of life for their citizens would increase dramatically. The countries themselves would benefit from investing in health care because their citizens would be healthier and live longer lives, which would then increase the overall productivity of the workers in those countries. Furthermore, in advanced countries such as the United States, where health care costs are a major cause of bankruptcy, governments could help relieve citizens of the burden of expensive health care. By spending more money on health care than on space programs, governments could create a healthier, wealthier, and more productive workforce.

In addition, many countries are spending large amounts of money on their space programs but are not getting a good return on their investments. There are very few people involved in space programs, yet, in some countries, they receive an incredibly high amount of money due to the expensive nature of sending rockets, satellites, and men into space. One example of this is the International Space Station. Several countries have contributed billions of dollars to the construction and maintenance of the space station. However, I cannot recall ever reading or hearing about any scientific discoveries made on the space station. Nor have I heard of any experiments being conducted there. It seems that astronauts often visit the space station, but they do not appear to be doing anything practical or useful to the large majority of the world's population. Instead, the International Space Station is just wasting billions and billions of taxpayers' dollars to increase the prestige of the nations associated with it. That money could be spent much more wisely and better back here on Earth.

In conclusion, I believe that governments should stop spending so much money on their space programs and should instead focus on investing their valuable financial resources here on Earth. Those funds could be better spent on health care and making the population healthier. In addition, since the space program is not producing any obvious benefits, the money spent on it could and should be spent on Earth, not in outer space.

여러 국가가 상당한 금액을 우주 탐사에 사용하고는 있지만 사실 이것은 그러한 국가의 국민들에게 그다지 많은 혜택을 주지 못한다. 대신에, 정부는 국민의 기본적 욕구 충족에 자금의 대부분을 사용하도록 노력을 기울여야 한다.

국민들의 가장 기본적인 욕구 중의 하나는 보건의료이다. 안타깝게도, 대다수 국가들은 국민들에게 양질의 의료를 보장하지 못하고 있다. 국가에서 더 많은 돈을 가장 기본적인 의료에 쓴다면 국민들의 삶의 질은 급격히 향상될 것이다. 그렇게 되면 국민들이 더 건강해지고 수명도 길어져서 그 국가의 노동자의 전반적인 생산성을 향상시키고 결국에는 국가 역시 혜택을 보게 된다. 게다가, 미국과 같은 선진 국가에서는 의료비가 파산의 주요 원인이 되고 있기 때문에 정부가 국민들의 비싼 의료비 부담을 덜어줄 수 있다. 우주 탐사 계획보다 보건의료에 더 많은 돈을 투자함으로써 국가는 더 건강하고 부유하며 생산성 높은 노동력을 창출해낼 수 있다.

그뿐만 아니라, 많은 국가에서 막대한 금액을 우주 탐사 계획에 쏟아붓지만 투자에 대한 수익은 그다지 좋지 않다. 몇몇 국가의 경우 우주 계획에 관여하는 사람은 아주 소수에 불과하지만 로켓, 위성, 우주인 등을 보내는 데는 비용이 많이 들 수밖에 없기 때문에 엄청난 돈을 받는다. 한 가지 예로 국제우주정거장을 들 수 있다. 몇몇 국가에서는 국제우주정거장의 건설과 유지에 수십억 달러를 쏟아부었다. 하지만, 우주정거장에서 별다른 과학적 발견이 있었다는 이야기를 읽거나 들어본 적이 없다. 또한 거기에서 어떠한 실험을 진행 중이라는 이야기도 들은 바 없다. 우주비행사들이 가끔씩 우주정거장을 방문하지만 전 세계인들에게 유용하거나 실용적인 무엇을 하고 있는 것 같아 보이지도 않는다. 그 대신에, 국제우주정거장은 관련 국가의 위상을 높이기 위해 수십억 달러에 달하는 납세자의 돈만 기다리고 있다. 그 돈은 이곳 지구상에서 훨씬 더 현명하고 바람직하게 쓰일 수 있다.

결론적으로, 나는 정부가 우주 계획에 그렇게 많은 돈을 쓰는 대신 이곳 지구에 소중한 재원을 투자하기 위해 노력해야 한다고 생각한다. 그러한 자금을 보건의료에 더 바람직하게 사용해서 사람들을 건강하게 만들 수 있다. 그뿐만 아니라, 우주 계획은 아무런 가시적인 이익도 가져오지 못하고 있기 때문에 우주 계획에 쓰는 돈을 우주가 아닌 이곳 지구상의 사람들을 위해 써야 한다.

Actual Test 01

Task 1 (Integrated Writing)

■ Reading

현대 사회로 접어들면서 사람들의 생활방식에서 많은 발전이 이루어졌지만 한 가지 부정적인 측면이 나타났다. 즉, 미국의 자녀 양육비가 급등했다. 사실, 미국에서 자녀를 양육하려면 세계 어느 나라보다도 비용이 많이 든다.

최근 조사에 따르면, 아이가 태어나는 순간부터 약 21세에 대학을 졸업할 때까지 먹이고 입히고 교육을 시키는 데 평균적으로 대략 26만 달러가 든다고 한다. 많은 가정의 경우 자녀를 비싼 사립 학교나 대학에 보내기 때문에 비용은 훨씬 올라가는데, 일부 학교는 등록금과 기숙사비로 연간 4만 달러가 들기도 한다. 이 수치에는 여행이나 장난감, 기타 완구 등은 포함되어 있지 않은데, 이것들 역시 비용이 만만치 않다.

믿기 힘든 이야기지만, 미국에서 자녀를 키우는 데는 프랑스나 스페인 같은 다른 유럽 국가들에 비해 3분의 1이나 비용이 더 많이 든다. 한 가지 이유는 많은 유럽 국가들에서는 제한된 사회주의를 실시하고 있어 부모들이 자녀를 학교에 보내는 데 등록금을 내지 않아도 된다. 또한, 이런 국가들은 생활 수준이 미국보다 낮은 반면 물가 역시 저렴한데, 이것은 부모 입장에서 더 많은 돈을 절약할 수 있는 큰 이점이 된다.

마지막으로, 부모가 돈을 어디에 쓰느냐의 문제가 있다. 대다수 국가들의 경우 부모들은 자녀들에게 할당된 돈의 대부분을 옷이나 음식 같은 필수품에 사용한다. 하지만, 미국에서는 다른 국가 사람들이 과도하다고 생각할 부분에 돈을 지출한다. 예를 들어, 미국의 부모들은 공부, 음악, 체육과 같은 사교육에 상당한 비용을 지출한다. 그뿐만 아니라, 미국 부모들은 자녀의 의료비에 막대한 비용을 지출한다. 이 모든 이유 때문에 미국에서 자녀를 양육하는 데는 많은 돈이 든다.

■ Listening

Narrator   Now listen to part of a lecture on the topic you just read about.

W: Everyone knows that raising children in America nowadays is expensive. Indeed, that's one reason why many couples are choosing to have only one child or none at all. However, I don't want to discourage any of you from having children of your own. There are some ways to get those expenses down.

For example, many families, even those with health insurance, spend huge amounts of money on medical expenses for their children. That's understandable. But, instead of treating illnesses when they occur, they ought to be practicing prevention, which, in the long run, will save them money. One way to do this is to practice extreme cleanliness. A clean child is a healthy child. Clean children become sick less often and have fewer allergies. That's money in the bank right there.

Another cost-reducing measure is also related to health. We often hear about kids that get burned in the kitchen or hurt themselves in other ways. Remember, even with health insurance, one trip to the hospital can cost tens of thousands of dollars. So parents should be educating their children on safety. Knowing about safety increases the chances that the child won't get hurt and will remain out of harm.

Finally, parents should be encouraging their children to pursue their own intellectual interests. Too many times, parents waste money on tutoring or lessons that their children aren't interested in. Why pay for piano lessons if your kid hates the piano? He's not going to become the next Mozart if he hates it. And parents shouldn't spend so much money on educational software if it's for something that their child has no interest in. Of course, these suggestions might only reduce a few thousand dollars off the total price tag, but, at today's rates, every dollar counts.

Narrator   방금 읽은 내용에 관한 강의의 일부를 들으시오.

W: 요즘 미국의 자녀 양육비가 만만치 않다는 것은 누구라도 알 거예요. 사실, 그것은 많은 커플들이 한 자녀만 갖거나 아예 자녀를 갖지 않는 이유이기도 합니다. 하지만 나는 여러분에게 자녀를 갖지 말라고 하고 싶진 않습니다. 그러한 비용을 줄일 수 있는 몇 가지 방법이 있습니다.

예를 들어, 많은 가정, 심지어 의료 보험을 든 가정에서도 자녀에게 막대한 의료비를 지출합니다. 이는 이해가 가는 일이죠. 하지만 질병이 발생할 때마다 치료를 하는 대신 예방을 해야 합니다. 결국에는, 이쪽이 비용이 더 절약이 되니까요. 이것을 할 수 있는 한 가지 방법은 극도의 청결을 유지하는 것입니다. 청결한 아이는 건강합니다. 청결한 아이는 질병에 걸리는 빈도가 낮으며 알레르기 반응도 적게 일어납니다. 돈을 절약할 수 있는 확실한 방법이기도 하죠.

또 다른 비용 절감 방법 역시 건강과 관련이 있습니다. 우리는 종종 부엌에서 화상을 입거나 다른 방식으로 다치는 아이들에 대한 이야기를 듣습니다. 의료 보험이 있더라도 병원을 한 번 찾게 되면 수만 달러가 들 수도 있다는 사실을 기억하세요. 그래서 부모들은 자녀들에게 안전에 대한 교육을 해야 합니다. 안전에 대해 알게 되면 자녀가 상해를 입지 않을 가능성이 커집니다.

마지막으로, 부모들은 자녀들이 각자 가진 지적 관심 분야를 추구할 수 있도록 격려해야 합니다. 자녀들이 관심을 갖지 않는 분야의 개인 과외를 시키거나 레슨을 받게 하는 데다 돈을 낭비하는 부모들을 너무 자주 보게 됩니다. 자녀가 피아노를 싫어한다면 피아노 레슨에 돈을 쓸 이유가 없잖아요? 피아노를 싫어하는 아이가 모차르트가 되는 일은 없을 테니까요. 그리고 부모들은 자녀들이 관심을 보이지 않는 교육용 소프트웨어에 그렇게 많은 돈을 쓰지 말아야 합니다. 물론, 이러한 제안들의 효과는 전체 비용에서 수천 달러를 절약하는 정도에 지나지 않겠지만 오늘날 지출로 볼 때 단 1달러도 무시할 수 없으니까요.

The reading passage states that the cost of raising children in the United States is higher than in other countries. The professor, however, claims there are many ways to decrease these costs.

The reading mentions that raising a child from birth to college averages $260,000. It declares that this number is often higher and does not include expenses like travel or toys. The professor notes that health care costs are enormous. She says that if parents practice prevention and keep their children clean and healthy, they can save lots of money.

The reading then argues that American tuition rates are much higher than in Europe, where many attend school for free. It also states that products in these countries are cheaper than in the U.S. However, the professor counters by saying parents should educate their children about safety. This will keep their children from getting hurt and will save thousands in medical expenses.

Finally, responding to the claim that American parents spend more money on excessive or unnecessary items, the professor declares that parents should first learn what their children enjoy before paying for it. For example, parents should not pay for piano lessons if their child hates playing the piano.

The professor comes up with several ways to decrease the price of raising a child, thereby making it more appealing to couples.

지문에서는 미국의 자녀 양육비가 다른 국가에 비해 높다고 말한다. 하지만 교수는 이러한 비용을 감소시킬 여러 가지 방법이 있다고 주장한다.

지문에서는 한 자녀를 출생에서부터 대학을 보낼 때까지 26만 달러가 든다고 한다. 이러한 수치는 종종 더 높아지기도 하는데, 여행이나 장난감 등의 비용은 포함되어 있지 않다고 되어 있다. 교수는 의료비가 엄청나다는 것을 지적한다. 그녀는 부모들이 예방법을 실시하고 자녀들을 청결하고 건강하게 키우면 많은 비용을 절약할 수 있다고 말한다.

또 지문에는 미국의 등록금이 유럽에 비해 훨씬 높다고 나와 있다. 유럽에서는 많은 학생들이 무료로 학교에 다닌다. 또한, 이러한 국가들의 경우는 미국보다 상품 값이 저렴하다. 하지만, 교수는 부모들이 안전에 관해 자녀들을 교육해야 한다고 말해 이 주장을 반박한다. 이렇게 함으로써 자녀가 다치는 것을 막고 수천 달러의 의료비를 절약할 수 있을 것이다.

마지막으로, 미국 부모들은 과도하거나 불필요한 부분에 많은 돈을 소비한다는 주장과 관련해 교수는 부모들이 돈을 쓰기 전에 자녀들이 배우고 싶어하는 것이 무엇인지를 먼저 살펴야 한다고 주장한다. 예를 들어, 부모들은 자녀가 피아노 치기를 싫어하는 경우에는 피아노 레슨을 시켜서는 안 된다.

교수는 자녀 양육비를 줄일 몇 가지 안을 내 놓았는데, 이는 커플들에게 더욱 호소력 있게 들린다.

Task 2 (Independent Writing)

Today, advertisers use various ways to make their advertisements more appealing. In most cases, they appear to be successful at making their products seem much better than they really are; thus they are able to tempt customers to purchase them. I have a number of reasons for feeling this way, and they are all based upon my own personal experiences.

First, my family has occasionally purchased products after seeing them advertised on commercials. Unfortunately, several purchases turned out to be misguided. For example, once we saw several advertisements for a new car. The advertisements stated that the car had excellent engineering, so it would never break down. My parents then purchased the car; however, after just a couple of weeks, it broke down because of an engine problem. We only kept that car for a couple of years, but, during that time, we had numerous problems with it and frequently had to get it repaired.

Another example of the exaggerating effects of advertisements is the many advertisements for restaurants on television. These are especially common for fast-food restaurants. The food in the commercials always looks delicious, and the people seem to enjoy eating it. Also, the appearance and presentation of the food in the commercials are amazing. These commercials have often prompted me to encourage my family to visit some of these restaurants. However, in many instances, the food was not as delicious as the actors in the commercials made it appear to be. Additionally, the helpings of food were smaller, and it did not look as appetizing as the food in the commercials did.

There is one more way in which advertisers often make their products look more attractive than reality. They often advertise a price that is not the correct one. Instead, it is much cheaper than the real price of the product. I saw this once in an advertisement for an airline. It was promoting very cheap fares anywhere in the country. However, when my father called to ask about the tickets, the operator told him there were many restrictions on those flights. According to them, we had to fly on certain dates and at specific times. And there were not many cheap tickets available. So, while there were some cheap tickets for sale, there were just a few, and we were not able to buy any.

I believe it is clear that advertisements show their products much better than they are in reality. Unfortunately, these commercials give consumers the wrong idea about the products being sold.

오늘날 광고주들은 광고를 보다 호소력 있게 만들기 위해 다양한 방법을 사용한다. 대부분의 경우 제품은 실제보다 훨씬 나아 보여 소비자들로 하여금 구매를 하도록 유혹하는 데 성공한다. 내가 이렇게 느끼는 데는 여러 가지 이유가 있는데, 이러한 이유들은 하나같이 내 자신의 개인적 경험에서 나온다.

우선, 우리 가족은 광고에 나오는 것을 보고는 제품을 구매하는 일이 종종 있다. 안타깝게도, 때로는 잘못된 정보였음이 밝혀지기도 한다. 예를 들어, 한번은 신차 광고를 몇 차례 보았다. 광고에서는 그 차에 탁월한 공학 기술이 사용되어 결코 고장이 나지 않는다고 선전했다. 하지만 부모님이 차를 구입하고 난 뒤 단 2주 후에 엔진에 이상이 생겼다. 우리는 그 차를 단 2년 동안 몰았는데, 그 시기 동안 여러 가지 문제가 생겨 수리를 받아야 했다.

과장 광고의 또 다른 예는 TV에 나오는 많은 식당 광고이다. 이것은 특히 패스트푸드 식당 광고의 경우에 흔하다. 광고에 나오는 음식은 항상 맛있어 보이고 사람들도 맛있게 먹는 것처럼 보인다. 또한 광고에 나오는 음식은 아주 그럴 듯해 보인다. 나는 이 광고들을 보다가 가족들을 졸라 광고에 나오는 식당으로 가게 만든다. 하지만 많은 경우 음식은 광고 속에 나오는 배우들이 그렇게 보이도록 했던 것처럼 그렇게 맛있지는 않았다. 게다가, 음식 양도 적고 광고 속의 음식처럼 식욕을 당기게 하지도 않았다.

광고주들이 제품을 실제보다 더 매력적으로 보이게 하기 위해 사용하는 한 가지 방법이 더 있다. 그들은 종종 정확하지 않은 가격을 광고한다. 대신에, 제품의 실제 가격보다 훨씬 저렴한 가격을 광고한다. 한번은 항공사 광고에서 이런 경험을 했다. 광고에서는 국내 어디건 대단히 저렴한 항공료로 여행을 할 수 있다고 선전했다. 하지만 아버지께서 항공권에 대해 문의하자 직원은 그 비행기편에 많은 제약이 있다는 것을 설명해 주었다. 그 사람들에 따르면 특정일, 특정 시간에 비행을 해야 했다. 그리고 저렴한 항공권도 그다지 많지 않았다. 그래서 할인 항공권이 있을 경우에도 너무 소수에 불과해 살 수도 없었다.

광고에서는 항상 제품이 실제보다 나은 것처럼 선전한다는 것은 분명한 사실이다. 안타깝게도, 이러한 광고들은 소비자에게 판매되는 제품에 대해 잘못된 생각들을 갖게 한다.

Actual Test 02

Task 1 (Integrated Writing)

■ Reading

요즘 시행되는 법률 가운데 가장 논쟁의 여지가 많은 부분 중의 하나가 과속 단속 카메라이다. 이 카메라는 여기저기에 설치되어 있어서 지나가는 차량의 속도를 측정한다. 카마라에는 레이더 감지기가 있어 과속 차량의 사진을 찍은 다음 운전자에게 과속 딱지를 보내 나중에 벌금을 내게 한다. 많은 사람들이 과속 단속 카메라를 싫어하지만 사실 이 카메라는

사회에 유익하다.

우선, 과속 단속 카메라 덕분에 도로가 더욱 안전해진다. 때로는 단속 카메라가 근처에 있다는 표시가 있기도 있지만 대부분은 보이지 않는 곳에 숨겨져 있다. 그래서 운전자가 근처에 단속 카메라가 있다고 느끼거나 아는 경우에는 과속 위반 딱지의 벌금이 200달러 이상이기 때문에 운전자는 대개 속도를 늦춘다. 속도를 늦춘다는 것은 사고가 준다는 것을 의미하므로 단속 카메라의 존재만으로도 이미 사람들을 보호하는 데 도움이 된다

두 번째로, 단속 카메라 덕분에 경찰들은 과속 운전자를 찾느라 많은 시간을 낭비하지 않아도 된다. 그래서 경찰들은 범인을 잡거나 대중의 안전을 도모하는 다른 중요한 일들을 할 수 있다. 사실, 단속 카메라가 성공적인 결과를 거두면서 점점 더 많은 카메라가 설치되어 미래에는 경찰관이 과속 위반 딱지를 떼는 일이 완전히 없어질지도 모른다.

마지막으로, 단속 카메라는 실제로 과속을 했다는 확실한 증거가 되기 때문에 법정에 와서 과속 위반 딱지에 항의하는 사람이 줄어 들었다. 이렇게 불만이 줄면서 끊임없이 사건이 적체되는 교통 위반 즉결 재판소의 일이 줄어들고 있다. 그래서 대다수 위반자들은 위반 장면이 찍힌 사진을 우편으로 받게 되면 딱지에 항의하는 대신 그냥 수표를 써서 벌금을 내는 쪽을 택한다.

■ Listening

Narrator　Now listen to part of a lecture on the topic you just read about.

M: I must say that I find speed cameras to be some of the most abhorrent devices that police departments all across the country are using. Not only do they infringe upon our basic rights, but they are also inherently dangerous. Here, let me give you a few reasons as to why I feel this way.

First of all, speed cameras actually don't make the roads safer. They make them more dangerous in many cases. Why? Let me explain. People are often worried about getting a speeding ticket since they cost so much money. So, if a person is speeding and suddenly notices a camera, what's he going to do? Slam on the brakes. That's what. And then the car behind him might just slam into him. There are numerous documented cases of accidents occurring because people tried suddenly to slow down upon seeing a traffic camera. So they aren't saving lives. In some cases, they are ending them.

Here's another thing. Now that fewer police officers are being tasked to catching speeders, they have more time to snoop around and bother law-abiding citizens. Just the other week I was harassed in the park by a cop when all I was doing was sitting on a park bench feeding the squirrels. And you'll notice that crime rates haven't decreased since these speed cameras have been installed. So what are the cops doing with their extra time?

Finally, cameras malfunction. Several people have received pictures in the mail that weren't even their cars. And others have gotten ticketed when they were definitely not speeding. Simply put, these cameras cannot be trusted to be completely accurate, and the government would be wise to ban their use before they cause any more problems.

Narrator 방금 읽은 내용에 관한 강의의 일부를 들으시오.

M: 나는 단속 카메라가 미국 전역의 경찰들이 사용하고 있는 가장 혐오스러운 장치 가운데 하나라고 생각합니다. 단속 카메라는 우리가 가진 기본적인 권리를 침해할 뿐만 아니라 본질적으로 위험하기까지 합니다. 그렇게 느끼는 몇 가지 이유를 말씀 드리죠.

첫 번째로, 단속 카메라 때문에 도로가 더 안전해지지는 않습니다. 많은 경우 더 위험하게 되는 하죠. 왜냐고요? 설명해 드리죠. 과속 위반 딱지는 적지 않은 벌금을 내야 하기 때문에 사람들은 종종 과속 위반 딱지를 받을까 봐 걱정을 합니다. 그래서 과속을 하다가 단속 카메라를 발견하게 되면 어떤 일이 일어날까요? 브레이크를 급히 밟게 되죠. 그게 문제예요. 뒤따르던 차가 그 차에 부딪힐 수도 있습니다. 단속 카메라를 본 사람이 갑자기 속도를 늦추는 바람에 교통사고가 발생한 기록이 많이 있습니다. 그러니 생명을 구하는 것이 아니죠. 경우에 따라서는 생명을 죽게 만드는 이유가 되기도 하죠.

다른 이유도 있습니다. 경찰관들이 과속 위반자를 잡는 일에 덜 투입되면서 시간적 여유가 생겨 여기저기를 기웃거리고 다니면서 법을 준수하는 시민들을 못살게 굽니다. 몇 주 전에는 내가 공원에서 다람쥐에게 먹이를 주고 있는데, 경찰관이 와서 저를 괴롭히더군요. 단속 카메라가 설치된 이후로 범죄 발생률이 줄지도 않았습니다. 그렇다면 남는 시간 동안 경찰은 무엇을 하고 있는 걸까요?

마지막으로, 단속 카메라는 오작동을 하기도 합니다. 어떤 사람들은 남의 차 사진이 든 사진을 우편으로 받기도 했습니다. 그리고 분명히 과속을 하지 않았는데도 과속 위반 딱지를 떼인 사람도 있습니다. 간단히 말해서, 이 단속 카메라를 완전히 신뢰해서는 안 되며 정부는 단속 카메라가 더 많은 문제를 일으키기 전에 사용을 금지해야 합니다.

Sample Answer

The reading passage makes the argument that speed cameras are beneficial to society. The professor, however, argues that they strip people of their rights and are actually dangerous.

First, the reading claims that speed cameras make roads safer because people will drive slowly for fear of paying heavy fines. Because they are driving slower, they have few accidents. The professor, however, says that speed cameras make roads more dangerous. According to him, people who are speeding will slow

down suddenly upon seeing a camera, thereby often causing accidents as they try to avoid getting ticketed.

The reading also states that speed cameras allow officers to spend more time catching criminals instead of watching for speeders. The professor counters this argument by mentioning that police are starting to harass law-abiding citizens like him. Also, he states that crime rates have not decreased lately, so the police are obviously not doing much with this extra time.

Finally, while the reading claims that the backlog of court cases is decreasing as fewer people protest their tickets in courts because of speed cameras, the professor says that many people are being improperly fined, so speed cameras cannot be trusted. For this reason, he believes they should be banned.

지문은 단속 카메라가 사회에 유익하다고 주장한다. 하지만, 교수는 단속 카메라는 사람들의 권리를 빼앗고 실제로 위험하기까지 하다고 주장한다.

첫 번째로, 지문에서는 사람들이 비싼 벌금을 내기 무서워하기 때문에 단속 카메라로 인해 도로가 더 안전해진다고 주장한다. 운전 속도를 늦추면서 사고가 적어진다. 하지만, 교수는 단속 카메라 때문에 도로가 더 위험해진다고 말한다. 그에 따르면, 과속을 하던 사람들이 단속 카메라를 보면 갑자기 속도를 늦추기 때문에 위반 딱지를 피하려고 하다가 교통사고를 유발하는 일이 종종 있다.

지문에서는 또한 단속 카메라 덕분에 경찰들이 과속 위반자 단속 대신 다른 범인을 잡는 데 더 많은 시간을 투자할 수 있다고 말한다. 교수는 경찰들이 자신처럼 법을 준수하는 시민들을 괴롭히기 시작한다고 말해 이 주장에 반박한다. 또한, 그는 최근에 범죄 발생률이 감소하지도 않은 걸 볼 때 경찰들이 이 남는 시간에 많은 업무를 하고 있지도 않은 게 확실하다고 말한다.

마지막으로, 지문은 단속 카메라 덕분에 교통 위반 즉결 재판소에 와서 위반 딱지에 대해 항의하는 사람의 수가 적어졌기 때문에 재판소에 적체된 소송이 줄고 있다고 말하지만, 교수는 많은 사람들이 부당하게 벌금을 부과 받기 때문에 단속 카메라를 신뢰할 수 없다고 말한다. 이런 이유로, 그는 단속 카메라 사용을 중단해야 한다고 생각한다.

Task 2 (Independent Writing)

Sample Answer

Although I believe the lessons students learn in classrooms are important, I do not think they learn the most important lessons there. Instead, I feel that the most important lessons learned in life are those taught outside of the classroom.

First of all, students learn many important lessons from their families. Students may spend several hours a day at school, but they spend even more time at home with their families. Families are easily the most important things in students' lives. Students can watch the relationships between their parents, brothers, and sisters. And they can also learn how to interact with each family member. When they get older, they will most likely have families of their own, so it is crucial for them to learn how to get along with their own family first.

Next, many students participate in sports and athletics. Sometimes they do this as members of a team. But all students at least participate in recess and physical education. When students play a game or sport, they are not just getting exercise. Instead, they are also learning about teamwork and how to work well with others. This is important because, in the future, almost everyone will find jobs after graduating from high school or college. People must work well together at their jobs in order to be as productive and efficient as possible. Learning how to work with others actually begins on the playground, not in classrooms, where individualism is often promoted rather than teamwork.

Finally, once school finishes, many students hang out with each other and engage in various group activities like doing their homework, playing computer games, or just watching movies. Basically, these students are learning how to get along with their peers. They are also developing friendships. Students learn early on that not everyone is the same and that people have different personalities. So, by hanging out and doing things together with their friends, students can learn how to get along with others. This is a very important lesson for life since students will meet hundreds or even thousands of people in their lifetimes.

It seems obvious that the best lessons for life are learned while students are outside of the classroom. Although they might not think of what they are doing as learning, students are in fact developing skills they will need and use for the rest of their lives.

나는 수업 시간에 배우는 것이 중요하다고 생각은 하지만 수업 시간에 배우는 것이 가장 중요하다고는 생각하지 않는다. 대신에, 인생에서 가장 중요한 것들은 교실 밖에서 배운다고 느낀다.

우선, 학생들은 가정에서 많은 중요한 것들을 배운다. 학생들은 하루에 몇 시간을 학교에서 보내지만 더 많은 시간을 가정에서 보낸다. 가정은 학생의 삶에서 가장 중요한 부분이 되게 마련이다. 학생들은 부모와 형제·자매들의 관계를 지켜보게 된다. 또한 가족의 각 구성원과 어떻게 상호작용을 하는지도 배울 수 있다. 그들은 나이가 들면서 자신만의 가정을 꾸리게 될 것이기 때문에 자신의 가족과 먼저 잘 지낼 수 있는 방법을 익히는 것이 중요하다.

다음으로, 많은 학생들이 스포츠와 운동 경기에 참여한다. 때로는 팀의 일원으로 경기에 참여하기도 한다. 하지만 모든 학생들은 적어도 쉬는 시간이나 체육 시간에 참여를 하게 된다. 학생들이 경기나 스포츠를 할 때 운동

만 하는 것은 아니다. 대신에, 학생들은 팀워크에 대해서도 배우고 다른 사람과 어울리는 법에 대해서도 배운다. 장래에 거의 모든 사람들이 고등학교나 대학을 졸업한 후에 직장을 구하기 때문에 이것은 중요한 역할을 한다. 가능한 한 생산적이면서 효율적이 되기 위해서는 직장 생활을 잘 해나가야 한다. 다른 사람들과 잘 지내는 법은 교실보다는 운동장에서 시작된다고 할 수 있다. 왜냐하면 교실에서는 팀워크보다는 개인주의가 추구되는 경향이 있기 때문이다.

마지막으로, 일단 수업이 끝나면 많은 학생들이 어울려 다니거나 아니면 숙제를 하거나, 컴퓨터 게임을 하거나 영화를 보는 등의 다양한 그룹 활동을 한다. 기본적으로 이런 학생들은 또래들과 잘 지내는 법을 익히는 셈이다. 또한 이들은 우정에 대해서도 배우게 된다. 학생들은 일찍부터 모든 사람이 다 같은 것은 아니며 사람마다 다른 개성을 지니고 있다는 것을 알게 된다. 그래서 친구들과 어울려 다니고 어떤 활동을 같이 함으로써 다른 사람들과 잘 지내는 법을 익히게 된다. 학생들은 살아가는 동안 수백 혹은 수천 명의 사람들을 만나게 될 것이기 때문에 이것은 인생에 특별히 중요한 가르침이 된다.

인생에서 가장 중요한 가르침들은 교실 밖에서 배우게 된다는 것은 분명한 사실인 듯 보인다. 학생들은 자신들이 하고 있는 활동을 배움이라고 생각하지 않을 수도 있지만 학생들은 사실 인생을 살아가면서 필요하고 사용하게 될 기술을 익히고 있는 것이다.

How to
Master Skills for the
TOEFL® iBT
Writing
Intermediate

How to Master Skills for the TOEFL® iBT Writing Intermediate is designed to be used either as a textbook for a TOEFL® iBT writing preparation course or as a tool for individual learners who are preparing for the TOEFL® test on their own. With a total of 16 units, this book is organized to prepare you for the test by providing you with a comprehensive understanding of the test and thorough practice of essential skills and question types to address the writing tasks on the TOEFL® iBT. Each unit provides a step-by-step program that can enhance your writing ability as well as familiarize you with the question types asked on the TOEFL® iBT. At the back of the book are a list of essential essay topics and two actual tests of the Writing section of the TOEFL® iBT.

Special Features:

- Intensive practice of the main question types for the Integrated and Independent Tasks
- Passages and questions that closely simulate the ones that have occurred on the TOEFL® iBT
- Step-by-step brainstorming, note-taking, outlining, paraphrasing, and summarizing practice
- A list of essay topics reconstructed from the ones that have so far been asked on the TOEFL® iBT
- Two complete tests that familiarize students with the actual test format
- Full answer key and Korean translations

How to Master Skills for the TOEFL® iBT Series:

How to Master Skills for the TOEFL® iBT Reading	Basic • Intermediate • Advanced
How to Master Skills for the TOEFL® iBT Listening	Basic • Intermediate • Advanced
How to Master Skills for the TOEFL® iBT Writing	Basic • Intermediate • Advanced
How to Master Skills for the TOEFL® iBT Speaking	Basic • Intermediate • Advanced